Family
and
Society

Also in the Series

Biology of Man in History

Family and Society

Selections from the

Annales

Economies, Sociétiés, Civilisations

Edited by

Robert Forster
and
Orest Ranum

Translated by

Elborg Forster
and
Patricia M. Ranum

The Johns Hopkins University Press
Baltimore and London

Manufactured in the United States of America

The Johns Hopkins University Press, Baltimore, Maryland 21218
The Johns Hopkins Press Ltd., London

Library of Congress Catalog Card Number 76-17299
ISBN 0-8018-1780-3 (cloth)
ISBN 0-8018-1781-1 (paper)

Library of Congress Cataloging in Publication data
will be found on the last printed page of this book.

Contents

André Burguière, *Introduction*   vii

1   **Nicole Belmont**, *Levana; or, How to Raise Up Children*   1
2   **Georges Duby**, *Lineage, Nobility, and Chivalry in the Region of Mâcon during the Twelfth Century*   16
3   **Christiane Klapisch and Michel Demonet**, *"A uno pane e uno vino": The Rural Tuscan Family at the Beginning of the Fifteenth Century*   41
4   **Emmanuel Le Roy Ladurie**, *A System of Customary Law: Family Structures and Inheritance Customs in Sixteenth-Century France*   75
5   **Micheline Baulant**, *The Scattered Family: Another Aspect of Seventeenth-Century Demography*   104
6   **Pierre Bourdieu**, *Marriage Strategies as Strategies of Social Reproduction*   117
7   **Jacques Depauw**, *Illicit Sexual Activity and Society in Eighteenth-Century Nantes*   145
8   **Witold Kula**, *The Seigneury and the Peasant Family in Eighteenth-Century Poland*   192
9   **Jean Cuisenier**, *Kinship and Social Organization in The Turko-Mongolian Cultural Area*   204
10   **André Burguière**, *From Malthus to Max Weber: Belated Marriage and the Spirit of Enterprise*   237
11   **Françoise Lautman**, *Differences or Changes in Family Organization*   251

Introduction

This special issue* became necessary and, in a sense, has composed itself. In the last few years studies of the family have flourished throughout the social sciences. For some of these sciences, particularly ethnology and sociology, family studies are a classic theme. For historians, it is a new problem. It may be the weakness—or the special calling—of history that it can only deal with an institution and measure its importance for the development of society when that institution is beginning to break down, when it is undergoing a crisis. Could it be that historical understanding, like the owl of Minerva, is condemned to take flight only at nightfall?

Instead of wondering what the historian's sudden interest in the problems of the family portends for contemporary society, we should ask ourselves why this interest was lacking for so long. Historical scholarship has crystalized around the notion of the state or the nation. This preference can be explained quite simply in practical terms. Historical sources, the raw materials of the historian, are more numerous and more accessible in public than in private archives. And history assumed its new role as a research discipline precisely at the moment when the first public archival collections came into being; indeed, it did so under their aegis.

In addition, however, the historian looked to the state on account of clearly ideological reasons. Unlike the natural sciences, which endeavor to break down what ordinary experience shows to be a whole in order to reach the constituent parts, history has operated on the basis of the romantic notion that man fully realizes himself only through a collective destiny. In order to fall within the historian's purview, man must rid himself of everything that pertains to his individual dimension. Such a romantic notion was not without practical use: the elaboration of national histories enabled nationalities and the various nationalist movements to justify their existence in terms of their origin. The high value attached

*Annales, E.S.C. 27 (July-October 1972).

to political history (conceived as history of the state) justified the strengthening of the state.

In such a context, the family was not only neglected; it was rejected as a mere by-product of reality, as something that stood in the way of change, in the way of history. Scholarship had no right to concern itself with the family, except to draw from it anecdotal and biographical information; but it was out of the question to use it as a means for finding generally applicable explanations. In this manner, genealogists and biographers imprisoned the family in a kind of lesser branch of history that was, furthermore, almost always of a reactionary persuasion. Ethnology and sociology eventually rehabilitated the family as a legitimate area of research; but the basic assumptions did not change. It was only when the society under study did not fall within the realm of history (and the expression used was "society without history" or "society without state") that the family not only furnished a proper framework for analysis but also became one of the factors that helped to explain that society.

It is therefore tempting to see this refusal to grant the family a place in the discourse of history as more than a simple rejection. Historical scholarship is a daughter of the bourgeois nineteenth century. I should like to put forth the hypothesis that historical scholarship conceived of itself as the history of the state and of nations not because it was uninterested in the family but, on the contrary, out of excessive deference to it and out of fear of subjecting to critical analysis an institution that was too closely tied to the whole system of values and the functioning of bourgeois society.

We should not underestimate the utopian component in the work of the historians of the nineteenth century. They hoped to recreate the past in the light of a future they envisioned in such a way that it would be possible to trace a straight line of progress from one to the other. And indeed, from Thomas More to Campanella, from Fourier to Cabet, all utopias exalt the state and reject the family. We now realize, of course, that the strengthening of the family during the bourgeois era—not only as the focal point of a new morality and a new way of looking at life but also as a shelter for property and a vehicle for capitalist accumulation—has by no means led to the decline of the state. And yet it is probably the single most important result of the recent preoccupation of historians with the problems of the family that the constant conflicts between the state and the family, the two competing institutions in the development of a society, have been brought to light. It appears that whenever the state no longer wields enough power to act and to protect its people, the family expands, assumes control of every aspect of the individual's life, and becomes a bastion. Whenever the state becomes stronger, the family shrinks, loosens the affective ties it had imposed on the individual, who is then more readily integrated into society as a whole. The strengthening of the lineage as Georges Duby has described it for the seigneurial class of the region of Mâcon around the year one thousand must be seen in the context of the uncertainties and the political vacuum of that period and in the context of the consolidation of feudal power. The strengthening of the lineage that Emmanuel Le Roy Ladurie has found among the peasants of fifteenth-century Languedoc corresponds, in turn, to the breakdown of that feudal power.

Are we, today, witnessing the surfacing of something that has been repressed? The family has again forced its way into the domain of history, thanks in large part to sociology, anthropology, and psychoanalysis, a field that historians are finally taking seriously.* We therefore felt no qualms about listening to these neighboring disciplines and about making room for them in this special issue. But essentially we were guided by the course taken by historical research itself. Twenty years ago now, Ernest Labrousse urged historians to undertake a systematic study of the notarial archives with a view to making a definitive investigation of the bourgeoisie.[1] The reconstitution of the family by means of marriage contracts, inventories after death, and other sources of this nature seemed to be the surest method of doing good social history. Today, this approach to the family as the supporting pillar of wealth and economic power is being so widely used in the writing of history that it seemed unnecessary to include it in this volume.

Instead, we felt that a large place should be given to historical demography.† Family reconstitution by means of a system of file cards, developed by Louis Henry, has provided a starting point for the analysis of family life, and historians are just beginning to exploit the possibilities of such an analysis. Originally conceived as a tool for the exact study of changes in fertility, family reconstitution has evolved into a body of sources that can be used for experimental purposes in such a way that the historian sometimes feels that he is seeing the social tissue, cell by cell, under the lens of his microscope.

---

*This last statement refers to an article by Edmond Ortigues, "Psychoanalysis and the Institutions of the Family" (pp. 1901–1104),which, to our regret, we were unable to include in this volume due to the limited space at our disposal.—Eds.

[1]At the Congress of the Historical Sciences, Rome, 1955.

†A number of the articles on historical demography in the special issue of *Annales, E.S.C.*, do not appear in this selection. Generally speaking, we feel that the techniques of historical demography are fairly well known to the English-speaking specialist; furthermore, some of the articles are available in English (Peter Laslett, R. S. Schofield). Certain other articles (David Sabean, Herbert G. Gutman) were excluded for the same reason. On the other hand, we included an article from another issue of *Annales, E.S.C.* (Nicole Belmont), in order to show the broad range of aspects under which the family can be considered.—Eds.

A number of areas remain to be explored. We must test the widely shared hypothesis concerning family structures (typology of the family according to size and degrees of kinship recognized within the kinship group, relationship between family size and the functioning of authority, etc.); we must also deal with behavior and understand its underlying moral norms. To this end, the family can be considered on three levels, for it is a biological entity (the conjugal family as it appears on the file card of the demographer), a social entity (since family structures determine the elementary social structures), and a focus of personal feelings. Historical demography in its widest sense thus presents us with an ambitious program, which the present volume hopes to submit to the reflection of all the social sciences.

André Burguière
Translated by Elborg Forster

1

Levana; or, How to Raise Up Children

Nicole Belmont

At the birth of a child the ancient Romans had a well-known custom of taking the newborn, "still red from his mother's blood," as Ovid says, and placing it on the ground at its father's feet. If the latter recognized the child and decided to take care of its needs, he would raise it up from the ground and take it in his arms. But if he doubted its legitimacy, if the child was misshapen, or if the birth had been accompanied by bad omens, then he would not raise it up. The child would be exposed and abandoned. Slaves would place it in a basket and carry it, by night, to a place destined for this use—the foot of the Lactaria column, for example. Sometimes the infant was picked up there by a stranger and either adopted or brought up to be a slave. I should like to shed some light on this gesture of raising up the newborn child, for there seem to be parallels to it in other systems of customs and beliefs, parallels that appear either as gestures or as words. What, then, do we mean by "raise up a child," aside from the ordinary sense of that expression?

This Roman custom has been noted by a number of ancient authors.[1] According to them, and in Gustave Witowski's free compilation of these texts,[2] "the midwife took the newborn, still red from the mother's blood, and placed it on the ground. This was done for three reasons: to make the child cry upon contact with the ground in order to invoke the god Vagitanus with this first cry; also to see if the child was straight

Annales, E.S.C. 28 (January–February 1973): 77–89. Translated by Elborg Forster.

[1]To cite a few: Ov. *Tr* 4.3.46; Varro *Antiq.,* bks. 1, 14, 15, 17, 24; Tert. *Ad Nat.* 2.2; Suet. *Ner.* 6; August. *De civ. D.* 4.2.

[2]Gustave Joseph Witkowski, *Histoire des accouchements chez tous les peuples* (Paris, 1887).

(*auspicaretur rectus esse*) and thus agreeable to the conjugal gods; and finally to make it greet Ops, or Earth, 'our common mother.' Further, under the auspices of the goddess Levana, the father was supposed to seize the child and raise it up from the ground. Yet he never lifted up a girl, being afraid of bad omens." This, then, was a juridical gesture in the sense in which the Romans understood it, namely, permeated with religious meaning. For a divinity, Levana (one of the *indigitamenta*), presided over the ritual, inasmuch as it took place under her auspices and inasmuch as she personified the father's gesture of recognition.

In his famous book *Mutter Erde*,[3] Albrecht Dieterich has studied this ritual, which is of great importance to his argument. This argument does not directly concern us here, for it is obviously somewhat outdated; but the author cites a number of similar practices from a more recent folkloric tradition. These may or may not be derived from the ancient Roman custom, but they are certainly its equivalent. In the Abruzzi mountains, "the midwife places the newborn on the ground as soon as it is washed and swaddled."[4] It is true that this account does not emphasize the act of lifting up the child, but we should note that the term for "midwife" in Italian is *levatrice*—"she who lifts." May we not assume that the Italian midwife has inherited this characteristic from the ancient Levana, since it appears in her name and sometimes in her ritual function, too? In the Abruzzi, we are also told, the child must be placed for an instant on the hearthstone, so that its bones may harden.[5] It was also said that it was the aim of the Roman custom to make the child strong and, in particular, to give him the strength he would need later when he wished to rise up from the ground.

Dieterich also cites some examples from Germany. He feels that this custom is part of the old Germanic-Scandinavian tradition. In Württemberg the midwife places the newborn on the ground and the father lifts it up.[6] In Herzogovina, the newborn is swaddled after its first bath, and then a woman places it on the ground at a crossroads. She hides nearby and as soon as someone passes, she presents the child to him, saying: "Receive, godfather, your godchild; may God and Saint John help you." If the individual is willing to stand godfather, he lifts up the child.[7] Here the godfather substitutes for the father, but the scheme of the ritual of recognition is the same. This practice is often justified by the reasons

[3]Albrecht Dieterich, *Mutter Erde. Ein Versuch über Volksreligion*, 2d ed. (Leipzig and Berlin, 1913).

[4]"Lavato e infasciato il neonato la levatrice lo posa in terra," in *Curiosità populari tradizionali*, ed. Giuseppe Pitré (Turin and Palermo, 1894), pp. 64 ff.

[5]Ibid.

[6]Elard Hugo Meyer, *Badisches Volksleben im 19. Jahrhundert* (Strasbourg, 1900), p. 15.

[7]*Wissenschaftliche Mitteilungen aus Bosnien und der Herzegowina* 6, no. 19 (1899): 612.

we have already noted: the child will grow up to be strong and hard working, but also intelligent, humble, and so forth.

Indeed, this ritual of recognition is a rather familiar ingredient of our "mythology of gestures." Newborn royal children were presented to the crowd in this manner. An obscure homonym of the famous accoucheur Dubois tells us that after the birth of the King of Rome, "Napoleon, yielding to one of his poetic inspirations, as he so often did, firmly grasped his son's body under the arms, lifted him up in his powerful hands and strode toward the door of the salon, where all the great notables of the Empire had assembled: 'Gentlemen,' he cried, 'here is the King of Rome!'"[8]

This custom does not seem to be peculiar to the Indo-European tradition. Equivalents can be found elsewhere in the world.

In Thailand, as soon as a child is born, the midwife cuts the umbilical cord, washes the child, and places it on a flat basket or, according to some authors, a winnowing basket.[9] Next to it, she puts a book and a pencil if it is a boy, a needle and thread if it is a girl, in order to conjure forth future talents. She also adds both the piece of bark from the tree (*thrysostadys siamensis*) that has served to cut the cord and the lump of earth on which it was cut. Then the midwife takes the basket and bounces it very lightly, though enough to shake the child. This she repeats three times, saying, "Three days a spirit child, four days a human child! What is this child? Take it!" One of the women present answers: "It is mine," and she lifts up the basket with the child. This woman is called *mee jog*, literally, "the mother or woman who lifts or lifts up." She gives the midwife a token payment and then places the basket next to the mother.

It is striking to find such similarity of gestures over such vast distances of time and space. The object of these two rituals—in ancient Rome and in Thailand—can be reduced to a common scheme if we make allowances for differences in social structures. In both cases the child must be integrated into the human world. In ancient Rome, a strongly patrilineal society, it was the paterfamilias who brought about this integration. In Thailand the ritual is more complex. Its first purpose is to seize the soul of the child, which is very volatile (*anima vagula, blandula*), and thus "finish" its person. The second purpose is to integrate the child into a human family. Simplifying matters somewhat, one might say that in ancient Rome—and this is not surprising—integration into the human

---

[8]Frédéric Dubois, *Eloges de l'Académie de Médecine*, cited in Gustave Joseph Witkowski, *Les accouchements à la cour* (Paris, 1890), p. 368.

[9]P. Anuman Rajhadhon, "Customs Connected with Birth and the Rearing of Children," *Southeast Asian Birth Customs* (New Haven, 1965), p. 147. See also, for China, the article by Marcel Granet, "Le dépôt de l'enfant sur le sol. Rites anciens et ordalies mythiques," *Revue Archéologique* 14 (1922): 305–61.

world was achieved by integrating an individual into a social unit by socialization; while in Thai society this integration involves, first of all, detaching the newborn from the world of spirits, an indispensible step toward making it into a human being.

On Eddystone Island, one of the Solomons, scholars have noted a connection between the act of climbing (especially climbing trees) and birth.[10] One of the indigenous words, *pondo*, designates a spirit who protects men from falling when they climb trees; but this word also means "to give birth, to be born." When a man falls out of a tree and dies, he is left to hang on the rope to which he had been attached (just like the fetus is attached to the umbilical cord), and the women have a ritual in which they come to insult him, calling him a "miscarriage." Furthermore, one of the funeral rites, that of the eighth day, is called *ake sage*, from *ake*, "to carry in one's arms," and *sage*, "to climb, to issue from the womb." The author concludes: "There is a parallel between being born and climbing trees." This was not the main point of the article, but it might be interesting to pursue this lead further.

Among the Tarahumara, "the shaman comes to take care of the child on the third day after birth. A great fire of cornhusks is lit and the child is placed on a blanket which the shaman lifts up with the help of the father. Three times he passes it back and forth through the smoke in the direction of the four cardinal points, finally holding it up into the air. This ceremony is supposed to make the child grow well and bring him luck, especially for growing corn."[11]

Fire also played a role in the ancient Greek rite of the child's integration, the *amphidromia*. This took place on the sixth day after birth, the father having decided to raise the child and not to expose it in a public place. During the ceremony, the naked father, carrying the child in his arms, described a circle around the hearth of the house. Many reasons for this ritual have been advanced.[12] Its purpose may have been to bring the child into contact with the purifying force of fire; it may have been to integrate the child into the family by contact with the domestic hearth; it also may have been to make the child a lightfooted and swift runner. Most authors feel, however, that this ritual gave the infant its human personality and integrated it into a social unit, the family. This gesture, unlike the Roman and Thai customs, did not emphasize the act of lifting up the child as much as that of making it describe a "magic circle" in the

---

[10]C. Barraud, "De la chasse aux têtes à la pêche à la bonite. Essai sur la chefferie à Eddystone," *L'Homme* 12, no. 1 (1972): 67–104.

[11]Karl S. Lumholtz, *Unknown Mexico: A Record of Five Years' Exploration of the Western Sierra Madre, in the Tierra Caliente of Tepic and Jalisco, and among the Tarascos of Michoacan* (New York, 1902), 1: 272.

[12]William R. Halliday, *Greek and Roman Folklore* (New York, 1963), p. 30.

arms of its father. This ritual may, in fact, have been the opposite of the Roman gesture, since the child does not seem to have been placed on the ground beforehand. Knowing as we do that some rituals and practices expressly forbade any contact with the earth, it would be interesting to contrast these with the Roman gesture that involved laying the child on the ground and having it lifted up by the father.

In the last part of the *Golden Bough* cyclus, Frazer has collected a large number of rites concerning the injunction against touching the earth and also the complementary prescriptions for being "suspended between heaven and earth."[13] Royal personages are often subject to this taboo. The Mikado of Japan was not permitted to touch his foot to the ground; he was always carried on men's backs or walked on mats spread before him. Chroniclers have reported the same fact about Montezuma. Under certain circumstances ordinary people, even things, can be subject to this prohibition. Among the Dayak, a newly married couple must not touch the ground for a certain period of time after the marriage. The Carrier Indians of British Columbia practiced cremation; the ashes of their chiefs were placed in a box and attached to the top of a mast, and that box was never allowed to touch the ground. Pliny reports in his *Natural History* that the way to speed up a slow delivery was to tear a spear from the body of a man without permitting it to touch the ground and to throw it over the house of the woman in labor. Frazer cites a number of prescriptions taken from the medical treatises of Marcellus of Bordeaux (fourth century A.D.): Colic can be treated with "a scrap of wool, taken from the forehead of a first-born lamb, if only the lamb, instead of being allowed to fall to the ground, has been caught by hand as it dropped from its dam."

Frazer has brought together all these rituals in the last phase of his cyclus in order to explain the presence of the mistletoe in the murder of Balder. Mistletoe has given rise to a great many beliefs and popular customs because of its peculiar position "between heaven and earth." But Frazer does not stop at what might be a "prestructuralist" interpretation. It is his aim to unveil gradually the symbolism of primitive thought, as one would remove, one by one, the more or less transparent masks from an image. According to Frazer, Balder is a personification of the mistletoe-bearing oak, and the mistletoe was considered to be the seat of life of the oak, perhaps because it was thought to be the visible emanation of lightning from the sky. The death of Balder, slain by a mistletoe, can be explained once it is understood that the mistletoe, his vital essence, has been torn from him.

[13]Sir James George Frazer, *The Golden Bough*, 3d ed. (London, 1913), vol. 7, *Balder the Beautiful*, pp. 1–17 (chap. 1). The examples in the following paragraphs are taken from this chapter.

Indeed, if mistletoe has been invested with magic power, it is precisely because it does not grow on the ground, but on a tree. (Frazer recalls that certain bushes and trees, such as the "flying rowan" in Sweden, also grow on walls or other trees.) The hypothesis I propose is the following: This position between heaven and earth is the visible image, not of lightning fallen from the sky onto a tree grown out of the earth, but of the child before birth carried in its mother's womb, where it, too, is suspended between heaven and earth. The symbolism of lightning, while not the last stage of the explanation, nonetheless plays a role in it. Being of an anagogical nature, the symbolism substitutes lightning for the paternal semen, the tree for the maternal womb, and the mistletoe, resulting from this conjunction, for the child that will start to grow. The belief that mistletoe was a product of lightning thus fits neatly into Frazer's framework; yet he was right to emphasize it. It is of a symbolic nature, like the entire framework, but it is special in the sense that it is the key symbol (or one of the key symbols, for there may be others) that provides access to the meaning of this belief.

Thus we notice that the rituals concerning royal personages consist of placing them in an intrauterine situation, like unborn children, who are suspended between heaven and earth. Having cited the prohibitions against touching the ground, Frazer cites those against seeing the sun.[14] This second taboo often applies to the same persons, which is easy to understand if we are speaking of an intrauterine position, for unborn children cannot see the sun. They are of this world but not in it. These prohibitions are sometimes applied during rites of passage, and it has long been known that these often involve a symbolic sequence of death, gestation, and birth.[15]

I shall now attempt to prove this hypothesis by using the various beliefs and practices surrounding mistletoe.

It is not surprising that mistletoe has excited people's imagination, for it possesses some rather unusual characteristics. It is a parasitic plant that can grow only on living woody plants. Its mode of germination has been noted since Antiquity: its seeds are transported by birds, particularly in their excrement. Pliny has this to say about it: "However one tries to sow it, it will not grow; it must be swallowed and then eliminated by birds, especially ring-doves and thrushes. It is in the nature of this plant that it can only grow after it has matured in the stomach of a bird" (*HN* 16. 93).

There is another connection between birds and mistletoe: it was from this plant that bird-lime for trapping birds was made ("to lime birds," it was called). A Latin proverb expressed this paradox: *Turdus sibimet ipsi*

[14]Ibid., pp. 17–19.
[15]A. Van Gennep, *Les rites de passage* (Paris, 1969).

malum cacat ("the thrush excretes its own misfortune"); it was applied to people who furnish the means for their own destruction, just as the birds transport the seeds of the plant that will furnish the substance used to snare them.

Once the plant has germinated, its root grows toward the center of the branch to which it is attached, while the stem grows in the opposite direction. Thus, the stem may grow vertically downward, or horizontally, or at an angle, contrary to the usual rule that plants grow vertically upward. The sprigs of the mistletoe multiply in a rather symmetrical, regular fashion, by twos, so that the tuft of mistletoe eventually comes to look like a ball.

Taking the step from a more or less mythological botany to a mythology that might be called botanical, we shall now examine the popular beliefs about mistletoe and, in particular, its use in the traditional pharmacopoeia. In the book *Flore populaire* by Eugène Rolland,[16] we are informed that in the French department of Cher, mistletoe was given to female domestic animals to induce an abortion or to hasten a delivery; it was used to bring down the milk in goats and was also given to goats so that they would not bring forth stillborn kids. In Belgium, mistletoe is hung on stable doors; people also like to "encase it in silver" and to make it into necklaces for children—in that case, the mistletoe must not have touched the ground. In Freiburg the proverb "a mistletoe-man can only suck" is used to stigmatize people who live as parasites. In many regions of Europe mistletoe was hung up over doors, for it was believed to ward off evil charms. More recently, this custom has been limited to inns, for which mistletoe has practically become the shop sign. Nor should we forget the contemporary custom of hanging a sprig of mistletoe over the threshold of a door during the Christmas season; everyone knows that walking or kissing under it will bring good luck and happiness.

But the most lively part of our historical mythology of mistletoe is its use by the ancient Gauls. Since our knowledge of the religion of the Gauls is extremely scanty, the religious aspect must remain secondary. We must concern ourselves with what we consider to be the historical aspects, even though these are actually only the myth that has come down to us. So we imagine the Gallic druids, clad in white, as they cut the mistletoe and drop it onto a cloth stretched out under the tree (so that it will not touch the ground). In fact, the image probably originated in a literary text, that of Pliny (*HN* 16. 95):

In treating of this subject, the admiration in which the mistletoe is held throughout Gaul ought not to pass unnoticed. The Druids, for so they call their wizards,

[16]Eugène Rolland, *Flore populaire* (Paris, 1967), 6: 227–37.

esteem nothing more sacred than the mistletoe and the tree on which it grows, provided only that the tree is an oak. . . . The mistletoe is very rarely to be met with; but when it is found, they gather it with solemn ceremony. This they do above all on the sixth day of the moon, from whence they date the beginnings of their months. . . . A priest clad in a white robe climbs the tree and with a golden sickle cuts the mistletoe, which is caught in a white cloth. . . . They believe that a potion prepared from mistletoe will make barren animals to bring forth, and that the plant is a remedy against all poison.[17]

All of these beliefs confirm our interpretation of mistletoe as the image of the child in its mother's womb, where it is suspended between heaven and earth. And indeed, the very peculiar type of germination that is attributed to it is reminiscent of the manner in which humans are conceived, since the bird swallows the seeds that are "matured" in its stomach, according to Pliny's expression. This mode of conception is precisely one of those found in myths and fantasies, where conception is often of an oral, and birth of an anal, nature. This is one of the most frequently found infantile theories of reproduction. In his article on infantile sexuality, Freud has shown that, given the child's ignorance of the existence of the vagina and his observation of pregnant women, particularly his own mother, he considers the intestinal orifice to be the only likely place for the baby's exit: "They are born through the bowel, like a passage". Furthermore, the "cloaca theory" also has the advantage of providing an answer to the question of where babies come from: "One gets children by eating something special (as in the fairy tale)."[18]

Another image no doubt competes with this one, namely, that of the egg. And indeed, the mistletoe berries look like tiny eggs, and eggs are also expelled through the anus. This is another mode of gestation and birth.

There may be another connection between mistletoe and birds, although it is more indirect and less obvious. The mistletoe sits in the tree like a nest; its position is the same (suspended between heaven and earth), and it has something to do with birds. There is no need to stress the symbolism of the nest: being a shelter, a refuge, a secure and warm place where one feels safe, it is, in a profound sense, reminiscent of the maternal womb. This association appears in the French terminology for mistletoe: *nid d'agasse* ("magpie's nest") in the region of Namur, *nid d'hiver* ("winter nest") in the Vosges mountains, and *ni d'jenatche* ("witch's nest") in the area around Belfort.[19] Furthermore, given the fact that mistletoe is a

---

[17]This translation is by Frazer, *Balder the Beautiful*, 2: 76–77.

[18]Sigmund Freud, "Three Contributions to the Theory of Sex," in *The Basic Writings of Sigmund Freud*, ed. and trans. A. A. Brill (New York, 1938), pp. 594–96.

[19]Rolland, *Flore populaire*.

parasitic plant, it is easily assimilated to the human embryo, which lives and grows at the expense of the mother, carried and nourished by her.

The use of mistletoe in the pharmacopoeia is not surprising, since it is a rare and unusual plant. We should note, however, that the first prescription concerning its use is a warning not to let it touch the ground (and, as we have seen, it is always preserved hanging, whether it is over doors or around the necks of children). Its "natural" position between heaven and earth, which led us to formulate the hypothesis that the mistletoe is analogous to the embryo, is therefore truly an important feature in the set of beliefs concerning it. It should also be noted that its use sometimes concerns the reproduction of animals—either positively, for example, when it is said that goats that have taken it will not bring forth stillborn kids or when, according to Pliny, an infusion of mistletoe imparts fertility to all barren animals—or negatively, when it induces abortion in domestic animals or hastens deliveries.

The etymology of the word brings the decisive proof that the image of the mistletoe as embryo is well founded in ancient beliefs. The French word *gui* ("mistletoe") is derived from the Latin *viscum,-i*, n., (which, in turn, is no doubt derived from the Greek ἰξός) and also means "lime"; we have already noted that bird-lime was made from the plant; hence the terms viscous, viscosity, and so forth.[20] But there was, in Latin, also the word *viscus,-eris*, n., whose different meanings are given as follows in Gaffiot's dictionary: "1. The internal organs of the body, viscera, intestines, entrails, particularly the womb and the testicles; 2. The flesh (under the skin of humans and animals), in the figurative sense, the flesh and blood of a woman, that is, the fruit of her womb, her progeny, her child; 3. In the figurative sense, the entrails, the heart, the womb." These two words, of course, are not identical, since they belong to different declensions,[21] but it is inconceivable that the meanings of these quasi-homonyms should not have exerted a mutual influence, which would have served to reinforce the subconscious image of the mistletoe as an unborn child: it had become a symbol that made it possible to elaborate beliefs and customs.

It is possible that this concept was paralleled by the image of the mistletoe as a nest (which is attested in the literature), although the nest does not refer to the embryo, but to the maternal womb, inasmuch as it is

---

[20]It should be noted in passing that lime was later made from holly, and this may be one of the reasons why these plants are now used together during the Christmas season, aside from the fact that both are still green at this season.

[21]Ernout and Meillet's *Dictionnaire étymologique de la langue latine* gives, on the one hand, "*uiscum, -i*, n. mistletoe, bird-lime; must have some connection with Greek ἰξός, although it is not clear"; on the other hand, "*uiscus, -eris*, especially *uiscera, -um*, n., entrails, viscera; without clear etymology." It is therefore impossible to determine whether these two words have the same origin.

inside the body (and this makes us think of nesting sets of Russian dolls). This image was probably less prevalent than that of the child in the womb, but it is interesting to note this shift from the content to the container.

The mistletoe has led us into a long, but useful, digression. We have noted that one of the prescriptions for its use demanded that it must never touch the ground. Whenever it was gathered, it was dropped onto a stretched cloth, and it was always hung up if it was to be kept. This prescription is derived from the peculiar position of the mistletoe among plants, which in turn gives rise to the symbolic image of the child in the womb, in other words, to the image of pregnancy. Returning to the topic of birth now, we shall show that birth is often seen as a fall.

The Tapirapé have one word, *aán*, to say "falling" and "to be born."[22] The Guayaki say "the child falls [or drops]" for "to give birth."[23] The Ifuago, a people of the Philippines, have a whole pantheon of divinities presiding over human reproduction.[24] "They have a beneficent role," the natives say, "for they carry us in the carrying blanket (as children are carried before they can walk)." One of the prayers addressed to these divinities says: "Hold tight the *oban* ("blanket"), for if it comes apart, the baby will fall." If it falls prematurely, it is a miscarriage. At the time of birth, however, they invoke Bolang, "who undoes the baby's shoulder straps" (this probably refers to the amniotic sac from which the child emerges), and Monliktag, "who does the dropping."

The Voguls of Siberia have a custom of tearing the mother's clothes from top to bottom after she has given birth, for the child has dropped out of her body and torn it.[25]

From all of these examples emerges an image of birth complementing the image of gestation we have established on the basis of the documents cited by Frazer. The child who had been "suspended between heaven and earth" drops when it is born. The delivery is a fall. It is not certain, of course, that all cultures have rituals and beliefs expressing this image. In some cases this image may be expressed negatively. Thus, the Pala of New Ireland are very careful to keep the child's head from touching the ground during birth, for such a contact would defile it.[26] (Dieterich would not be

---

[22]H. Baldus, "Os Tapirapé, tribu Tupi no Brasil Central", *Revisto do Arquivo Municipal*, Vol. [?], pp. 96–105, 107–24, 127.

[23]Paper given by P. Clastres in the seminar of Claude Lévi-Strauss.

[24]Roy F. Barton, *The Religion of the Ifuagos*, American Anthropological Association Memoir no. 65 (Menasha, Wis., 1946), pp. 43–47.

[25]E. I. Rombanjejewa, "Einige Sitten und Bräuche der Mausen (Wogulen) bei der Geburt der Kinder," in *Glaubenswelt und Folklore der Sibirischen Völker* (Budapest, 1963).

[26]P. K. Neuhaus, *Beiträge zur Ethnographie der Pala, Mittel-Neu-Irland* (Cologne, 1962).

too happy about this.) The Pala feel that it is cause for rejoicing when the birth is such that this contact cannot take place—namely, when the child is born with a "caul," that is, with its head covered by part of the amniotic sac so that it cannot directly touch the ground, or when it is born feet, rather than head, first. These two kinds of birth confer upon children a privileged, almost aristocratic, status. The women, in particular, treat children born in these ways with a great deal of respect. It is a well-known fact that the normal presentation is by the head and that the delivery is much more difficult when the child is presented feet first (breech birth) and even impossible when it is presented athwart. One is tempted to feel that the image of birth as a fall from the mother's body does not apply if the child is born feet first. The Chinook, for example, according to the report by Franz Boas,[27] thought that the child would be born "standing up," that is, feet first, if someone stood up behind the pregnant woman. When it is born head first, the child falls to the ground. In many cultures, it is prescribed that the child must be caught on a mat by the person acting as midwife. The image of the child who is born feet first reverses that of the fall: such a child is a being who stands up from the moment of birth.

In *Les signes de la naissance* I have attempted to give an explicit account of the meaning attached to feet-first birth.[28] As a general rule, this was considered to be a bad sign, a belief that appears to be rooted in an old Indo-European tradition. In ancient Rome, a child born in this manner was called *Agrippa*. J. Vendryès has studied the etymology of this name, which he splits into **agri-ped*, thus revealing the Sanskrit word *agra* = forward.[29] *Agrippa* would thus mean "feet forward" and would be derived from the oldest sources of the Indo-European vocabulary. The baneful connotations of this presentation are explained by its association with death. Pliny says so explicitly: "It is in the order of nature that we come into the world head first and go out of it feet first."[30] This statement is confirmed by many beliefs, customs, and tales. Thus, the dead are always carried out of the house feet first, as indicated by the familiar French saying *"partir les pieds devant."* In a certain region of Hungary, if people wanted to know whether there would soon be a birth or a death in the house, they would throw a shoe across the room. If it came to rest with the heel pointing toward the door, it would be a birth; if it was the front of the shoe, they could soon expect a death. One of Grimm's fairy tales, *The*

---

[27]Franz Boas, *Chinook Texts,* Smithsonian Institution, Bureau of American Ethnology Bulletin no. 20 (Washington, D.C., 1894), p. 242.

[28]Nicole Belmont, *Les signes de la naissance. Etude des représentations symboliques associées aux naissances singulières* (Paris, 1971).

[29]J. Vendryès, "Agrippa et Vopiscus," in *Misceânea scientifica et literaria dedicado ao Doutor J. Leite de Vasconcellos* (Coimbra, Port., 1934), 1: 428–33.

[30]Pliny, *HN* 7.8.

Godfather,[31] tells how a poor man received from a stranger a vial with water that would permit him to heal the sick: ". . . Only thou must see where Death is standing. If he stands by the patient's head, give the patient the water, and he will be healed; but if Death is standing by his feet, all trouble will be in vain, for the sick man must die." Life then is associated with the head and death with the feet. The axis of life runs from the head to the feet in birth, but from the feet to the head in death, and also in a feet-first birth. Such a birth, therefore, violates the order of nature: if death is the inversion of the order in which a person is born, this inversion has already taken place when a child comes into the world feet first.

Now, if birth is a fall, this is the case only if the child is born head first. If it is born feet first, it does not drop, but is born "standing up," as the Chinook say. In many populations, the "bodily technique" of delivery (to use Mauss's expression) is a standing position for the mother, who often holds on to the branch of a tree so that the child will present itself by the head. This, for example, is the custom of the Tarahumara, whose ceremony after the delivery we have already described. The women give birth standing up, holding on to a branch over their head. The child drops into a nest of grass that has been prepared beforehand.[32] A nineteenth-century traveler reports that in Loango in French Equatorial Africa the women give birth standing up, leaning against the walls of their huts, or else on their knees, with their head resting on their arms, so that the child will be born head first.[33] Here the vertical position of the mother appears to be taken as the prerequisite for the head-first birth of the child, which is taken to be horizontal.

The gesture of the Roman paterfamilias is analogous, though in the opposite sense. The father is called upon to take the child that is lying in a horizontal position and to raise it up following the axis of his own body, in other words, to give the child a vertical position. The "natural" birth of the child thus takes place in horizontality, the "social" birth in verticality. The gesture by which the father—as we have pointed out—brings the child into the family and into society consists of giving it a vertical dimension. This also sheds light on the phrase *ut auspicaretur rectus est*, which is not completely translated by "to see if it is not deformed (or sickly)." It must also be taken quite literally: a straight child will be a man able to stand up, a vertical being. It is only after the child has passed this test that the father decides to admit him into the family, by conferring

[31]*Grimm's Household Tales*, ed. and trans. Margaret Hunt, 2 vols. (London, 1910), 1: 168–79.

[32]Wendell C. Bennett and Robert M. Zingg, *The Tarahumara. An Indian Tribe of Northern Mexico* (Chicago, 1935), p. 234.

[33]Cited by George Julius Engelman, *La pratique des accouchements chez les peuples primitifs* (Paris, 1886).

upon him the status of human being in the gesture of raising him up. At the same time, this gesture is also a commitment to "raise,"[34] that is, educate him. It should be recalled that the Latin verb *tollere*, like the French verb *élever* [and the English verb *to raise*] was used in a literal as well as a figurative sense: it meant both "to lift" and "to educate." This metaphorical sense was perceived by a nineteenth-century writer, Jean-Paul Richter, who published a treatise on the raising of children under the title *Levana*, the name of the Roman divinity who presided over this ritual.

It is striking to note that this vertical position of man, eminently natural though it be, is also charged with cultural meaning. Within the framework of his semiotics and semantics of gesture, J. A. Greimas sees gesticulation as a social phenomenon.[35] Of particular interest to our problem is the fact that he stresses "the weight of gravity in the human body which, in a sense, emphasizes two spatial axes":

1. The vertical axis, being the direction in which gravity exerts itself, is the condition for the categories of contact versus non-contact of the human mass in relation to other masses. This axis can either stress non-contact, by making the body appear liberated from the laws of gravity (as in ballet), or it can make use of certain of its possibilities by deviating from the norm (as in walking on the hands in acrobatics).

2. As for the horizontal axis, it constitutes the solid (or liquid, in the case of swimming) surface which "naturally" calls for movement, as opposed to the "natural" posture of standing still. However, the articulation "horizontal ground" versus "vertical man" is generally seen as the inchoative position preceeding mobility, even though this view is only partially justified.

Recall that one of the peculiarities of mistletoe is its ability, not present in most other plants, to grow in every direction—horizontally, downward, or obliquely. This shows very clearly that the image of mistletoe is the opposite of man, whose vertical stance is directed against gravity, just as the growth of most other plants resists the influence of gravity. Mistletoe, however, is like the child in the womb, which is free to adopt all possible orientations, since it is floating in the amniotic fluid.

We also know that the acquisition of the vertical position was one of the most important stages in the process of human evolution. "The first and most important criterion common to all men and their ancestors is

[34]The Latin verb *tollere* points to the root *tela-*, which is also found in the Greek word τελαμών = "holding-strap." Cf. the birth divinities of the Ifuago, who keep a tight hold on the carrying blanket during pregnancy and drop it at the time of birth (Barton, *Religion of the Ifuago*, p. 17).

[35]A. J. Greimas, "Conditions d'une sémiotique du monde naturel," *Langages* 10 (June 1968): 10. This article is a brilliant introduction to an entire issue on "practices and languages of the gesture."

their vertical stance. . . .All the human fossils known to science, even those that are as strange as Australopithecus, possessed the vertical stance," asserts André Leroi-Gourhan.[36] Even better: "As soon as a creature has established its vertical stance, it is no longer an animal, nor even a half-man." And indeed, "human existence in a vertical position leads to neuro-psychic developments by which the development of the brain becomes more than mere growth in size. The development of face and hand remains as closely interrelated as ever during the stage of brain development. The use of the tool by the hand and of language by the face are the two poles of the same mechanism."[37]

It is fascinating to note that the Roman gesture symbolically reproduces the scheme of the evolution of man as described by Leroi-Gourhan, for it involves the act of "verticalization," the freeing of the upper extremities for prehension, and the acquisition of language. These are the three striking features of the ritual: the two-fold gesture of taking and raising the child, in conjunction with the verbal element of calling it "to raise a child." This ritual invokes a symbolism that recalls, as it were, the entire history of the race. A newborn child is integrated into society in a ritual that symbolically reenacts man's accession to full humanity in its most essential features: verticality, the ability to grasp with the upper extremities, and language—all of which also imply that a society exists. As a symbol for the history of the race, the Roman gesture also symbolizes speech; but the relationship between the two is difficult to interpret. Their meaning is the same, and it can only be expressed in the tautological form, "to raise a child." It is this very tautology that gave the Roman ritual its "symbolic effectiveness."

We might be able to distinguish between what is expressed in the gesture (and thus is not said) and its meaning (which may be given a verbal expression) by describing the former in the passive form "a child is raised," after the manner in which Freud elucidates the fantasy "a child is beaten."[38] This formulation, thanks to its grammatical rigidity, its opaqueness, as it were, would make it possible to translate what the gesture wishes to convey, whereas the expression "to raise a child" is more specifically related to language because of its many flexional possibilities.[39] The obscure connections between this gesture and this verb may enable us to state the difficult and perennial question as to the relationship between myth and ritual in somewhat different terms.

[36]André Leroi-Gourhan, *Le geste et la parole,* vol. 1, *Technique et langage* (Paris, 1964), p. 32.

[37]Leroi-Gourhan, *Technique et langage*, p. 34.

[38]Sigmund Freud, "On bat un enfant," *Revue française de Psychanalyse* 6, nos. 3–4, 274–94.

[39]For the theory of these problems, the reader is referred to the article by J.-P. Valabrega, "Le phantasme, le mythe, et le corps," *Topique* 9 (1972).

It seems clear that there is no such thing as a ritual gesture that is totally independent of any verbal element. The minimal expression "verbal element" was chosen purposely, for it may simply be a matter, as in the Roman gesture, of one verb and its complement. On the other hand, it may also be a myth whose narration takes several days. But at times, this verbal element seems to be missing: while certain rituals are founded on specific myths that they serve to illustrate, so that there is a continuous reciprocal relationship between them, others appear to the observer to stand on their own. The fact is that in these cases the verbal element is not missing but is to be found elsewhere. Claude Lévi-Strauss has shown, for example, that a series of myths of the Pawnee (North American Plains Indians) stands in a close relationship of correlation and opposition with the ritual of certain other tribes of Plains Indians, particularly the Mandan and the Hidatsa.[40] In other cases, the verbal element may not be so far removed; it may be present in the same cultural context as the ritual but appear unrelated to it. If this is the case, we must try to discover it where it is, present and hidden at the same time. In the example we have chosen to examine here, it was so near that one was apt to miss it; it was nothing more than the shift from the literal to the figurative sense, a matter of "going beyond"; in short, a metaphor.

---

[40]Claude Lévi-Strauss, "Structure et dialectique," in *Anthropologie structurale* (Paris, 1958), pp. 257–66.

2

Lineage, Nobility, and Chivalry in the Region of Mâcon during the Twelfth Century

Georges Duby

Twenty years ago I was putting the finishing touches to my book on society in the region of Mâcon during the eleventh and twelfth centuries. The recent reprinting of this work has made me realize the necessity of reexamining the text on more than one point and especially on one specific question. Steeped as I was at that time in the work of Marc Bloch, I interpreted chivalry in southern Burgundy as the progressive crystallization during the eleventh century of a much less clearly defined social stratum which, prior to the year 1000, had been designated as the "nobility." During the last twenty years, the problem of the relationships between chivalry and the nobility has been posed in another manner as a result of research carried out in other French provinces. For Léopold Génicot, in particular, nobles and knights in the region of Namur during the twelfth century formed two superposed strata that were clearly isolated from one another. Unsettled by these assertions, I was eager to reread the documents I had used earlier. This article is the result of my reexamination.

Annales: E.S.C. 27 (July–October 1972): 803–23. Translated by Patricia M. Ranum.

Southern Burgundy offers very few narrative sources for the eleventh century. None of the genealogical texts can be found there which, in the case of other provinces, permit us to perceive the idea that contemporaries had of their family's antiquity, that is to say, of their nobility. On the other hand, for the tenth and eleventh centuries, the cartularies of religious establishments—particularly of the abbey of Cluny—provide documentary material that is richer and more abundant than anywhere else, thus permitting us to observe the higher levels of the social hierarchy more clearly there than elsewhere. To make this picture even more precise, I have chosen to limit this reexamination to a more restricted geographical area than the one included in my first study. I have concentrated upon the region where the documentation is the richest and most unbroken, an area of less than two hundred square kilometers in the immediate vicinity of the abbey of Cluny, a zone in which property acquisitions by the monastery were the earliest and most numerous.

Comprising about forty rural townships today, in the year 1000 the region included forty-five parishes, about a hundred hamlets and peasant settlements, and four castles—Lourdon, which belonged to Cluny, and three others, Berzé, Uxelles, and la Bussière, which were in the hands of lay lords who were at that time busy building up around each of these fortresses an autonomous territory which was blocked along one of its borders by the "*ban de Cluny*," that protective zone which attempted to establish the institutions of the Peace of God around about the monastery. Such was the region of my research.

The aim of this study was to take a cross section of society and go back to the end of the eleventh century and pick out all the male owners of lay property who were active between 1080 and 1100 and whose descendants are known to have borne the title "knight" during the twelfth century. As much as possible I restricted my male landowners to a single generation, thus excluding uncles and fathers who were still living and sons who were already adults during the period of the sample. I also eliminated certain men who were present in the region but held only marginal possessions and appeared only occasionally in written sources. (This is particularly true in the case of the three other masters of castles—Bâgé and Montmerle in Bresse, and Bourbon on the Loire—and of a few families from the aristocracy of the Charolais region.) In this manner I was able to track down five hundred individuals in all, individuals belonging to thirty-four family groups—thirty-four "houses," seven of them broken down into two or three branches of cousins. In all this makes forty-one *fraternitates*, or groups of brothers. Beginning with this sample, I set out first of all to fit these individuals into a genealogy and, by following the generations backward, to find their most distant ancestors. Next I attempted to see—by noting down all the social attributes of these five hundred individuals and their ascendants in the charters and notices that refer to them—whether these lineages were at the time considered to be noble or knightly.

In the documents dating from 1080–1100, family groups were clearly set apart by a *cognomen*, a family name that brothers and cousins bore in common. Actually, three of these *cognomina* were each borne by two distinct groups; property holders in the same places, they were related, but very distantly, and had by that time formed separate lineages. Let us also note that of the thirty-one family names used, seven were nicknames that had become hereditary; two of them, which merit our attention, were those of two of the three castle owners. The twenty-seven others were names associated with the land, that is, with the family's landed patrimony, its inheritance.

Anyone starting from this solid base and attempting to set off in search of ancestors is sure to encounter serious difficulties. First, the documentation is far from being consistently rich. Very plentiful around the year 1000, the documentation becomes increasingly scarce as the eleventh century progresses. There are two principal reasons for this. First of all, the flood of alms offered to religious establishments progressively waned while written records of donations gradually became less common. Thus, the cartularies of the monastery of Cluny and of the cathedral of Mâcon, our chief sources, are markedly poorer as we approach 1100 than they were a century earlier. Second, the expansion of ecclesiastical property in the region under study gradually eliminated lay proprietors; the latter were pushed back bit by bit to the land they still held on the outskirts of this zone; as a result they slowly drift out of our purview. If we add the increasing vagueness of the chronology of the records, and especially of the charters and notices of Cluny, in the second half of the eleventh century, the difficulty of linking the generation that is the subject of the initial study to the one that was active a century earlier, around the year 1000, becomes evident.

To succeed in our task we must use three sorts of evidence: specific mention of kinships found in the documents; surnames; and individual names which in many cases had been inherited from ancestors, but according to rules that perhaps were not absolutely inflexible at the period or that are in any case not clear to us. The first clue becomes weaker as the search goes farther back into time. In acts guaranteeing the transfer of rights, the indication of kinship was more frequent, since blood links were stronger and the individual felt less free, vis-à-vis men of his blood line, to dispose of his inheritance. But kinship structures—I will return to this point—were apparently modified during the eleventh century in the direction of a progressive narrowing of lineal solidarity. As a result, the indications of filiation or of kinship were much more numerous in 1100 than in 1000, and it is therefore more difficult at the earlier date to connect the members of the aristocracy to a family group and to link them to their descendants.

The second group of indications also begins to break up rather rapidly. In 1100, adding a family surname to the name of an individual making a contract was a recent innovation. Of thirty-one surnames, only fourteen appear in acts before 1070, eleven before 1050, five before 1035, and none are mentioned before 1000, when we find only the individual's name. But the use of this documentary material is itself hampered by modifications that occurred during the eleventh century as a result of a very important development that merits a thorough study but to which we can only allude here. I am referring to the progressive reduction in the number of names. The forty-seven male laymen, active in the year 1000 and identified as the ancestors of the five hundred individuals who form the basic sample, shared thirty-five names among them. Although namesakes already existed among them—seven *Bernard*s, for example, and three *Josseran*s—they were few. But for their five hundred descendants of the year 1100, only thirty-nine names were used; in other words, the name-sakes were twice as frequent. There were still seven *Bernard*s, but now there were ten *Josseran*s, fifteen *Hugues*es, twelve *Geoffroy*s, and five *Humbert*s. The phenomenon is closely related to increased use of the family surname. It also resulted from a double trend that affected kinship relations, a trend that involved both the spreading of the family tree into divergent branches and the drawing together of lineages through marriage alliances. All the same, if we consider that seventeen of the thirty-five names used in the year 1000 disappeared altogether shortly afterward and that, as a result, twenty-one of the thirty-nine names used in 1100 were newly adopted by the families under consideration, it appears that the evolution of the family name is complex and involves the combined phenomena of condensation and innovation, thus enriching further its psychological and social meaning. Indeed, of the five most common names in 1100 (they are borne by forty-nine individuals, that is to say, by more than half of the total number), one, *Hugues*, is that of the man who had been abbot of Cluny since 1049; another, *Geoffroy*, belonged to the lineage of the counts of Mâcon; while the remaining three, *Josseran*, *Bernard*, and *Humbert*, were hereditary in the two very powerful families that owned the strongest castles. Thus, of all the names that ancestors had borne, those that continued in use recalled the most prestigious roots of the ascendance or showed a relationship to the most glorious lineages of the region.

New names can be explained first of all by the exogamy to which aristocratic families were forced, being obliged to marry their children increasingly farther outside the restrictions of cousinship. But certain innovations can only be ascribed to a change in mental outlook. Thus, the intrusion of names borrowed from the New Testament—the four *Etienne*s and the two *Pierre*s found in 1100—doubtlessly result from a gradual evolution in religious iconography, while a fascination with epic heroes also may be involved, since *Girard, Roland,* and *Olivier* appear among the new names. In any event, the repetition of masculine names plays its part in smudging the surest and most direct clue provided by genealogical research.

And finally, the persons most frequently appearing in the documents I am using are unmarried or childless individuals, who were the most generous donors to the Church. The families whose history is the least obscure are those who donated the most, to the point of becoming impoverished or extinct, in any event of disappearing from our purview. On the other hand, the family groups that were the most vigorous and the most solidly anchored to their land holdings were the least generous almsgivers. As a result, they appear less frequently in cartularies. It is therefore understandable that my reconstitution of ascendants remains incomplete and uncertain.

The documents and the direct and sure indications found in them are, however, sufficiently rich to justify my efforts. Indeed, the picture becomes clearer if we also use less obvious signs which, when we encounter them linked to one another, lend solid support to a presumed kinship. We are justified in asserting that two individuals are blood relatives when they bear the same unusual name and when their hereditary possessions are on adjoining lands. The presence within a patrimony from generation to generation of certain unusual elements—a certain precarium held from a religious establishment, a certain domain composed of one compact tract of land, or a certain parish church—is a sure indication of filiation among their successive owners. Naturally, after a centuries-long sequence both of inheritances shared among heirs and of marriage alliances, land ownership in this region of allodial lands became atomized. This atomization reached such a point that, in the majority of the tracts in which the abbey of Cluny gradually developed its landed wealth, we see a mass of heirs owning land side by side. These heirs are undoubtedly related, but so distantly that it is practically impossible to untangle the skein of kinships that binds them.

I will cite as an example the lands of Sercie, eight kilometers north of Cluny. In about 1090, the cellarer of the abbey, Hugues de Bissy, a second cousin of three of the knights involved in this study, undertook to acquire these lands bit by bit by means of *conventiones* or *comparationes* concluded, says the text, "with his uncles, with other relatives, and with other men."[1] In the monastery's name he then had to deal with thirty-

---

[1] *Recueil des chartes de l'abbaye de Cluny*, ed. Bernard and Bruel (Paris, 1876–1903), nos. 3034, 3066, 3642.

seven groups of owners, among whom were ten peasant holders of allodial lands. Twenty of the hundred and five individuals included in our study are represented in these transactions, and they belong to nine family groups; three of them held their land in fief, two others in their wife's name. But five family groups, including the family of the lords of Uxelles, seem to have inherited their share of this land from a distant ancestor. This lends strength to the impression already created by the study of individual names that a close cousinship united the entire aristocratic society into a homogenous block. Because it inextricably tangles the bonds of kinship, this very coherence increases the difficulty in establishing genealogies, but it strengthens presumed kinships. In short, I believe that for any European region during this period, the results of this inquiry are the best we can expect.

Our first question must be: just how far back can we trace the genealogies of these thirty-four family groups? In other words, on the eve of the twelfth century, what was the antiquity of these families, that is to say, their "nobility," since nobility was above all a question of distant and well-established ancestors? In about 1100 was the aristocracy in this region formed by those who had inherited the old wealth? Or, on the contrary, was it composed of social climbers who had recently left behind the rank of commoner as a result of serving a master or as a result of someone's gift?

1. For four groups of brothers (families 4, 16, 17, 34 in fig. 2.1) we lack any indication of formal filiation. We do not know the father of the twelve individuals who represent them at the end of the eleventh century. But actually, for two of them (4, 34) multiple indications authorize us to reconstitute in complete safety a genealogical chart spreading over four generations. Thus, only eight persons remain whose ascendance is unknown.

2. Next come four other groups (9, 13, 24, 26), or fourteen individuals, whose fathers and uncles we can trace with certainty. Nevertheless, with the greatest degree of probability we can project the family for one of them (26) over four generations and even do likewise for two others (9, 13) over six generations.

3. Out of thirty persons representing nine other groups (6, 10, 15, 18, 20, 21, 28, 29, 33), we can clearly locate certain grandparents and, for four of these groups (6, 15, 18, 33), the genealogical chart can be prolonged to include a fourth generation.

4. Then come fourteen groups whose filiation is completely certain over four generations (1, 2, 3, 5, 8, 11, 14, 19, 23, 25, 27, 30, 31, 32); for five of them (1, 2, 3, 8, 23) a fifth generation can be added without hesitation.

5. This extension over five generations is sure for two groups (7, 12).

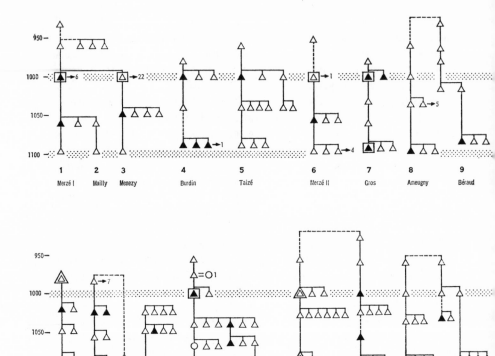

Δ adult male layman   ▲ miles   L sure filiation

O heiress   □ nobilis   ⌊. probable filiation

                        △ dominus   = matrimonial bond

                                      →₇ alliance with family 7

Figure 2.1. Genealogies of Families in This Study

6. For the thirty-fourth group (22) this extension is certain for six generations.

We can draw four conclusions on the basis of the above data. First, twenty-eight of the thirty-four families that formed the upper level of lay society at the end of the eleventh century, or more than 80 percent of the whole, appear to have already been firmly settled on the rich allodial lands before the year 1000. Without exaggerating, we could raise that figure to 95 percent. In other words, keeping in mind the amount of documentation available, we might propose that the entire aristocracy of

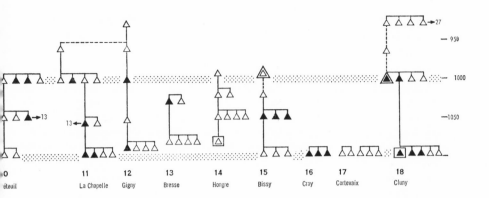

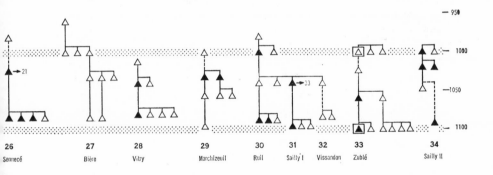

the year 1100 had been well established for more than a century at the
minimum. For twelve families, that is to say for more than a third, the
antiquity of their hold upon the land can be increased by another fifty
years.

Second, I have said that three of the thirty-four family groups each
controlled a castle and the powers of command attached to it. These three
families are among those whose ancestry can be traced furthest back. The
most distant known ancestor of the masters of the castle of Berzé and of
the castle of la Bussière were active in about 960, and probably as far back

as 940, while that of the masters of the castle of Uxelles was active in about 980. However, our research does not permit us to trace deeper roots for these family trees, which were more powerful than the others in the twelfth century. The family known to be the most ancient of all is not among them; the first representative of the dynasty commanding the castle of Uxelles appears in written sources later than that of eight lineages, and probably later than eleven. Of course, we must take into account the gaps in the documentary material upon which this data is based, for members of the lay aristocracy step out of the shadows only because of their contacts with religious establishments. Indeed, three-fourths of the genealogical charts that go furthest back into the past involve families owning land in the region in which the landed fortune of Cluny first spread, and the family of the lords of Uxelles is not among them. The important point here is that the line of men who, in about the year 1000, set about building an independent castellany around the fortress in which they had become established, do not appear to have had any allodial wealth going further back than that of many of the neighboring lineages. In other words, we cannot assert that it was because their family position was better established locally that these three families were able to begin the climb—implemented by appropriating for themselves the powers of the ban and its profits—that placed them clearly above the others in the hierarchy of power and wealth by the end of the eleventh century. On the contrary, it is possible to propose that the progressive emergence of these lineages resulted from the fact that one of their ancestors, through the good luck of having been delegated authority in some manner we cannot discover, had become settled in a preexisting castle.

Third, the oldest branches of these families (one, without doubt; nine, in all probability) appeared on the stage of history only a very short time after the county of Mâcon had become hereditary and considerably earlier than the founder of the most powerful lay principality of the region, the seigneury of Beaujeu, made his appearance. Half, if not two-thirds, of these family groups were firmly established before the great political and social change which, toward the year 1000, made the masters of castles autonomous, caused the feudal seigneury to develop, and saw the growth of the movement for the Peace of God—before the time, by the way, when the word *miles*, a chivalric title, appeared in the legal vocabulary and spread. This permits us to assert that the aristocracy in the region about Cluny was by no means the result of that mutation. Indeed, the entire aristocracy seems already to have been firmly established on its allodial possessions when, in the middle of the tenth century, the rapid growth of the early land endowment of the Cluniac abbey began to shine a first spotlight on the neighboring social milieu. We do not witness the birth of this aristocracy; it appears completely formed once the shadows of unrecorded history have dissipated.

Lastly, on the basis of the combined evidence provided by specific references to filiations and marriage ties, the manner in which individual names were spread through family groups during different generations, and the way in which the lands of the aristocratic patrimony were divided, we can reasonably conjecture that twenty-eight of the thirty-four family groups, and eighty-three of the five hundred individuals recorded at the end of the eleventh century—that is to say, 80 percent of the aristocratic milieu—were actually connected to six original ancestors. To one of them, whose early holdings spread up into the mountains of the Beaujolais and to the upper valley of the Grosne—from which came the lords of Beaujeu and a number of aristocratic families who settled outside the zone we have chosen to study—we can attach eight bloodlines(1, 2, 3, 24, 22, 23, 27, 5). Two of these and six others (4, 19, 14, 20, 21, 26) come from another stock or trunk, the Evrard and the Alard families, whose oldest known representative in the region of Mâcon lived in the entourage of Charles the Bald and whose ancestral fortune was located between Cluny and the Saône valley. A third family stock can be found to the west of Cluny, and a fourth on the wooded hills that tower above the monastery to the east. From each of these two trunks come five bloodlines (31, 34, 32, 33, 30, 7, 8, 9, 15, 4), one of which is also related to the Evrard stock. From the last two branches, both located along the Grosne River downstream from Cluny, four and three groups seem to have sprung, two of which are also related to the Beaujolais branch.[2]

In any event, there is no doubt that the aristocracy of 1100 was a society composed of heirs. The majority of its members descended from men who had possessed the land of this region in great tracts during the

---

[2]Moreover, there is no doubt that to these cousinships, determined by a common ascendance, we must add others resulting from more recent matrimonial alliances and that the latter weave an even tighter network of relationships among these families. For example, the use of the name *Wichardus*, which shows kinship with the lords of Beaujeu, also establishes a link between six groups descending from the Beaujolais stock (1, 2, 3, 23, 5), two groups descending from the Evrards (19, 21), and three others descending from another common stock (8, 9, 15). In like manner the use of the name *Humbertus* apparently shows relationships not only with the lords of Beaujeu but with those of Sailly II, Sennecé, Barberèche, Hongre, and Berzé as well. In addition, we have found that Gros, Bissy, Taizé, Cortevaix, and Besornay apparently inherited lands from a common ancestor at Sercie. Lastly, in the generation we have taken as our point of departure, that of the late eleventh century, and in the generation that immediately preceded it, the texts reveal a certain number of marriages that tangle the skein still farther. Thus, Geoffroy II de Merzé became related to the Ménezy family through his wife and to the Burdins through his brother-in-law; Dalmas de Gigny and Letaud d'Ameugny married sisters of the lords of Uxelles; the Créteuils and the La Chapelles were united by marriage with the Bresses. A certain degree of endogamy, practiced despite censure by the Church, seems to have made all of these five hundred persons cousins to some degree.

preceding century, before the patrimony of Cluny had begun to spread; of
this we have proof. At the end of the eleventh century these people still
retained possession, or had done so until very recently, of a good number
of parish churches—the Bérauds had Chazelle; the Ameugnys, Taizé; the
Créteuils, Chassy; the Bières, Berzé-la-Ville; and the La Chapelles,
Bragny—from which their patronymic surnames originated. It is as if
toward the middle of the tenth century, at the latest, six very large
patrimonial properties—whose previous use is unknown to historians
—had been broken up through shared inheritances to create the landed
fortune of the various branches of the local aristocracy. Yet this process
of fragmentation, which in its entirety eludes the historian's grasp, appears to have gradually slowed down. Indeed, by the end of the tenth
century we can attach twenty-four individualized branches to these six
original trunks. Subsequently, during the eleventh century, only four
more new family groups broke off through the triple ramification of two
of these branches. At the same time, six branches that we cannot with any
certainty attach to these original stocks emerged from the shadows, while
four family groups known to us by documents from the year 1000 died
out. Thus, a period of dispersion, dissociation, and proliferation was
succeeded by a period of rigidity during the eleventh century. Why? Were
kinship patterns changing? This is the second question we must ask.

Twenty years ago I hypothesized that a change in family structures
within the aristocracy occurred during the eleventh century. Since then
the best students of the post-Carolingian aristocracy and the best specialists in genealogical research—I am referring to Gerd Tellenbach's students
—have been led to formulate the hypothesis that within the Holy Roman
Empire there was a progressive crystallization of kinship patterns into
patrilineal dynasties, that is, into lineages.[3] Moreover, since such phenomena are closely connected to the question being discussed here, the idea
of nobility, I thought it would be useful to reexamine the documentary
material I had previously used. On this point, I feel I have not completed
the reexamination. Indeed, such a study is difficult because the sources
are so defective, primarily because they are not abundant. In the absence
of any specific formulation of rules or customs, we must begin with
official documents and try to discern through them what the customs
were. Such indications are, however, infrequent, and their interpretation
is generally a very delicate matter. In addition, the documentation has the
more serious weakness of having been affected during the period with

---

[3]Especially Karl Schmid, "Zur Problematik von Familie, Sippe und Geschlecht, Haus
und Dynastie bein mittelalterlichen Adel. Vorträge zun Thema: Adel und Herrschaft im
Mittelalter," *Zeitschrift für die Geschichte des Oberrheins*, 105, 1957.

which we are concerned by a development that may well distort our observations.

First of all, the format of legal acts was transformed. The strict framework used in the tenth century when drawing up charters for donations, sales, or exchanges of property disintegrated rapidly after the year 1000 and subsequently was abandoned completely. At the same time, in the cartularies of ecclesiastical establishments, written acts drawn up between laymen concerning properties or rights later acquired by the Church became rare and then disappeared, either because the archivists failed to keep these deeds once a certain date had expired or because lay society abandoned the practice of drawing up such acts. The decisive turning point in this deterioration seems to have occurred in about 1035. In other words, the deterioration is closely related to the disappearance of public jurisdictions, to the abandonment of written proof, and to the adoption of other procedures guaranteeing property ownership. Faced with the modification in sources, we must ask whether the statistical data supporting the hypotheses I shall offer reflect a real change and not merely external changes in the documents themselves. If we add to this the fact that the documents allow us to glimpse only one aspect of the kinship relationship, the aspect involving economic relationships and the patrimony, the fragility of our conjectures is evident.[4]

A perusal of genealogical tables encourages us to suppose that between the middle of the tenth and the end of the eleventh centuries the biological expansion of families slowed markedly. Our basic hypothesis consists in relating this phenomenon to a contraction of the bonds of kinship within the framework of a strictly male bloodline, and to the appearance on the scene of specifically lineal structures. To verify this hypothesis, I will ask three successive questions: During this period can we observe whether the solidarity of blood relatives closes ranks about the heritage? Can we discern a progressive affirmation of male primacy? Does the eldest appear to have been granted certain privileges?

The first of these three aspects of the kinship relation is the most visible and lends itself best to statistical treatment. Here we see indisputable changes in the direction of greater group cohesion. Yet these changes are complex and can be broken down into four distinct trends: the increase in joint possession among heirs; the increased presence of kin as witnesses in legal acts; the increasing frequency of parental agreement to alienation of property; and lastly, the increase in familial usurpations of charitable donations given by ancestors. I shall study each of these four developments

---

[4]In order to reduce this fragility, on this question I used sources concerning not only the very restricted area selected in order to study the most visible aristocratic families but the whole of southern Burgundy as well.

separately. To simplify matters, I shall break the period into four chronological segments: the first and the second halves of the tenth century, the first half of the eleventh century, and the period between 1050 and 1120. For each of these segments I shall indicate the percentage of legal acts extant in which the various manifestations of each of these developments are discernible.

1. Infrequent before 950, joint possession subsequently became a way of ownership whose frequency remained almost constant. The change —which reveals the increasing coagulation of the bonds of kinship—lay in the progressive growth after the mid-tenth century of joint ownership among brothers, which the texts call *fraternitas* or *frereschia* (28 percent during the second segment, then 33 percent, then 50 percent). Perhaps more significant is the fact that more distant blood relatives shared increasingly in the jointly owned property (2 percent, then 6 percent, then 14 percent).

2. The study of the eschatocol, or conclusion, of legal acts reveals a clear and progressive intrusion of relatives among those signing the acts (from 4 percent, to 10 percent, then to 16 percent, and finally to 20 percent). The phenomenon certainly cannot be isolated from the simultaneous disappearance of public assemblies. In addition, it is accentuated by the fact that during the tenth century explicit indications of kinship are found more and more rarely in the formal signatures at the end of the documents. But the very fact that during that period scribes did not judge it useful to identify relationships, as they did rather often in subsequent years, is in itself noteworthy. In any event, the father's or mother's presence among signing relatives continually decreased until it almost completely disappeared (28 percent, 7.5 percent, 4 percent, 3 percent). This proves that by the year 1000 sons no longer possessed autonomous rights to their share of the inheritance during their parents' lifetime. On the other hand, we must note the increased role of the *proximi*, that is, of blood relatives more distant than children or brothers (from 3 percent, to 10 percent, 14 percent, and 18 percent). Finally, I should like to point out that the development appears to have been very even, with no break in the rhythm.

3. The intervention of relatives—as the texts say, *laudare, concedere*, and to give *consilium* when hereditary property was leaving the family —also became increasingly frequent (4 percent after 950, 7.7 percent, then 33 percent of the acts), with a sharp increase between the first and the second halves of the eleventh century. Let us add that in about 1080 we find the first reference to fees paid in coin in return for this approval. Also, though the proportion of sons remained the same (about one-third), that of proximi increased from 3 percent between 950 and 1000, to 14 percent, and then to 16 percent.

4. Almost unknown before the year 1000 (I have found only three cases), the *querella* and the *calumpnia*—both of which involved the lineage's claim to an old family possession then owned by a religious establishment—remained rare during the eleventh century. Subsequently such claims became more frequent (increasingly from 1.6 percent to 3 percent by the final period). The important point here is that in disputes—described as *consanguinatis objectione vel cupidatatis illectione* in a document of 1030[5]—the role played by proximi as compared to that of sons or brothers increases gradually. Their role in such disputes as a whole increased from 12 percent to 35 percent.

Thus, these four statistical sketches supply convergent indications that clearly show the progressive strengthening of the solidarity of the bloodline as far as the inheritance is concerned. This slow, continuous development appears by the second half of the tenth century. If the change in the external appearance of the acts, a change I mentioned above, is not deceptive, it accelerated during the second third of the eleventh century.

Anyone asking my second question immediately finds himself on much shakier ground. Did the rights of sons or of brothers increase at the expense of their sisters? In other words, did society, at least in regard to hereditary possessions, become increasingly male-oriented? Indeed, evidence concerning the practices followed for inheritances is scarce and uncertain. Reference is occasionally made to these procedures in acts recording donations and in acts attempting to end a quarrel between heirs. But an inheritance is never described in its entirety, nor is the manner in which it is shared. Thus, we can never evaluate with any certainty the portion which any one heir received and compare it with that received by the others. Lastly, the evidence is so spotty that we must give up trying to see any pattern of development.

It is clear that a woman could inherit from her father. However, references to a transfer from mother to daughter or from sister to sister of allodial property coming from the maternal side of the family are more frequent and more explicit.[6] Moreover, though certain texts lead us to believe that women's rights to inheritances could be equal to those of their brothers, these texts are rare and their interpretation is open to debate. Indeed, most references imply that the male heirs received a larger

---

[5] *Recueil des chartes de l'abbaye de Cluny*, no. 2906.

[6] Alexandra made a gift in *locum divisionis* to her daughter Landrée; a little later, Landrée, through an identical act, bequeathed the property to her sister (*Cartulaire de Saint-Vincent de Mâcon*, ed. Ragut [Mâcon, 1864], nos. 467 and 468 [960 and 997–1031]); Elisabeth gave "a piece of land that came to me through my mother and my ancestors," "my part of the inheritance" (*Recueil des chartes de l'abbaye de Cluny*, no. 2860 [1031–48]).

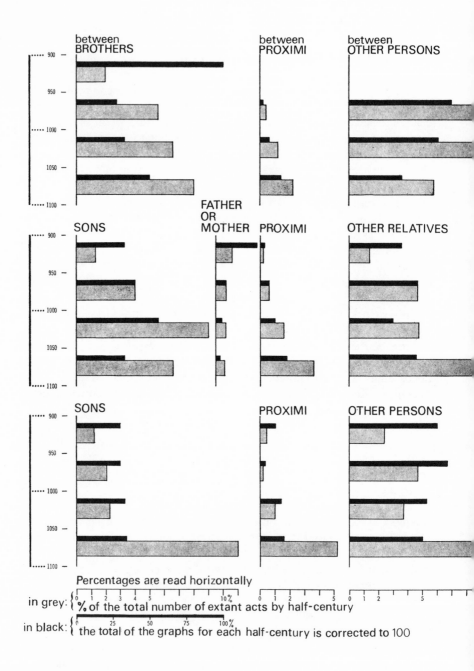

Figure 2.2. The Clustering of Blood Relatives around an Inheritance

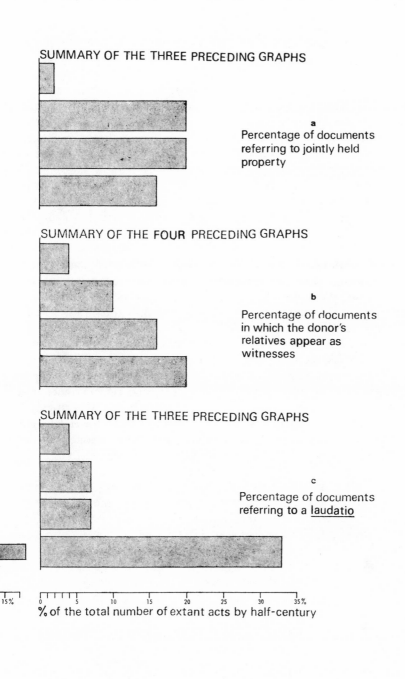

SUMMARY OF THE THREE PRECEDING GRAPHS

a
Percentage of documents
referring to jointly held
property

SUMMARY OF THE **FOUR** PRECEDING GRAPHS

b
Percentage of documents
in which the donor's
relatives appear as
witnesses

SUMMARY OF THE THREE PRECEDING GRAPHS

c
Percentage of documents
referring to a <u>laudatio</u>

15%

0   5   10   15   20   25   30   35%
% of the total number of extant acts by half-century

portion.[7] Could this superiority lead to a total exclusion of daughters from an inheritance? The frequency of joint possession of property among brothers alone, and of divisions in which the number of portions equaled the number of boys in the family, would tend to keep us from rejecting categorically such a hypothesis. Moreover, we can base our hypothesis upon explicit documents. Take the couple with five children, "four sons and a daughter. . . . One became a monk at Cluny; they gave him his share of the inheritance." After his father's death, another son, the eldest, gave himself to abbot Odilon, who had ransomed him. When he in turn died, he bequeathed the whole of his possessions to the monastery "before his sons and daughters." "Next, the third brother . . . became a monk at Cluny and gave his share to the church of Saint-Pierre in Mâcon, the fourth, the last-born, remained alone and kept all the shares of the inheritance as a fief during his lifetime." After his death the entire property was turned over to Cluny. Never was the least reference made to the fifth child, a girl. The same sort of exclusion was in store for the married sister of a donor (one of the five hundred persons in our sample) who offered "the quarter of the inheritance which came to [her] as a hereditary right after sharing with [her] three brothers."[8]

Of all the models of society that could be constructed on the basis of these documents, the least nebulous would doubtlessly be that of a society in which disposing of the inheritance is a matter for men; in which women play only a minor role; in which unmarried sisters remain under their brothers' guardianship and at the very most receive only a small part of the jointly held inheritance as their funeral alms, a small part generally taken from the property inherited by their mother; and in which married daughters who have left the household with their dowries no longer have any claims to the family's allodial holdings.

This general impression is confirmed by an examination of matrimonial laws. Here a perceptible change occurred between the tenth and the eleventh centuries. The husband's control of the couple's fortune was strengthened. Indeed, before the year 1000 the wife could maintain a clear legal autonomy within the conjugal group. She administered her own hereditary properties; her husband gave her what was called the *sponsalitium*, that is, a third and sometimes even a half of his share of the inheritance, "to do what she wishes with it," "to have it, to sell it, to give it." This gift was so complete that we encounter women who remarried

[7]A man possessed one-half of a manse, and the other half belonged to his sisters (*Recueil des chartes de l'abbaye de Cluny*, no. 1899 [991]); a donor had received two-thirds of a domain from his father, and his aunt had received the other third (no. 3574) (the division occurred in about 1050); a donation of two-thirds of a church, "which comes to me by hereditary right; the other third belongs to my sisters . . ." (no. 2860 [1031–48]).

[8]Ibid., no. 2118 (about 1030) and no. 3304 (about 1080), in which the brother-in-law is included among those signing the act.

and passed on to the children of their second marriage property that had come from the ancestral patrimony of their first husband.[9] During the eleventh century everything changed. The husband, backed by his lineage, expressed the desire to maintain strict control over the *sponsalitium*. Every precaution was taken to see that there would no longer be any risk of its falling into hands other than those of blood relatives. And now it was the husband who administered his wife's hereditary property—that is, the dowry, that small portion of the family fortune that her father or her brother had given her, a portion that had, moreover, come from the least precious part of the patrimony. This dowry might be made up of alms that had been willed by a dead relative and that the heirs were not eager to cede to the Church, and in many cases, of property in the mother's own dowry. But as often as possible, care was taken to avoid removing anything from the heart of the inheritance, that is, from that property passed on by the most distant ancestors.[10] This indisputable strengthening of the husband's power appears to reveal the defensive gesture of a family group that had been brought together in a different manner than in the past. Now it clustered about a patrimonial property that was destined more specifically to support the male offspring and that must therefore be protected from the threat of atomization resulting from the economic effects of matrimonial alliances. Such a reaction must be viewed in relation to a more conscious mental attitude, that of the image of the lineage, which we can see stated clearly for the first time in about 1025—the date is important—in one of the clauses of an act recording a donation: "If the children born of my loins from my legitimate spouse die without a legitimate *son*," my heirs [*heredes* and *proheredes*] will have no right to succeed me. "And likewise, as the years pass, legitimate sons issuing from my seed and succeeding one another by direct and legal *line* of generation, cannot have any of these possessions transferred into the possession or the seigneury of our other heirs."[11]

My third and final question is, in this lineage of "sons," of males, were the eldest in any way privileged? To the contrary, the bulk of the texts I have used paints a picture of equal rights to the inheritance for brothers.

[9]*Cartulaire de Saint-Vincent de Mâcon*, no. 210 (tenth century); *Recueil des chartes de l'abbaye de Cluny*, no. 2265 (994), no. 254 (925–26), nos. 370, 798, and 953.

[10]*Cartulaire de l'église collégiale Notre-Dame de Beaujeu*, ed. Guigue (Lyon, 1864), no. 12 (1087). *Cartulaire de Saint-Vincent de Mâcon*, no. 463 (997–1034); portion given to Saint-Vincent de Mâcon "by the hand of Bernard, her husband" (no. 477 [late eleventh century]). *Recueil des chartes de l'abbaye de Cluny*, no. 3301 (1049–1109): a portion made up of former alms; no. 2528 (early eleventh century): the aunt had given two manses to God, and "my mother, when I was married, snatched away these two manses and gave them to me for my dowry. . . ."

[11]*Recueil des chartes de l'abbaye de Cluny*, no. 2493. Likewise, in 1100 (no. 3030), "if my two sons whom I am leaving in the world outside the Church die without heirs, none of my heirs can claim any of this allodial land."

However, throughout this entire period, fathers in this region were entitled to determine personally how their possessions would be divided among their heirs. Direct references to "charters of divisions" are followed, after 980, by direct references to "divisions," which undoubtedly were no longer committed to writing but whose continuity was assured by custom during the interval between the written dispositions of the tenth century and the earliest extant written wills, drawn up in the Beaujolais region in about 1090.[12] Unfortunately, these are merely references; no evidence permits us to measure whether the eldest were given lesser or greater advantages by such divisions, or by the donations made by living parents to their children, which were frequent until the beginning of the eleventh century but which subsequently disappeared, perhaps in the face of strengthened family solidarity. Of course, we do find in our sources two rather blunt instances of the privileges of primogeniture. However, on the one hand these examples occur at the very end of the period, on the eve of the twelfth century, and on the other hand, they occur in a very limited social milieu, that of castle owners, that is, among those holding an office which, although it was the object of familial appropriation, had maintained its public nature and as a result was undoubtedly considered indivisible.

Let us look at two lords of castles. One of them, starting off in 1100 for the Holy Land, distributed legacies and established one of his four sons as the "heir to the rest of his honor." The other, at approximately the same date, asserted that his father, while still living, had already made him a "gift of his honor," forbidding him "to give or sell anything to anyone, either his sons or his daughters."[13] What are we to conclude from such limited and late evidence? Our knowledge of later inheritance procedures in southern Burgundy would authorize us to see them as the first manifestations of a movement that later gained full momentum. I have, however, some reservations on this point. Nevertheless, even if we agree that the principles which obliged a father to leave an equal share of the inheritance to each son persisted, the genealogical tables indisputably show that from the beginning of the eleventh century at the latest, family bloodlines tended to crystallize around a single branch, a single axis, in which sons apparently succeeded one another by order of primogeniture. Fostered by the increased solidarity among blood relatives, by the privileges of masculinity, and undoubtedly even more so by the new trends in matrimonial customs, this crystallization nevertheless appears to have resulted chiefly from a prudent restriction of marriages. All sons

---

[12]Published in the *Cartulaire lyonnais, documents inédits pour servir à l'histoire des anciennes provinces de Lyonnais, Forez, Beaujolais, Dombes, Bresse, et Bugey*, ed. Guigue (Lyon, 1893), no. 10.

[13]*Recueil des chartes de l'abbaye de Cluny*, nos. 3737 and 3031.

undoubtedly possessed the same rights to the succession, but upon their father's death they did not share the inheritance. Only one of them married and fathered legitimate sons who, thanks to the practice of prolonged joint possession, later had no difficulty in succeeding to the rights of their unmarried uncles and to the entire heritage, amputated only by any property the uncles may have given the Church as funeral alms.

There are abundant indications that marriages were restricted to one, or at the most to two, sons. I return to the example I gave above of the family with four sons, two of whom were monks at Cluny, while only the eldest had children and the youngest died unmarried. To this I add the case of the lords of the castle of Uxelles. In 1070 there were five sons, two of whom entered Cluny, while two others disappeared without leaving a trace. Only one had children. I also wish to point out that, among the donations inter vivos, that is, between living persons, those made by an unmarried uncle to one of his nephews are the most numerous and remained customary the longest. In addition, there is the incontestable testimony of the men who drew up acts in their brothers' names, who acted alone while the other males merely gave their "counsel" or agreement. And further, I cite the results of my genealogical research. These results are only partial. We cannot hope to trace all the adult members of a family group, and the very ones who escape our observation are those of the collateral branches. Yet we must keep the following facts in mind. There were thirty-four lineages. Only three of them became individualized during the eleventh century by breaking off from two of the original ancestral stocks. There were no more than eight others in which, during any one generation, several sons had children. That leaves twenty-three distinct families whose adventitious branches wilted without proliferating. If we look at the masters of castles, we can see the superiority of the eldest over his brothers very clearly after 980, that is, at the beginning of the process that gave birth to independent castellanies. For example, in about 1030, Gauthier, at the castle of Berzé, had five brothers. He was a canon, and yet he commanded the castle alone, as did fifty years later his grandson Hugues, who had at least three identifiable second cousins. Lastly, let us note—and this is final proof of the privileges granted the eldest—that the principle of the superiority of direct descendants over those of collateral branches, when combined with the effects of restricted marriages, frequently resulted, if a son were lacking, in a daughter's succession to the paternal inheritance even if she had uncles and cousins. In such an event her husband would "hold" it. Thus the castle of Berzé was on two separate occasions, in about 1060 and again in about 1090, controlled by two sons-in-law, men who were strangers to the region and who may have been social climbers, although the collateral branches of the lineage were well supplied with males.

All these indications are tenuous, but they are convergent. This reexamination thus permits me to remain steadfast in the opinion stated in my book on society in the region about Mâcon: there was a condensation, a gathering together about the male line, a progressive affirmation of a dynastic state of mind, which undoubtedly became more marked among those possessing castles but which was nonetheless common to the entire aristocracy.

The last problem still remains, but it takes us back to our initial question. Did the aristocracy, in its gathering self-awareness, refer to the notion of nobility or to that of chivalry? Indeed, the preceding presentation has attempted to show more clearly and at closer hand the relationship between the social vocabulary and what it reveals about psychological attitudes, and the living reality, that is, specific individuals, or more precisely those thirty-four family groups that became the most individualized during the eleventh century.

Concerning vocabulary, I will repeat what I have said in the past; but a more strictly statistical treatment of the sources permits me to be more specific and to make stronger assertions:

1. In order to show that an individual belonged to the aristocracy in the mid-tenth century, the adjective *nobilis* (or one of its equivalents, *clarissimus, illustris*, etc.) was used. But this usage was rare, and in 80 percent of the cases it appears to have been linked to the requirements of certain traditional, formalized texts: texts of contracts for precarium and of acts involving property exchanges, when the word was used to designate individually the person benefiting from the act, and texts of the records of the judicial assembly, when it was a matter of collectively designating the judge's assistants.

2. After about 970, a double change occurred. First it gradually became customary to distinguish those men who belonged to the dominant social group of lay society. The spread of aristocratic titles into the vocabulary of records and charters shows that scribes increasingly felt the need to express the superiority of certain personages. This was because the aristocracy was developing more coherence and importance, because a chasm was deepening at a certain level of the hierarchy of social conditions. Thus, among all the acts in which we find terms indicating membership in the aristocracy, the proportion using the old format in which these words were traditionally employed became progressively smaller, slowly at first, then much more rapidly after the second half of the eleventh century, dropping from 76 percent between the years 970 and 1000, to 56 percent from 1000 to 1030, to 29 percent between 1030 and 1060, and to 10 percent during the final period.

At the same time one term, the word *miles*, appeared among the titles and soon supplanted all the others. In the extant documents it appears for

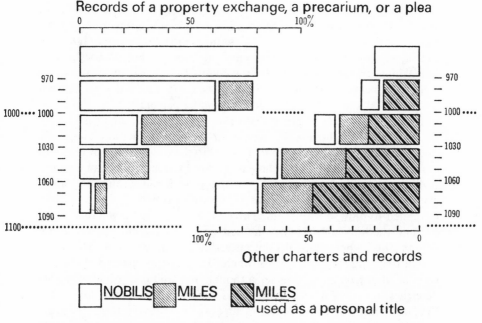

Figure 2.3. Distribution of Noble Titles in Records of a Property Exchange, a Precarium, or a Plea, and in Other Charters and Records (per 100 documents in which this title occur)

the first time, used in this sense, in 971. It was inserted into the old traditional phrasing, where it increasingly won out over such words as *vassus* or *fidelis*, which expressed the vassal's subordination, and even more markedly won out over *nobilis*. It is found in 20 percent of the acts of this type between 970 and 1000, in 53 percent between 1000 and 1030, and in 70 percent between 1030 and 1060. Then the percentage falls to 50 percent between 1060 and 1090, but at that time formularies specifying certain phrases had almost ceased to be used.

The triumph of the chivalric title is more evident in other acts: two-thirds of the uses between 970 and 1000, four-fifths between 1000 and 1030, and 87 percent and 85 percent in the two subsequent chronological segments. In addition, it was increasingly used here as an individual title attributed to the person who was supposed to deliver the act or to the one who intervened as a witness (16 percent, 23 percent, 33 percent, and finally 48 percent of all acts).

3. Here it is indeed a matter of a veritable substitution, as proved by two examples from among many, one dating from the year 1002, the other from 1000. In an account of a judiciary plea presented by the count of Mâcon, there is successive reference to *ceterorum nobilium hominum qui ante eos stabant* and to *ceterorum militum qui ibi aderant*. A formula

for an exchange of property throws the spotlight on a certain Bernard, lord of Uxelles. He is designated as *"vir clarissimus* according to the high rank of the century"; but his signature reads, "Bernard, *knight*." Of course, *miles* did not completely eliminate *nobilis*, but its use became increasingly frequent after 1030. It accounts for 31 percent of the terms used to indicate social superiority between 970 and 1000, 64 percent between 1000 and 1030, and 81 percent and 82 percent subsequently.

However, in order to prove that those who are called noble and those who are called knights are the same persons, we must do more than study titles. We must attach the men themselves to their names. Let us return to our five hundred individuals, three of whom, I remind you, commanded a castle, ninety-six of whom were indisputably of old wealth, and all of whom were cousins. The adjective *nobilis* (in its superlative form at that) is applied to only four of them. Three of these four are given this title in one and the same act; yet they are neither among the most powerful nor among those whose most distant ancestors are known to us. Moreover, two of them are called knight elsewhere. The fourth is the lord of Uxelles, who is *noblissimus*, of course, although the obituary of Mâcon that describes him thus adds: *"noblissimus miles."*[14] Let us turn to another title, *dominus*, which also indicates superiority. I found it three times, but its use undoubtedly indicates an increased concern for expressing the social hierarchy, since of the three persons bearing this title, two were masters of castles, the castles of la Bussière and Berzé.[15] Lastly, let us look at the title *miles*. It is attributed to thirty-four individuals. Its usage was clearly more widespread, although it involves only 32 percent of the persons and twenty of the thirty-four lineages in my study. In four of these family groups, all brothers who had remained laymen bear this title. In twelve others it is applied only to the eldest. Is this another privilege extended to the firstborn? Among those described as knight or calling themselves knight are two of the lords of castles and the cousin of the third. However, along with them we find people whose fathers are unknown, for example, the three Cray brothers. That leaves seventy-one individuals without titles, of whom thirty-nine are, it is true, brothers or nephews of a knight.

Having established this basic data, let us follow these lineages as far as possible into the past and go back to the year 1000. Of the forty-seven male laymen found to be the ancestors of the five hundred individuals of the year 1000, fifteen bear the title of knight (this is 34 percent, a little higher than at the end of the eleventh century, although the use of the word *miles*, as we have seen, had spread during the intervening years).

[14]Ibid., no. 3104 (about 1090); *Necrologium Ecclesiae Sancti Petri Matisconensis . . . , ou, Notice des bienfaiteurs de l'Eglise Saint-Pierre de Mâcon,* ed. Guigue (Bourg, 1874), p. 28.
[15]*Recueil des chartes de l'abbaye de Cluny,* nos. 3671 and 3565.

Among these forty-seven persons, there are proportionally more *domini* (four) and above all more *nobiles* (six, that is, 13 percent instead of the 4 percent found in 1100). Of these six "nobles," two possess a castle, but three, including these two castle owners, are also called knights elsewhere or in the same act.

Finally, if we view the genealogies as a whole, we find that in the documents at our disposal only three of the thirty-four lineages failed to have at least one member bearing the title of knight in one or another generation. Of these three families, one has just stepped out of the wings (it is the only one upon which we can base the fragile hypothesis of social climbers joining the aristocracy). The other two are old and powerful families; the representative of one of them in the year 1000 is described as *prepotens amicus* of the count of Mâcon, while one of the males of the other family is called noble in 1080. That leaves all the others, that is to say, 92 percent of the entire group. For seven of them, the chivalric title only appears in the generation living between 1080 and 1100; for seven others it appears in the preceding generation; while for eighteen (or 53 percent), including two of the lords of castles, it is found in about the year 1000.

On the other hand, the title *nobilis*—or its equivalents—does not appear to have been restricted to members of a small elite. Not only did the owners of castles lack the most ancient genealogies, they were also not described as being more noble than the others. Their particular situation is indicated by another term, *dominus*.[16] Therefore, the words *noble* and *knight* appear to have been interchangeable everywhere: titles show a universal continuity. In all families, as in that of the lords of Uxelles, it seems that one could use any title indiscriminately and that in the year 1000 as in the year 1100, a male representative could be called *vir clarissimus* or *noblissimus miles*. Thus we can unhesitatingly conclude that aristocratic society was homogeneous. Its members had been joined into a single coherent group ever since the second half of the tenth century, that is, before the great changes that are indicated by the birth of the feudal seigneury and the diffusion of the institutions of the Peace of God. They had common ancestors, a cousinship that exerted pressure to maintain the old endogamic practices, an economic superiority that tended to protect the strengthening of lineal structures, and lastly a common vocation to power and to military service that accentuated the masculine nature of this social class. It is this common vocation that undoubtedly explains how, in a world in which the fief was of little consequence when compared with allodial lands, it was so easy to move

[16]At Berzé in the year 1000, the lord was called *miles* and *dominus*, and in 1100 he was called *dominus*. The opposite was true for the lords of la Bussière, who were *dominus* in 1000 and *miles* and *dominus* in 1100.

from the notion of "nobility," supported by the image of antiquity of race combined with the idea of native authority and power, to the notion of "chivalry," so closely bound to the notion of public military service.

This reexamination has therefore permitted me to assert even more surely what I formerly proposed. In an area that is brought into focus by unusually rich documentation, there was in the eleventh century a landed aristocracy well established upon a patrimony which, from generation to generation, had been held by bloodlines that were chiefly descended from wealthier ancestors, although the lack of sources cannot permit us to go back beyond the mid-tenth century. Before the year 1000, inheritance practices and the relative economic independence of individuals threatened the cohesion of these fortunes. However, so that the superiority of the social group would not be compromised, kinship relationships were slowly modified within the framework of very flexible customs in a direction that emphasized lineal traits. This contraction occurred earlier in those families holding "honors," that is, having a castle and the mission to command and to punish. Among the "masters" who had been invested with a power that had originally been a public one, "houses" or noble families took shape. Here we can see the influence of political structures upon family structures.

Nevertheless, these men—who, breaking free about the year 1000 from all effective subordination to the count, built up about their fortress a small, independent principality—came from lineages similar to the others, lineages neither richer nor more ancient. It is only because the evolution of political relationships permitted them to become wealthy through the "extortions" they levied on the peasantry and to become the leaders of the local *militia* that, during the eleventh century, a certain differentiation began to take shape within a homogeneous social body. It gradually isolated at the summit of the aristocracy a small, dominant group, that of the "sires." Richer and more powerful, granted—but not seen as more noble than their cousins, the other aristocrats, since after the year 1000 they bore the same chivalric title as the latter. This title apparently was not used for social climbers, men who had risen rapidly through fidelity, military service, or the granting of a fief. It designated a preexisting social group in a surer and more explicit manner. The modification that is revealed by the rapid acceptance of this term did not affect the material structure of society but rather men's image of it. It remains for us to explain why they preferred a noun that stressed the military function and service over adjectives that expressed the glory, in varying degrees of intensity, of an individual's birth. The date of this change in vocabulary prompts us to see a relationship to changes in the political order—the construction of the feudal seigneury and the diffusion of the ideology of the Peace of God.

3

"A uno pane e uno vino": The Rural Tuscan Family at the Beginning of the Fifteenth Century

Christiane Klapisch and Michel Demonet

"A *uno pane e uno vino*"—sharing food and drink. Does this phrase express an unusual situation in the Tuscany of the early Quattrocento? Such does not appear to be the case, for these words are often used by the taxpayers and the scribes of the *Catasto* of 1427 to describe families—"extended" in some cases to include an old mother, an uncle, a brother, or an isolated relative, and in others to include couples or entire families assembled under the same roof in large aggregates.

The answer to this question is not unimportant, since some scholars view the end of the Middle Ages as the moment in which Western Europe may have passed from a "medieval" model of marriage and family

Annales, E.S.C. 27 (July–October 1972): 873–901. Translated by Patricia M. Ranum.

This research was part of the series of projects involving the Florentine *Catasto* carried out in close collaboration with David Herlihy, formerly professor of history at the University of Wisconsin. We have worked together on this inquiry since 1967 and have been given financial support by the University of Wisconsin and the National Science Foundation on the American side, and by the Ecole pratique des hautes études, VIe section, and the Centre national de la recherche scientifique (initially as part of the Recherches coopératives sur programme 181, headed by Professor P. Wolff) on the French side. Our study of the rural Tuscan family, based on the data in the *Catasto* and programmed for the computer, complements Herlihy's work dealing with the same problems in urban Tuscany during the

structures to a "European" model, with delayed marriages, a sizeable amount of permanent celibacy, and small conjugal families.[1]

In the following pages we intend to examine whether Tuscany, a southern province of that Europe in transformation, fits the model proposed for the regions situated farther to the north. A sort of chronological and geographical surveyor's staff, the Florentine census of 1427–30, called the *Catasto*, is especially interesting since it permits us to avoid the sort of samplings taken from urban groups and from the upper levels of society which have been used in many of the best studies on the subject.[2] Such groups are not very representative of a population that is in the main essentially rural. On the other hand, of the 60,000 households described in the *Catasto* of 1427–30, approximately 37,000, composed of some 175,000 persons, were rural.[3] In this census each individual was listed by name, sex, age, and relationship to the head of the household. Thus, this entire enormous rural population is available for use in studying the family, since certain of the variables that determine scope, structure, and duration are at our disposal—although we must keep in mind any distortions inherent in a census that is decided upon and organized by the tax authorities.[4] Compensating for the absence of

---

Quattrocento; cf. D. Herlihy, "Mapping Households in Medieval Italy," *Catholic Historical Review* 58 (April 1972). [For a summary of the results of research involving both the rural and the urban portions of the *Catasto* and also details concerning the compilation of this fifteenth-century census, see Christiane Klapisch, "Household and Family in Tuscany in 1427," in *Household and Family in Past Time,* ed. Peter Laslett (Cambridge, 1972), pp. 267–81.—Trans.]

[1]Cf. especially J. Hajnal, "European Marriage Patterns in Perspective," in *Population in History,* ed. D. V. Glass and D. E. C. Eversley (London, 1965); and on the problem of family size, the studies of Peter Laslett, "Size and Structure of the Household in England over Three Centuries," *Population Studies* 23 (1969); "The Comparative History of Household and Family," *Journal of Social History* 4 (1970); and Laslett, ed., *Household and Family in Past Time,* introduction.

[2]Cf. L. Henry, *Anciennes familles genevoises: Etude démographique, XVIe-XXe siècles* (Paris, 1956); L. Henry and C. Lévy, "Ducs et pairs sous l'Ancien Régime," *Population* 15 (1960); J. C. Davis, *The Decline of the Venetian Nobility as a Ruling Class* (Baltimore, 1962); T. H. Hollingsworth, "The Demography of the British Peerage," *Population Studies* 18 (1964); L. Stone, *The Crisis of the Aristocracy, 1558–1641* (Oxford, 1965); R. B. Litchfield, "Demographic Characteristics of Florentine Patrician Families, Sixteenth to Nineteenth Centuries," *Journal of Economic History* 29 (1969).

[3]Agglomerations of more than 1,000 inhabitants include a total of approximately 81,000 inhabitants, or 30.8 percent of the population. If to them we add the populations of those localities that comprised between 650 and 1,000 inhabitants and that seem to show "urban" characteristics—about 8,100 inhabitants in all—we find that a third of the total population described in the *Catasto* lived in an urban setting.

[4]On the fifteenth-century Florentine *catasti*, see E. Conti, *I catasti agrari della repubblica fiorentina e il catasto particellare toscano (secc. XIV–XIX),* Instituto storico italiano per il Medio Evo (Rome, 1966); see also the bibliography on the subject in Christiane Klapisch, "Fiscalité et démographie en Toscane, 1427–30," *Annales, E.S.C.* 24 (November-December 1969), and the discussion of the demographic value of certain aspects of the *Catasto*.

literary works, journals, genealogies, and parish registers, which might have shed light on the structure of the medieval peasant family, this census permits us to elucidate the characteristics of the rural family group in Tuscany and the developmental cycle that it followed. In addition, beyond the limits of the province, this census undoubtedly provides a few answers to the problems posed by Western European population history as a whole.

At first glance, the peasant home as described by the *Catasto* seems to have been very small, although it was, on the average, larger than the urban family in all regions. In the principal cities of Tuscany the family was marked by an undeniable "urban" stamp.[5] It was very small (3.9 persons per household), and its predominant forms were the conjugal family, an enormous mass of truncated families, and a crowd of isolated individuals who had come to try their luck in the city.[6] The demand for manpower, the mobility of individuals, and the high mortality rate undoubtedly explain the collapse of urban family groups and the break-down of solidarity among generations and relatives, at least among the lower classes. The difference between the average sizes of urban and peasant households is not excessive, however, since the average rural home included only 4.7 persons. Are these limited sizes compatible with a complex family structure and a family group that has extended beyond that of the simple conjugal family?

Here we will use as an example the *contado,* or countryside surrounding the city of Pisa, an exclusively rural region in which 3,900 families lived at the time of the *Catasto.* This province was rather heterogeneous and extended from the lower valleys of the Arno and the Serchio, through the hills located to the south of this river basin, and as far as the region of the Maremma, those low, almost deserted hills stretching along the shore toward the south which served as pasture for transhumant herds.

The average rural family of this region included 4.7 persons, which was a little larger than in a region of pure maremma such as the adjoining contado of Volterra (4.4 persons) but clearly smaller than in other regions of the Florentine territory such as the area southwest of the contado of Florence itself—a region of hills and *mezzadria,* that is, sharecropper farms—that adjoined the Pisan countryside and in which the peasant family averaged 5.1 members. This average figure is higher than that for the urban family of Pisa (4.2), and it is much greater than that of the small Florentine family (3.8); but, although half the population lived in a

[5]On "urban" characteristics, see W. J. Goode, *World Revolution and Family Patterns* (New York, 1963).
[6]Herlihy, "Mapping Households."

household including 6 or more persons, houses with 3, 4, or 5 persons remained the most common (15 percent of the total number of households for each category) (see fig. 3.1 in Appendix).

This average has in itself only limited significance, as anthropological and demographic research has shown.[7] One and the same statistic reveals very different demographic and social realities—for example, a high birthrate in a society in which conjugal families dominate, or a preponderance of "extended" families where the mortality rate is high. A statistic showing the "average" family represents more than a typical household, for it masks households that have reached various stages in their development within societies that are characterized by very different family structures.

In order to determine the value of this data, we can first relate it to the age of the head of the household. In the countryside about Pisa, until he was about forty years old a man directed a household whose size was smaller than the general average[8] (table 3.1). But a striking degree of stability is evident in the average size of households headed by a man over forty.[9] Until nearly the end of his life, a *capo di famiglia* presided over an approximately constant number of individuals. This was not the case for an urban Tuscan family, as we see in table 3.1;[10] the family generally reached a maximum size when its head was forty-five to fifty years old and then decreased until the end of his life. Is the developmental cycle of the urban family therefore a relatively short one, which stopped when its head died, although his counterpart's death did not interrupt the more slowly developing transformation occurring in the rural family?

The aggregate percentages of the various types of rural households confirm this first impression. The conjugal family, or what remained of it after the death of one of the partners, constituted only a little more than half (about 52 percent) of the 4,000 households in our study;[11] to which we add 12 percent for the households composed of isolated individuals,

[7]M. Fortes, in *The Developmental Cycle in Domestic Groups,* ed. J. Goody, Cambridge Papers in Social Anthropology, no. 1 (Cambridge, 1966), introduction; L. K. Berkner, "The Stem Family and the Developmental Cycle of the Peasant Household. An Eighteenth Century Austrian Example," *American Historical Review* 77 (April 1972).

[8]This involves 90.8 percent of the households; the percentage of homes headed by a woman remains low in the countryside and is generally less than 10 percent of the total.

[9]As Herlihy emphasized in "Mapping Households," especially in table 3.2. The author does not find exactly the same characteristics in the second half of the fifteenth century in Florence.

[10]Households headed by a woman remained on the average very small, more than three times smaller than those headed by a man. Their maxima are displaced toward the top, between twenty and fifty years, an age when widows were still raising children. But these large families have little effect on the total, since women reaching or passing their sixtieth birthday represent 62 percent of all the female heads of households in this region.

[11]This figure includes solitary couples or those living with unmarried children, and widowers or widows with unmarried children.

Table 3.1—Size of Household according to Age of the Head

Age of Head	Countryside around Pisa		All Rural Areas			City of Pisa		All Cities		
	Male	Female	Male	Female	Total	Male	Female	Male	Female	Total
Under 18	2.1	1.5	2.5	1.7		3.1⎫		2.6	1.7	
18–22	2.8⎫		3.1	3.1		3.1⎬ 2.1		2.7	3.1	
23–27	3.4⎭ 4.5		3.7	2.8		3.3⎭		3.1	2.4	
28–32	4.8	2.1	4.4	2.8		3.7	2.7	3.7	2.8	
33–37	4.7	2.5	4.9	2.7		4.4	2.8	4.2	2.7	
38–42	5.1	2.2	5.4	2.6		5.3	2.7	4.8	2.6	
43–47	5.2	2.2	5.5	2.4		5.6	3.4	5.2	2.4	
48–52	5.4	1.9	5.7	2.2		5.3	2	4.9	1.9	
53–57	5.3	2.2	5.4	1.6		5.3	2	4.9	1.8	
58–62	5.7	1.3	5.2	1.6		5.1	1.6	4.6	1.7	
63–67	5.2	1.1	5.1	1.5		4.7	1.5	4.5	1.4	
68 and over	5.4	1.4	5.3	1.4		5.1	1.7	4.5	1.4	
Unknown	2.7	1.2	2.5	1.2		2.3	1.3	2.5	1.3	
Total	5	1.6	5	1.7	4.7	4.6	1.8	4.3	1.7	3.9

who were the residue of former conjugal families or who had been cast off by extant families. Therefore, a little more than a third of all households would belong in the broadest sense of the word to the category of "extended families," which were composed of several nuclear families living "*a uno pane e uno vino*" (22 percent), or which had added one or several individuals to the central nucleus as a result of either an agnatic [male kinship] or a collateral relationship (11 percent). This total percentage of extended families is markedly higher than the usual rates for Western Europe in the early-modern period.[12] The rate for our rural Tuscan family comes close to that of the models for Eastern Europe, where nineteenth-century anthropologists thought they recognized, in reconstructing the *zadruga,* the archetype of the archaic European family community.[13]

These complex households bear the distinct stamp of the agnatic relationship through direct male descent since, in more than 70 percent of them, individuals or secondary groups were connected to the principal nucleus by the ascendant-descendant bond and since only 30 percent were cemented together by a purely lateral solidarity that prompted several brothers to live together after their parents' deaths.

[12]Cf. Laslett, *Household and Family.* By "nucleus" I mean the widower living with one unmarried child (or several children) who lives with another couple.

[13]Cf. the work of E. J. Hammel, "Preliminary Notes on the Cycle of Lineage Fission in Southern and Eastern Yugoslavia"; P. Laslett and M. Clarke, "Household and Family Structure in Belgrade, 1733–34"; and J. Halpern, "The Zadruga," all in Laslett, ed., *Household and Family.*

This brief description reveals imperfectly a much more fluid reality that will no more allow itself to be embodied in a statistical summary than the household would allow itself to be reduced to an average size.[14] Can we go beyond this aggregate numerical evaluation and interpret the structural relationships among the various types of families?

A histogram combining the types of households, classified according to their structures for each age-group of heads of households, permits us to project the probable cycle of family development by indicating the successive forms a household could take as its head aged (fig. 3.2 in Appendix).

Before the age of twenty, a young peasant male of this region had few chances of becoming his own master. If he succeeded, he rarely lived alone after both parents had died for he usually had to provide for his brothers and sisters who were still minors. Most often he had a surviving parent with whom he lived, usually his mother.

The great majority of adolescents in rural areas, however, lived in a home in which the adolescent did not bear the responsibility as head, although twice as many children or adolescents were their own masters in the cities.[15]

By the age of twenty-five, not even a third of the young men in the countryside around Pisa had been able to set up a home of their own. Among those who were independent—be they bachelors or married men—a majority still had to support an aged mother or younger brothers and sisters.

After that, and until the head of the household was approximately forty-five or fifty years old—the point at which the household reached maturity—the development of the family was characterized by (1) a rapid increase, both in absolute and relative terms, in the number of families composed of couples with children; (2) a decrease in the number of families composed of a widower and his unmarried children, while those composed of a married couple with a widowed parent remained stationary; (3) an almost total disappearance of individuals living alone, while the number of childless couples remained stationary; and (4) a steady increase of "multiple" households cemented by a horizontal or collateral relationship, which accounted for up to 15 percent of those households headed by a forty-year-old man.

After the head of the household had passed the age of fifty, there was a decrease in the number of couples with unmarried children, an increase in the number of solitary couples whose married children had left them, and

---

[14]Cf. Hammel, "Preliminary Notes."

[15]Such children accounted for 1.4 percent in the entire rural region in the western half of the Florentine territory, a little more in the Pisan contado (1.9 percent), but less than the 2.7 percent in the Tuscan cities as a whole.

an increase in the number of multiple families of the patriarchal sort in which sons and their families remained with the parents.

By the end of this cycle, when the old head of the household had reached or exceeded sixty-five years of age, more than 35 percent of the households were living under a patriarchal regime, with grandparents or even great-grandparents and the families of married sons living together year in and year out. Nearly 12 percent of the entire population lived in one of these "great families" ruled by an old man who was more than sixty-seven years old.[16]

The distribution of households in this region of Tuscany according to the age and matrimonial status of their head confirms that the greatest chances of becoming the head of the family group occurred rather late, after one had reached approximately the age of forty. The position of *capo di famiglia*, as they described themselves with some degree of pride, could be claimed by 90 percent of all sixty-year-old men and 70 percent of all forty-year-olds, while only 45 percent of the men in the thirty-year-old group could do so, and only 30 percent of all twenty-five-year-olds.

Marriage was surely not the means to authority. The ratio between males who were heads of households and the total number of men in their age group is similar to that between married or widowed heads of households and the total number of married men or widowers; and for each age group the chances of becoming the head of a household seem to have been totally independent of matrimonial status. Age, however, seems to have been a contributing factor to gaining control of the family rudder. In this region in which nearly half the men were already married at twenty-five, married or widowed heads of households constituted only 15 percent of the male population in this age group. At about forty years of age, when almost all men had married, a third still did not head the households in which they lived, and a sizeable number (about 10 percent) of old men, both married men and widowers, were still subject to another man's authority or at most were only able to share authority with him. It can be assumed that 87 percent of all male heads of households were married men or widowers;[17] yet this statistic actually conceals another that is more important for social history: of all married men or widowers, of all these aspiring "heads of families" who hoped for complete authority over a family cell that they had founded, only 72 percent were successful during their lifetime (see table 3.2 and fig. 3.3 in Appendix).

[16]In this region 23 percent of the households were directed by a head who was sixty-eight years or above (22 percent by a man of that age), and more than 24 percent of the total population lived there.

[17]A woman's marital status evidently opened the way to authority, since 75 percent of the heads of households of this sex were widows. But this marital status was obviously a result of age; 31.5 percent of widows were more than sixty-seven years old. By the age of forty, 5 percent of the women were their own mistresses, 8 percent at fifty, and 15 percent after sixty.

Table 3.2—Distribution of Male Heads of Households, Both Married and Widowers, by Age and Percentage of Total (Contado of Pisa, 1427–30)

| | % of All Heads of Households | | | % of Heads of Households, Married and Widowed | |
Age	Heads of Households	Men of Same Age Group	% of Married Men and Widowers of All Men of Same Age Group	Of All Heads of Households of Same Age Group	Of All Married Men and Widowers of Same Age Group
Under 18	1.6	1.5	0.2	0	0
18–22	3	13.7	15.3	21.5	19.3
23–27	5	29.9	52.9	51.4	30
28–32	7.5	45.6	73.8	79.1	48.9
33–37	6.1	56.5	85	85.5	56.7
38–42	12	70.5	93.3	94.3	71.4
43–47	7	74.1	96	97.1	75
48–52	11.3	83.9	95.2	96.6	85.1
53–57	6.7	85.8	93.4	96.1	88.3
58–62	10.8	90	95.2	96	91.2
63–67	5.4	87.5	97.6	98.3	88.2
68 and over	22	85.9	93.1	95.4	88
Unknown	1.5	54.1	28	40.2	77.7
Total	100	37.6	45.4	87.1	72.3

A factor analysis taking into consideration the sex, age, and matrimonial status of the head of the household by township, by wealth and profession, and by various indications of the size and structure of the household reveals that the percentages of the total population by large age groups or by matrimonial status remain approximately constant and consequently do not appear discriminative.[18] Male heads of households, whether married or widowed, adult or elderly (over forty-five and over sixty-five years of age), remain near the center of gravity for the whole. However, young unmarried heads of households or those whose status is undetermined are found to have been characteristic of certain large villages that stand apart from the central cluster. These same atypical localities also include a sizeable number of households headed by women. Although the disparity between the number of married men or widowers

[18]The statistical technique of a factor analysis of relationships consists of seeking out in the whole at *n* dimensions the principal axes of inertia for the system. Its originality rests on the relationships existing between the two "clusters," that of characteristics and that of individuals. One single analysis is necessary, while other methods would necessitate two; and the graphic comparison is much easier to interpret and "speaks" to the reader. In addition, this method takes *relative* frequencies into account and consequently analyzes profiles, while stressing the differences (cf. J. P. Benzecri, *Distance distributionnelle et métrique du X² en analyse factorielle des correspondances,* Institut statistique de l'Université de Paris, 1969 [mimeographed]).

who are heads of households and the number of married men or widowers as a whole remains only slightly noticeable and does not clearly indicate any one group of localities, the isolation of townships characterized by an unusual frequency of young heads of households reveals an atypical situation in these rural areas (see fig. 3.4[1] in Appendix). We shall return to this point later.

Once the peasant of the region of Pisa—and this is undoubtedly valid for rural Tuscany as a whole—had reached a position of authority late in life, he did not loosen his grasp until the very end and gradually filled his house with his sons' children[19] as his own family let daughters marry and leave the family group.[20] Toward the middle of the long and slow cycle in the development of the household, there was a marked increase in the probability that several generations would overlap for an appreciable period of time, despite a high mortality rate, as we can see by the percentages of households comprising three generations in table 3.3.[21]

Less than one rural household out of four, therefore, included a grandfather, or more often a grandmother, and grandchildren, but in the city the probability fell to a rate of one out of five. Although men were married at a relatively late age compared with girls, the sons of rural families do not appear to have postponed their marriages until they could "set up housekeeping" thanks to the retirement or death of the person holding the family inheritance or until they received a portion that would make them independent.[22] The father's voluntary renunciation of author-

[19]We obtain a very clear indication of this by comparing the distribution of children under fourteen years of age according to the age of the head of the household in which they lived, with that established on the basis of their own father's age. The first table involves a double maximum, the first point corresponding to the biological maximum reached at about forty or forty-five years of age, the age at which a man exerts his full power as father; this maximum, of course, is found in the second table as well. The second point, which only appears in the first table, represents the number of grandchildren living in a household comprising at least three generations and headed by an elderly man: 41 percent of the households directed by a head who was more than sixty-seven years old included between one and four children, and 7 percent had five children!

[20]There was a very clear tendency for newlyweds to choose to live in the house of the groom's father. Sons-in-law are almost never mentioned in the *Catasto*; I found only two in our 4,000 Pisan homes. The return of the widowed daughter and her children to her father's house was also rare in this region; she generally remained with her parents-in-law, who would reluctantly return her dowry; when she finally managed to obtain it, she would remain independent.

[21]In this table, established on the basis of a computer program worked out by Herlihy, the percentages for the city of Pisa are used as a standard of comparison. Households including four generations, rare though they were, often sheltered a "centenarian." Thus, in the Pisan contado, Giovanni di Nardo, a sixty-nine-year-old head of a household, supported a father who was a hundred and three (Archivio di Stato, Pisa, Ufficio Fiumi e Fossi, 1542, f° 143).

[22]For this region the average marriage age for males, calculated by the method described by J. Hajnal in "Age at Marriage and Proportions Marrying," *Population Studies* 17 (1953): 111–36, was 26.3 years; in the *Catasto* the average age of bridegrooms, fifteen in all and

Table 3.3—Number of Generations per Household (city and countryside of Pisa, in %)

Number of Generations per Household	City of Pisa	Countryside around Pisa
One	29 %	23.3%
Two	49.8	52
Three	20.4	23.5
Four	0.8	1.2
Total	100	100

ity over his household was only on rare occasions recorded in the *Catasto,* which lists an insignificant number of retired fathers who lived in the house of their son, who was officially considered to be the fiscally responsible individual.[23]

Did the death of the head of the household and the accession of the new heir therefore mean the beginning of a new family cycle? This event did not really break up a major number of households, and married brothers who continued to "live in common" formed a rather sizeable proportion of the total number of homes (8.1 percent in the contado of Pisa). Equality among heirs was the general rule in rural Tuscany, as it was throughout Italy at that time;[24] and the chief recourse against

---

described as such, was slightly higher: 27.1 years. The average age for women at marriage was much lower, 17.3 years, both according to Hajnal's methods and according to a sample from the *Catasto.* In the city of Pisa, the masculine age climbed to 28.8 years and the feminine age to 18.6. For Florence, see D. Herlihy, "Vieillir au Quattrocento," *Annales, E.S.C.* 24 (November–December 1969).

[23]Of almost 4,000 homes, 66, or 1.65 percent, included a retired father and 17 percent an elderly mother. In the city of Pisa, 8.5 percent of the households supported a retired father, 16.5 percent a widowed mother.

[24]Cf. A. Pertile, *Storia del diritto italiano* (Turin, 1896); E. Besta, *La famiglia nella storia del diritto italiano,* 2d ed. (Milan, 1962); and Besta, *Le successioni nella storia del diritto italiano* (Padua, 1935). Primogeniture or ultimogeniture appeared later in the rural world, and during the Middle Ages the transfer of peasant possessions was rarely made exclusively in favor of a single son, who either excluded his other brothers by means of portions for minors established once they had agreed to renounce their inheritance, or who agreed to support them on the family property on condition that they remain unmarried. The "stem family" as it existed in the Pyrenees and the Alps (cf. Berkner, "The Stem Family") does not appear to have been a widespread system of family structure and inheritance in the region we are studying, nor, apparently, in the rest of the Florentine contado. The average age of adult, unmarried brothers living with a married head (twenty-nine to thirty years) shows that they still had the possibility of marrying and establishing an independent family or else of remaining on the paternal property. The ratio of adult brothers to heads of households is, moreover, lower in the Pisan countryside than in the chief towns. At Pisa, there were ten adult brothers per hundred heads of households; in the contado only seven. A stem family system would imply a higher percentage of permanent celibacy than the maximum of 6.5 percent that we have found in the rural population described by the *Catasto* of this region.

breaking the peasant inheritance into pieces remained joint ownership, which generally went hand in hand with co-residence and joint cultivation of the land.[25] An inheritance therefore did not automatically imply the division and fission of the family group.[26] Co-residence remained firmly entrenched as long as the replacement rate for families remained low (since a small number of sons reached adult age during their father's lifetime) and as long as the maximum size of the family group (beyond which coexistence became intolerable or impossible on a property that was too small) was as a result reached at a late date. At that point fission would eventually appear the only way to resolve the problems raised by divided authority and by shared means of subsistence among families that were too distantly related.[27]

[25]But not always, and enough examples are found in the *Catasto* to justify raising the question. "Division" generally involved the separation of families which until then had been welded together into a single home. Yet on many occasions division also followed upon the heels of a family separation, and in any case the *Catasto* was slow to record this event, since it meant a revision of the fiscal rates for rural parishes. It was, however, the approval of the employees of the *Catasto* and the recording of the event in their registers that rendered family schisms legal. Cf. C. Fumagalli, *Il diritto di fraterna nella giurisprudenza da Accursio alla codificazione* (Turin, 1912), pp. 116, 127, 139. Cf. also examples of recent property and family divisions for this region in the Archivo di Stato, Pisa, Ufficio Fiumi e Fossi, 1540, f° 350, 355, and 448; 1545, f° 145; 1559, f° 385 (in all three cases, the recorded division of property apparently followed an earlier separation of the families). According to jurists of the day, if two relatives were inscribed in the *Catasto* under a common name, and if the fiscal burden was shared, they were presumed to hold the property in common. Thus, many factors come into play in an attempt to discover the actual situation within a certain number of extended families as they appear in the fiscal registers. Even though the persons are listed as co-residents, we encounter the problem of whether the individuals really lived in common; the phrase indicating such an arrangement assumes that the same table was shared (*a uno pane e uno vino*), but many large families nevertheless declared several distinct dwellings, though they might be very close to one another. (Cf. for example, Tommeo di Stefano, who lived with his three married nephews in "case due coniuncte insieme . . . le quale case elli habitano con la sua famiglia" [ibid., 1542, f° 657].)

[26]Less than in the city at any rate; in Pisa, only 4.4 percent of the households were formed by joint families of co-resident brothers.

[27]For demographic factors influencing the size of the household, see the discussion of A. J. Coale et al., *Aspects of the Analysis of Family Structure* (Princeton, 1965, in T. K. Burch, "Some Demographic Determinants of Average Household Size: an Analytic Approach," *Demography* 7 (1970): 61 ff. This author stresses that in a regime of the extended family, a low mortality rate increases the probability that an adult son will remain in his father's household, thus increasing the size of that family. On the other hand, in a stem-family system, where a maximum of only two couples belonging to two successive generations can co-reside, and a greater number of sons survives until adulthood, only one will remain with the father once he has married, and the others will go off to increase the number of isolated households and will as a result decrease the average household size. In a system of extended families, a multiple household's increase in size depends essentially upon fertility and mortality rates or, in other words, on the number of children reaching adulthood. In Tuscany, the marriage age for women, although early, undoubtedly was not sufficient to increase fertility since the considerable difference in ages between husband and wife contributed to early widowhood (in this region at least 23.7 percent of women were widows by the age of fifty) and since women generally did not remarry.

Indeed, if we follow a group of families through the Quattrocento,[28] we note that the multiple families of 1427 tended to preserve their characteristics from one generation to another. It is clear that during the course of their development multiple families were more likely to form complex units in the years or decades to come, since two married brothers living together could each hope to see a son reach adulthood, marry, and found, on the same patrimony and under the same roof, a family that would live next to its cousins. The bursting point generally came during the third generation, between cousins or between an uncle and nephews too numerous to survive within the narrow framework provided by the family property. As in the Serbia described by Hammel, co-residence in family groups rarely continued after the marriage of the cousins—*fratelli cugini*, as they described themselves.[29] While the division that occurred at that time did not necessarily result in the appearance of simple conjugal families, we can nevertheless view this division as the point of departure for a new family cycle.[30]

Joint ownership among male heirs was the frequent solution to the threat of broken-up property inherent in the egalitarian customary law dealing with the transfer of property. Treatises by jurists of the day confirm this in their discussions of tacit, that is, unofficial joint ownership.[31] Canon lawyers of the fourteenth and fifteenth centuries devoted an abundant literature to the problems of "two brothers." Their chief

[28]In San Lorenzo al Corniolo, a parish of Mugello to the north of Florence, the fifteenth-century *catasti* compiled between 1428 and 1480 (the *catasto* of 1487 is missing for this parish) indicate seventy-nine family groups, 17.7 percent of which were composed of lineages in which several co-resident fraternal couples were jointly responsible for taxes at one time or another during this period. Now, four of them continued this type of fraternal alliance over two generations at least, and perhaps even beyond 1480. Seven others remained stable units throughout the lifetime of the married brothers. In seven other lineages, one or several unmarried brothers joined the head and his wife; two later married and remained in the same house, thereby moving up into the first category.

[29]Cf. Hammel, "Preliminary Notes." The proportion of cousins who were co-heads of adjoining households was at the most 1 percent of the total number of households. Taxpayers often insisted, in order to justify their claims, that joint ownership of this sort really existed, although it was unusual; thus Andrea di Puccio, who at sixty-seven was still living with his sixty-five-year-old cousin, declared, "Nostri padri non partitteno mai e chusi noi none abbiamo partito" (Archivio di Stato, Pisa, Ufficio Fiumi e Fossi, 1559, f° 121). The bond between cousins seems to have been considered by these households of cousins as a fraternal one rather than one between distant relatives, and the term *"fratello cugino,"* which designated such households, was often replaced by the word *"fratello"* through a slip attributable either to the taxpayer or to the scribe.

[30]Schisms occurring in the most complex families, those composed of brothers or cousins, occurred more frequently than among married sons and fathers. These schisms therefore gave rise to the appearance of more "multiple" households, although they were actually another type, since their predominant relationships were those between an ascendant and a descendant.

[31]The study by Fumagalli, *Il diritto di fraterna,* is the most detailed; cf. also N. Tamassia, *La famiglia italiana nei secoli decimoquinto et decimosesto,* 2d. ed. (Milan, 1971).

concern was the urban family and the lawsuits resulting from the breakdown in family ties that had, until then, meant cohesion; but the large peasant family does not yet seem to have raised problems of this sort for the jurists of the period. In Tuscany, as in Venice or in Lombardy,[32] under certain conditions the male descendants of the deceased head of the household who still lived together in rural areas legally remained owners-in-common, or "*fraterna compagnia*"; and the principles established in the fourteenth and fifteenth centuries regarding the presumption and proof of jointly owned property would be repeated endlessly until the eighteenth century in the case of peasants, even though they had long since ceased to be applied to nobles or businessmen.

Was this cleavage, which lawyers of the period described, between occupational or social groups to be found in parishes and families in the region under study? First let us point out that artisans, small shopkeepers, and "services" comprised only a small minority (4.5 percent) of taxpayers in the large villages of the Pisan contado, a minority even smaller than in the Florentine rural areas as a whole (5.7 percent). Through factor analysis, using the township as a common unit, we have been able to draw a clear distinction between the families of these occupational groups and those of the peasants. In addition to the occupational pattern of families in those townships encompassing the greatest number of families from the "secondary" and "tertiary" sectors* (Livorno, Castiglione della Pescaia, and a major portion of the parishes in the *podesterie* of Campiglia and Palaia), we also encounter a greater number of very rich families (assessed on the basis of more than 400 florins), a greater than normal number of households directed by a woman or by an unmarried man, and an unusual number of small households composed of one person (see fig. 3.4[3] in Appendix).

If we then take the occupational groups themselves as units of analysis, we can verify that the distribution of family types is very different among artisans and tradesmen from that found among peasants[33] (see table 3.4 [2] and [3]). Everything seems to indicate that each generation of shopkeepers and artisans broke up the expanded solidarity so dear to the peasants, since they were incapable of expanding their means of production. Their family cycles, much shorter and more "individual" than those of the peasants, did not benefit from the conditions that helped the latter

*The French divide the economy into three "sectors"; the primary sector, which includes economic activities producing raw materials (chiefly agriculture); the secondary sector, which transforms these raw materials; and the tertiary sector, which includes all activities not directly involved in producing consumer goods.—Trans.

[32]Fumagalli, *Il diritto di fraterna,* pp. 89, 106.

[33]Respectively, 12 percent among isolated individuals as compared with 3 percent among peasants; 57 percent among conjugal families as compared with 53 percent; and 18 percent of multiple households compared with 30 percent (table 3.4[3]).

Table 3.4(1)—Size of Rural Households on the Basis of Taxable Wealth (western half of Florentine territory) (in % of total households in each category)

Size of Fortune (in florins) / Size of Household	0	1-25	26-50	51-100	101-200	201-400	401 and over	Total
1-3 persons	34.8	46.6	43.3	35.1	25.7	18	16.1	37.4
4-5	33.4	27.2	26.3	26.8	27.6	22.6	21.7	28.1
6-10	28.9	23.8	27.8	32.3	37.4	39.2	37.3	29.2
11 and over	2.9	2.3	3.6	5.8	9.2	19.8	24.8	5.2
Total	100	99.9	100	100	99.9	99.7	99.9	99.9
% of all households	23.4	30.7	15.3	13.4	9.8	5.1	2.3	100

NOTE: The columns totaling slightly less than 100% are due to the presence of declarations of patrimonies which have no dependent "mouths" to feed but which have nonetheless been included in the total.

rebuild their families. Wealth being equal, townships predominantly composed of landowners working their land themselves are located along an axis of the factor analysis at the pole opposite that occupied by artisans. Their families are large (6–10 persons), extended to include several nuclear ones; their heads are firmly established men, either married or widowers. If we then look at those townships in which cultivators predominate (whatever the manner by which they hold their land), we find them grouped about the variables that are characteristic of extended and large families, although they are all at very different levels of wealth (fig. 3.4 [3] in Appendix).

Table 3.4(2)—Size of Households on the Basis of Occupational Category (same geographical region) (in % of total households in each category)

Occupational Category / Size of Household	Mezzadri (Share-croppers)	Affittuari (Persons Renting Land)	Small Landowners Operating Farm	Artisans, Tradesmen	Without Specified Occupation
1-3 persons	20.3	25.3	30.5	37.9	48.2
4-5	32.5	29.5	30.3	30.1	25.1
6-10	40.5	37.1	31.8	27	22.9
11 and over	6.6	8.1	7.4	4.8	3.6
Total	99.9	100	100	99.8	99.8
% of all households	21.2	4.7	18	5.8	50.2

Table 3.4(3)—Typology of Rural Households on the Basis of Occupation (same geographical region) (in % of total households in each category)

Occupational Category / Type of Household	Mezzadri (Share-croppers)	Affittuari (Persons Renting Land)	Small Landowners Operating Farm	Artisans, Tradesmen	Without Specified Occupation
Isolated households	1.4	2.8	4.6	12.2	19.9
Conjugal families Not extended	54.9	54.5	51.8	57.2	52.2
With one ascendant member	11	11.7	11.9	10.2	9.2
With one collateral member	1.3	1.1	2	2	1.3
Multiple households With vertical principle	22.6	21.3	21.1	13.4	11.7
With horizontal principle	8.8	8.5	8.5	4.8	5.5
Total	100	99.9	99.9	99.8	100

Thus, rural taxpayers with a few fields appear to have maintained solid family structures. We see no fundamental difference between the family structures of the sharecropping *mezzadri* and those of small landowners cultivating their own fields.[34] The abundance of land left vacant by the

[34]See above, tables 3.4. At the most we can find more isolated households or nonconjugal ones in the second group than in the first (4.6 percent as compared with 1.4 percent), and as a result, slightly lower percentages of conjugal families (51.7 percent / 55 percent) or of multiple households (29.6 percent / 31.3 percent), while at the same time there is on the average a slight decrease in the families of small landowners cultivating their land. (These percentages are applicable to the western region of the Florentine territory and not specifically to the contado of Pisa.) The greatest family aggregates are found chiefly among small landowners and the *affittuari,* who took over *poderi* through a *mezzadria* when their homes became too crowded. Yet what sort of life-in-common and co-residence could this be, since the *mezzadro* was supposed to inhabit the peasant house on his landlord's property? Take the example of the household of Antonio di Fanuccio, in the territory of the township of Colle, near the contado of Pisa. Antonio described himself as "de' fratelli della corte di Colle" and, indeed, he theoretically lived in a household composed of six families and twenty-seven persons; but one of his brothers lived in a separate house, and the head of the family also declared two residences "nella quale abitano i dette fratelli carnali et cugini stanno tutti insieme" (Archivio di Stato, Florence, *Catasto*, 251, f° 54). In the household of a neighbor, Bartolo di Nardo, which comprised five families and twenty-three mouths to feed, the eldest son was really a *mezzadro* in the region and probably lived on the *podere* (ibid., 251, f° 156). Many examples are also found in the contado of S. Gimignano, where very large families rented *poderi* and were undoubtedly at least temporarily reduced in size as a

demographic decline and thus available for cultivation directly favored those attempting to gather together lands and indirectly favored "family regrouping." The bourgeois would piece together *poderi* ["small farms"] or sharecropping farms, while established peasant families would round out their patrimony when a child was born or some member reached an age at which he could contribute new manpower. In the cases of both the *mezzadri*, who went from parish to parish in search of the best *podere*, and the families of small farmers, this "family regrouping" permitted the members to gather the strength needed to cultivate land that was more profitable for the owner and less risky for the cultivator. The "master" of the sharecropping farm asked that his *lavoratori* ["laborers"] form a complete unit of production, from small children up to grandmother, in order to assure the complete exploitation of his property. The small landowner found that the best protection of his inheritance lay in the cohesion of his family group, and he sought to delay the moment of fission as long as possible.

However, persons farming their land constituted a minority of the population described in the *Catasto*. About half the households in the western portion of Florentine territory and three-quarters in the Pisan contado stated that they had no occupation or gave no indication that they personally worked the land. For the most part these taxpayers were humble people, many of whom worked as hired laborers, lived frugally on the income from a few fields, or were domestic servants elsewhere. The family structure of this group is related to that of rural artisans, though the characteristic traits are more accentuated, at least in the western sector of the Florentine state.[35] Within the Pisan contado those villages characterized by a major number of taxpayers with no declared occupation seem closer to other peasant townships than to the group of large villages conspicuous for the high percentage of artisans and "services."

On the whole, wealth appears to differentiate family structures more effectively than does occupational category. Family structures obviously varied enormously according to the household's wealth. Thus, the number of simple conjugal families and the number of multiple households differed considerably according to whether the household possessed from 1 to 25 florins, or had a capital of more than 400 florins—an enormous sum for these rural areas, where the average fortune was about

---

result of settling a portion of the family on these lands (ibid., 266, f° 453, with a theoretical household of thirty persons, and f° 530, with twenty-two persons, f° 534, etc.).

[35]A high percentage of very small households (48.2 percent have from one to three persons) and of isolated individuals (20 percent; 17.8 percent were multiple households, in other words, far fewer than among small agricultural landowners or *mezzadri,* who averaged between 28 percent and 31 percent.

55 florins.[36] The number of such families ranges respectively from 50 percent to 25 percent and from nearly 16 percent to 57 percent of the total number of households in the category, while the average size of the family increases noticeably with the wealth.[37] These contrasts are at least as clear in rural areas as in cities, and even in Florence, where multiple households and those adding an ascendant or a collateral member to the nuclear family (respectively 9.6 percent and 7.4 percent on the average) are found much more frequently among persons taxed on more than 400 florins (15.3 percent and 8.7 percent) than among poor or middle-income families (see fig. 3.6 in Appendix).

By factor analysis, we can clarify this link between wealth and the enlarging of the family group on the village level. The first axis, the horizontal axis of figure 3.4(2), is an axis indicating wealth; along the second axis, which is primarily an axis indicating the size of the households, we find associated with this variable other family characteristics, such as the number of nuclear families included in it, the type of association among these nuclear families, and the characteristics of the head of the family himself. Peasant townships show a tendency to increase in size and complexity of structure as their wealth increases; but the clusters linking wealth and large families split into two groups when we come to townships characterized by the presence of large fortunes. These same townships are also those which are set apart from the purely rural localities by the relative importance of the secondary and tertiary sectors.

These associations define certain regional groups that are representative of the diversity of functions and of wealth in villages. The poorest parishes of the Pisan province, situated in the low regions along the lower Arno (the *podesterie* of S. Maria al Trebbio and part of Cascina and Calci) show a connection between material poverty and family size, which is markedly below average. They form a very special group when compared with comfortable peasant townships to the north of Pisa (*podesteria* of Ripafratta), where extended families predominate, and with the villages of the "Pisan hills" south of the Arno, which, with their average-sized families and their moderate wealth, form the middle of the central "cluster." In the large villages of the Maremma, we find smaller families, despite the presence of unusually large fortunes. More diversified employment, a greater degree of mobility within the population as a result of transhumance or of maritime activities, and perhaps malaria contributed to reduce the number of large families and to counteract the influence of their wealth (figs. 3.4 [3] and 3.5 in Appendix).

[36]In the contado of Pisa the average was 42 florins.
[37]Cf. table 3.4 (1).

We must therefore qualify the idea that wealth and the extension of the family group always went hand in hand. In the townships of the Pisan contado, the nature of the occupational activities carried on and of the wealth possessed was a major discriminative factor that gave rise to considerable differences in behavior within social groups of equivalent wealth. The long cycle of family development is therefore not characteristic exclusively of well-to-do and rich families, but rather of those with lands to cultivate. Men who hired themselves out for the day obviously saw no advantage in maintaining co-residence and joint fiscal responsibility with persons other than members of their very close family. As soon as they were old enough to work, their sons went off as the labor market beckoned. These observations cast a light on the special role played by the sharecropping *mezzadria*. Although the families that worked a property through this sort of contract were stripped of any other source of income, the vast majority of them showed a strong tendency to form large and extended groups. Although the contract implied residence on the land of the *oste* ["landlord"] and frequently obliged families to move from one parish to another, this incessant transplanting did not destroy the cohesive bonds of these "family associations for production." The very instability of the *mezzadria* contract and the relative uncertainty about the future that consequently hung over the peasant's head did not prevent the extended family from persisting in a social stratum of peasants who had been stripped of any other resources, in contrast to the rest of the agricultural and industrial proletariat. Using taxable capital as our only criterion does not fully take into account the contrary trends that strengthened the extended structures of the family group among the sharecropping *mezzadri* and weakened them among the common laborers. In the diversified society of fifteenth-century Tuscany—a society that was in addition turned upside down by declining population and military conflicts—social hierarchies and class conflicts masked and distorted a family structure that varied according to the total social picture.

We might ask ourselves what implicit model of the family and of the authority exerted over it fits, as an ideal, the structures we have described and the demographic and economic constraints that influenced the family group. After all, it is not clear that the extended family was still considered the ideal family by the average peasant of this region, despite the great possibility that he would spend his entire life in such a family. But how can we discover the peasant's own view of the domestic group of which he was a part? An indirect method is to determine the hierarchies that peasants spontaneously introduced among members of the *famiglia*, by examining the place assigned to various members of the household on the list of the *Catasto*. Such an attempt would be based on the assumption that the head of the household had personally dictated his family's composition to the scribe and that, in copies made subsequently, the order he had established was respected.[38] If we accept this premise, we can determine both the degree of respect due each individual and those internal relationships that were considered preeminent. A sampling of the first 1,000 families of the Pisan contado provides some interesting indications.

Assuming that the taxpayer whose name appears at the top of the declaration was indeed the head of the household,[39] we first discover that almost without exception his name appears at the top of the list of household members. If he was married, his wife was named immediately after him and before any other person in 87 percent of the cases in which the family also included children, ascendants, or collateral relatives. In the remaining 13 percent, she is listed after one or more of the latter, especially after her mother-in-law,[40] and on rare occasions—although apparently more frequently than in an urban setting—after her own children.[41]

In the rare cases (1.7 percent of all households) in which the father "has retired" and has ceded his authority to one son with whom he continues to live, the transfer of power was real. The old couple is listed before the son—who in such a case is always unmarried—only 12 percent of the time in this type of household. Otherwise, the elderly parents, always named together, are listed after the son and his family and even after the

[38]With rare exceptions, the *campione,* or scribe copying the official register, was only recopying the list of household members as it appeared on the original declaration written or dictated by the taxpayer. On the other hand, it is possible that the peasant, without realizing it, had a certain hierarchical order imposed upon him as the result of the mental categories of the scribe, who by his questions influenced the order of the replies. (Likewise, the scribe would be following a traditional order in the general form of the declaration and in the description of the household property.) Our research therefore runs the risk of defining hierarchies within the peasant family as the scribe saw them rather than as the peasant himself lived them.

[39]He is thus the head of the "fiscal household." The most striking discrepancies between fiction and reality in tax records appear in the families of minor orphans who had inherited paternal property that was now in their name and who declared their own mother as a dependent. In the list of *bocce,* or dependent "mouths," to feed, the mother was often listed first, thus regaining the prestige commensurate with the authority she was actually exercising.

[40]In two-thirds of the households that included an aged mother, the head's wife, her daughter-in-law, preceded her. In an urban setting, at Arezzo for example, it seems that the prestige of the head's wife paled before that of her mother-in-law, for in half the cases the latter was listed before her daughter-in-law. The brother-in-law allowed his sister-in-law to appear before him on the list in 56 percent of the cases in the region of Pisa, and half of those in our sample for Arezzo.

[41]In households in the Pisan countryside composed of a couple and its unmarried children, the mother was listed after her children in only 3.4 percent of the cases; but the percentage was even lower in the city (1.5 percent). The husband-wife order was almost never reversed, but husband and wife were sometimes separated by the head's brother or, more rarely (in 4 cases out of 106), by a married son.

grandson's family or that of a second married son, if they exist. On the other hand, unmarried grandchildren are always listed after their grandparents.

In multiple households in which several married brothers live together, the lists make a clear distinction between the various subgroups of the family in more than two cases out of three (70 percent). This is implicit evidence that distinct "families" were juxtaposed. In the very few cases in which a married son and a married brother live together with the head of a family, it is impossible to discern which of the latter is preeminent.[42] The hierarchies of age win out among ascendant or descendant couples and, secondarily, among collateral groups. There is no doubt that the fraternal bond that kept *frèrèches* [married siblings in co-residence after the death or retirement of their elders] united was primarily considered a link between groups that had become slightly dissymmetrical through the difference in the ages of their respective heads. In any event, the eldest son of either family head was merely the chief among the children owing obedience to their father.

The place granted to women largely depended upon their matrimonial status. The wife of the old retired father met exactly the same fate as her husband and was either honored at the head of the list or relegated with him to the very end. But once widowed, the woman found that the respect due her was greatly diminished, at least in rural families. In only one out of three occasions is she listed immediately after her son, the head of the family, and before her daughter-in-law, her grandchildren, and her own unmarried children.[43] The widowed sister-in-law of the head of the family would seem to have been considered the equal of her late husband while her children were still minors and she served as their spokeswoman before their uncle; but once they were of an age to claim their share of authority and their part of the inheritance, their mother was apt to be moved down, like the grandmother, to the end of the list. Even while married, women did not always share in the authority and prestige due their husbands. The married son rarely preceded his mother, but the married brother of the family head was listed before his sister-in-law in 30 percent of the cases, while unmarried sons were listed before their sister-in-law 25 percent of the time. We know that a patrilineal system often results in the disparagement of women and girls, by whom property is not transmitted. The

[42]Of these, 1,000 rural households, 10.6 percent included at least one married son of the head of the household, at least 1.6 percent included two sons, and at least 1 percent included a married brother and a married son. These percentages seem a little lower than those for the 4,000 families as a whole (12.8 percent of households included at least one married son, and 2.6 percent at least two).

[43]Our sample shows that in the city of Arezzo, she would have one chance out of two to precede all these relatives.

Catasto reflects this tendency to discriminate between the sexes to the degree that certain individuals described their children by listing boys first although they were younger than the girls, while the inverse never occurred. Using a sampling of 200 homes in which the presence of children of different sexes permits us to discern this preference,[44] we find that only one of the twenty-four urban households considered the boys preeminent as compared with seven of the forty-two rural households. If a study of a larger proportion of the population were to confirm this tendency, we could consider it a secondary characteristic of patrilineal rural society.

The preceding remarks are only preliminary work in a more extensive and detailed research project we would like to carry out. At best these remarks permit us to discern within the family group the existence of subgroups hierarchically arranged according to the age of their respective head. In *frérèches* in which several *fathers* coexisted, the eldest seems to have been considered to a certain degree the head of the family community; but the threat that the property might be divided certainly must have tempered his authority in households of small landowners, if not among the *mezzadri*, and the younger son could attenuate his elder brother's authority over his own sons by evoking his title as coheir. The description in the *Catasto*, therefore, generally makes a clear distinction between two parallel groups, subordinating sons to fathers and women to their husbands. In households of this sort, the entire younger generation is occasionally shown as submissive to the older generation as a whole, or all the women are listed after all the men. However, these tendencies are seen more often in the country than in our small urban sampling, and they indicate both an accentuation of the structural characteristics we have attempted to elucidate and a more deeply rooted sense of the agnatic bond of male descent.

On the other hand, these relatively rigid hierarchies of age operated fully in patriarchal households, and they made the sharing of authority by different generations impossible. If by chance authority was ceded, the direction of family affairs was no longer shared with the individual who had abdicated. This rapid decline of the old retired couple and, even more markedly, of the surviving grandparent or great-grandparent, is striking in

---

[44]In addition to the families having only children of the same sex, we are excluding those in which children of both sexes are listed by age regardless of sex and in which it is therefore impossible or of no interest to try to determine the strength of the sexual criterion. In the contado of Pisa, where numerous corrections were made on the original list during the two years that followed the compilation of the register, during which time employees would add taxable sons who had been "forgotten" by their father, we have also eliminated such families since the list was not drawn up at one sitting (and since they are the only ones to list girls first before an older brother whose name was added later).

rural areas. As a general rule, the great majority of aged men made no concessions in exercising their authority; at times it was shared with a brother or a nephew, but never with a son.

We have described briefly the family structures in which the magnitude of the great, undivided, agnatic, patrilineal, and "patrivirilocal" family can unequivocally be seen. The fact that only a minority of the households studied represents such a family does not prevent the system from also including the other types of families in a complex cycle in which this copy of the "medieval model" of the family remained sensitive to economic and demographic conditions. The predominant developmental cycle among landowning rural classes was one that continued over several generations, during the course of which these generations overlapped to the degree permitted by the mortality rate. But the family characteristics of the sharecropping *mezzadri* show that the economic criterion of the family patrimony was not the sole and absolute guiding force. Indeed, this type of contract preserved an extended-family system within a class of the rural population whose lack of possessions would more properly oblige it to limit the size of the domestic unit.

Within this rural society in which the peasant family maintained a solid numerical base and an extended structure, the atypical families—as factor analysis shows—were those usually found in cities. In some places they were numerous enough to train a spotlight on a number of especially wretched townships—or especially rich ones—that were not exclusively agricultural. Yet as a whole, the population of the Pisan countryside follows the general model we have described.

The average size of the household, which remained rather low despite these structural characteristics, confirms empirically what demographers have been seeking to establish through their computations: a high mortality rate combined with a moderate or relatively low fertility rate effectively limits the average size of the family group, even in a regime where the extended family predominates.[45] Their theoretical calculations of average sizes roughly correspond to those we have found in rural Tuscany, where the great agnatic family based upon male descent was predominant, and in the cities of that province, especially in Florence, where the conjugal family and its remnants prevailed in the vast majority

[45]Cf. Coale et al., *Aspects of the Analysis of Family Structure,* commented upon by Burch, "Some Demographic Determinants." Since the life expectancy at birth was between twenty and forty years, under the same demographic conditions, the average size of households in a system of extended families would be 30 percent to 73 percent greater than that reached in the system of conjugal families. Thus, for $e_0 = 20$, we can compute a theoretical average of 3.6 per household in a system of nuclear families, and of 4.7 in an extended system; with $e_0 = 40$, we move to 4.2 and 7.2 respectively. The actual situation in Tuscany seems to have fallen between these two groups of figures at a level corresponding to an intermediate e_0.

of the population and where more distinct and impermeable social categories prevented the "extended" model of the upper classes from spreading further down the social ladder.

Consequently, this rather low average size, observed within a society of the late Middle Ages, cannot lead us to conclude, in the absence of other data, that the "European" model of marriage and family structures had spread. The originality of Tuscany, when compared with Western Europe at the beginning of the early-modern period, lies in the fact that a numerical decrease in the population and in families went hand in hand with very low female marriage ages, reduced percentages of permanent celibacy, and extended family structures—all characteristic traits of the "non-European" model. Recent research has shown that certain sectors of Tuscan society, the Florentine aristocracy in particular,[46] came close to the "European" model during the sixteenth and seventeenth centuries. Did identical tendencies also appear in the rural population, and at what period? In any event, the *Catasto* proves that the process had not yet started at the beginning of the fifteenth century, with the exception, perhaps, of the proletarianized rural classes or among those engaged in the process of urbanization.

[46]Cf. Litchfield, "Demographic Characteristics of Florentine Patrician Families."

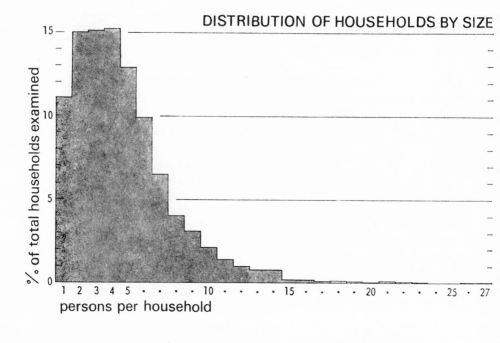

DISTRIBUTION OF HOUSEHOLDS BY SIZE

% of total households examined

persons per household

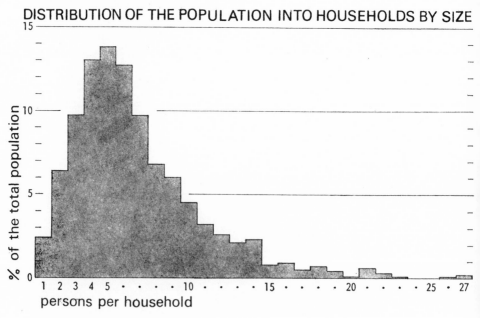

DISTRIBUTION OF THE POPULATION INTO HOUSEHOLDS BY SIZE

% of the total population

persons per household

Figure 3.1. Size of Households (Contado of Pisa, 1427–30)

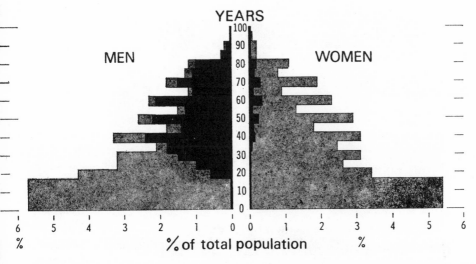

Figure 3.2. Proportion of Heads of Household by Age Group in the Contado of Pisa (in black: heads of households; in grey: total population)

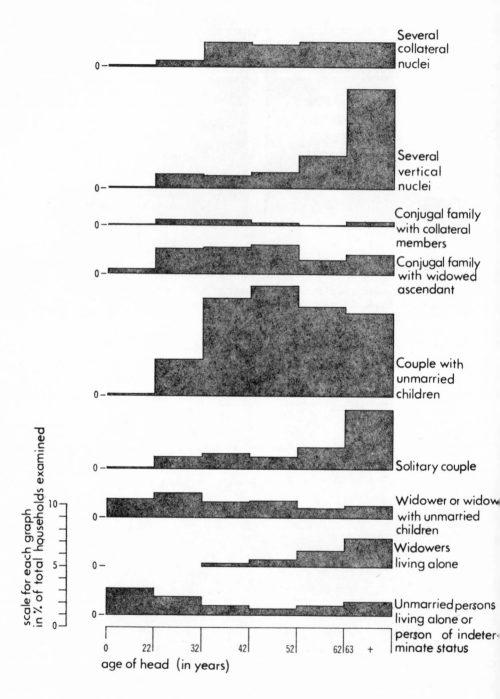

Figure 3.3. Typology of Households by Age of Head (Contado of Pisa, 1427–30)

3.4(1). Clusters of characteristics and villages.

The two clusters, that of "characteristics" and that of "individuals"—in this case the 147 localities of the contado of Pisa—are arranged in relationship to one another according to the first three axes of gravity, which, combined, convey the inertia of 38 percent of the total data. (20.8 percent, 10 percent, and 7.2 percent respectively).

On both diagrams, the first axis, a horizontal one, indicates wealth; more specifically, it separates, on the left, the poorest individuals, those who possess no real estate and who are burdened with responsibilities, from all those on the right who possess something, however modest.

The second axis, indicated by a vertical arrow, goes from the largest and most complex households, at the bottom, to the smallest and simplest, at the top. Other characteristics are closely correlated to the size of the households: structure of household and social position of the head. They are therefore included in the same group of data symbolized by this second axis.

The third axis, represented here in perspective by the size of the dots (the largest are closest to the reader and the smallest are the most distant from the central point at which the three axes cross), is a sort of second axis indicating wealth and distinguishing property owners from one another according to the size of their fortune. It separates characteristics of unusual wealth within the rural setting (200 florins and over) from the common lot, i.e., the slender resources of small peasants and quit-rent holders grouped about the central point.

The first cluster therefore represents a selected group of 106 characteristics as related to the 147 rural localities in the region of Pisa that they describe; the second cluster represents these 147 localities as related to the cluster of characteristics. Although these two graphs can be superimposed, we have juxtaposed them to make them more readable. (In the following pages we have isolated a few of the "families" of characteristics whose arrangement permits us to define the "factors," and we have also indicated the regional groups of villages that can be set apart owing to a certain number of common characteristics.) In figure 3.4(1), the most general characteristics (and consequently the least discriminative ones) and the principal villages delineated by these characeristics are concentrated about the central point. The more eccentric characteristics are isolated, since the localities that are marked by their presence are located at some distance from the central cluster. As a result we can understand why the shapes of the two clusters are not identical: poverty, to the left, and the small size of households, at the top, mark a long, oblique trail of localities stretched out across the upper left portion of the village graph. On the other hand, characteristics unusual in these rural areas—such as fortunes greater than 400 florins, the presence of artisans and "services," major migratory exchanges, etc.—which are found grouped in the upper right quadrant of the cluster of characteristics, cause only a slight extension of the cluster of localities in that direction, while a single characteristic, such as households including more than ten persons, is sufficient to pull a large number of the villages down to the bottom of the graph.

3.4(2). A few families of characteristics.

In this figure we have isolated the most significant characteristics by presenting them in families.

In (a) and (b) we show two inverted representations of wealth. In (a) we show in increasing order the gross wealth (that is to say, before legal deductions) and the taxable wealth. The influence of the third axis, which makes a distinction between the rich and the less rich, is seen at the right, where the dots stand out clearly and stay away from the central point. The abrupt bend of the line joining these two points toward the top, on the side of the greatest wealth, reflects the socioprofessional differentiation among upper classes of the peasantry, which are pulled toward the bottom by the size of their households, and those even wealthier sectors of the population that have a more diversified economic activity and include smaller families.

In (b) we move, from left to right, from the heaviest responsibilities burdening the family to the lightest: this representation of the deductions authorized by the Florentine tax administration appears to be roughly the opposite of the preceding graph.

In (c) the spread of occupational categories moves from the poorest, the braccianti *("day laborers") and hired farm workers, to farmers and sharecroppers* (mezzadri) *on their right. Toward the center of gravity of the whole are the numerous persons "with no declared occupation." In the right portion, close to the wealthiest individuals, we find landowners doing their own farming, who are clearly set apart near the bottom, and artisans, shopkeepers, and "services" at the top, although they are all on very similar levels of fortune (100 or 200 florins). This "fork" suggests, as in (a), that these two occupational groups present very different family profiles.*

In (d) the characteristics of the size and structure of households, indicated by the second axis, are strung along rather evenly from the bottom to the top until we reach households of two or three persons. But the very marked bend to the right and the horizontal line joining these points when we reach households with one person show in a remarkable manner how the presence of very small households, of solitary individuals, and of vacant patrimonies is clearly correlated with other "urban" characteristics (occupational activities, economic independence of women and young persons, more accentuated concentration of wealth).

Graphs (e) and (f) isolate characteristics concerning heads of households in terms of their age and their marital status. In (e) mature men, either married or widowers, who are responsible for a famiglia, *are grouped about the central point. This is where the authority resides in the great majority of households. Toward the top and to the right we find a separate group of young men who are already independent and who are associated with "urban" characteristics, both occupational and economic. Women appear in their turn in graph (f) in a very eccentric fashion; their presence at the head of a household can be indisputably observed in the less "rural" milieus of the Pisan contado but only in a completely marginal fashion within the agricultural population.*

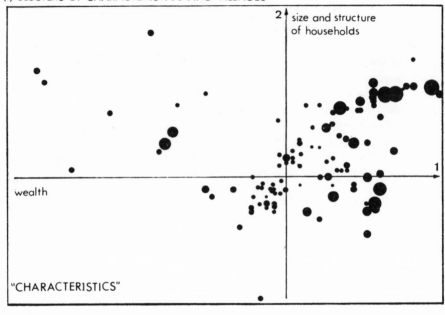

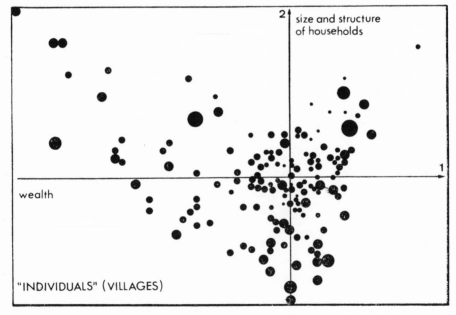

Figure 3.4. Factor Analysis of Localities in the Contado of Pisa

(2) A FEW FAMILIES OF CHARACTERISTICS

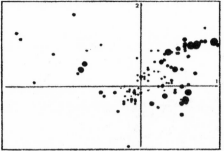

→ THE CLUSTERS OF CHARACTERISTICS

A FEW FAMILIES OF CHARACTERISTICS
↓
(the line which joints the points indicates the
direction taken by each family of characteristics)

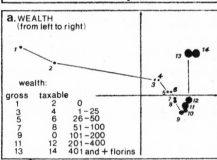

a. WEALTH
(from left to right)

wealth:

gross	taxable	
1	2	0
3	4	1 – 25
5	6	26 – 50
7	8	51 – 100
9	0	101 – 200
11	12	201 – 400
13	14	401 and + florins

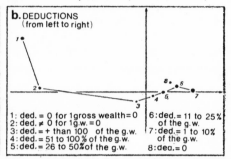

b. DEDUCTIONS
(from left to right)

1: ded. = 0 for 1gross wealth=0
2: ded. ≠ 0 for 1g.w.=0
3: ded. = + than 100 of the g.w.
4: ded. = 51 to 100 % of the g.w.
5: ded.= 26 to 50%of the g.w.
6: ded.= 11 to 25 %
    of the g.w.
7: ded.= 1 to 10%
    of the g.w.
8: dea.= 0

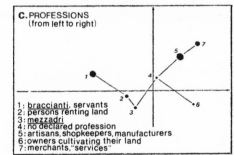

c. PROFESSIONS
(from left to right)

1: <u>braccianti</u>, servants
2: persons renting land
3: <u>mezzadri</u>
4: no declared profession
5: artisans, shopkeepers, manufacturers
6: owners cultivating their land
7: merchants, "services"

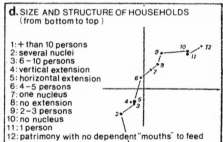

d. SIZE AND STRUCTURE OF HOUSEHOLDS
(from bottom to top)

1: + than 10 persons
2: several nuclei
3: 6 – 10 persons
4: vertical extension
5: horizontal extension
6: 4 – 5 persons
7: one nucleus
8: no extension
9: 2 – 3 persons
10: no nucleus
11: 1 person
12: patrimony with no dependent "mouths" to feed

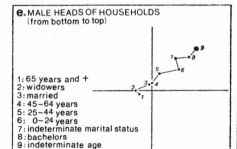

e. MALE HEADS OF HOUSEHOLDS
(from bottom to top)

1: 65 years and +
2: widowers
3: married
4: 45 – 64 years
5: 25 – 44 years
6: 0 – 24 years
7: indeterminate marital status
8: bachelors
9: indeterminate age

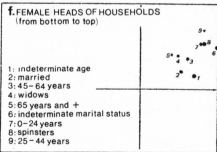

f. FEMALE HEADS OF HOUSEHOLDS
(from bottom to top)

1: indeterminate age
2: married
3: 45 – 64 years
4: widows
5: 65 years and +
6: indeterminate marital status
7: 0 – 24 years
8: spinsters
9: 25 – 44 years

(3) REGIONAL GROUPS

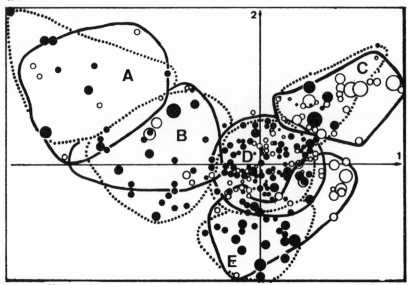

Above, the two clusters of figure 3.4 (1) are superimposed

A SANTA MARIA A TREBBIO (in part)

Gross and taxable wealth nil
Mobile population
No houses belonging to occupants
Indebted households
Reduced sizes of households,
directed by men

B SANTA MARIA A TREBBIO (in part)
CALCI (in part) + CASCINA

Taxable wealth nil, overburdened
household
No houses belonging to occupants,
or rented houses
Rented oxen
Salaried farm workers and small
farmers cultivating rented fields
Mobile households
Sick persons

C PALAIA (in part), LARI (in part)
CAMPIGLIA (in part), LIVORNO:
CASTIGLIONE DELLA PESCAIA

Large fortunes
Secondary and tertiary professional
sectors
Households of reduced size and of
simple structure, headed by young
men, bachelors, persons of indeterminate status, or by women
Families bearing one name, mobile

groups of villages   groups of corresponding
                      characteristics

D CALCI ⎫   PESCOLI
       LARI ⎪ (in part) VICO
       RIPAFRATTA ⎬ +ROSIGNANO
       PALAIA ⎪   MARTI
       CAMPIGLIA ⎭   VALLE DI BUTI

Average or modest wealth
Indebted to an average or sizable
degree
Stable population
Agricultural workers, either small
landowners or sharecroppers, and
others, without declared occupation
Oxen and small livestock owned
House owned
Households of average or large size
(4-10 persons), extended either
vertically or horizontally, directed
by male heads who are mature or elderly, married or widowers

E RIPAFRATTA (in part)
LARI (in part)

Same socioprofessional characteristics
as D, but households large or of
complex structure

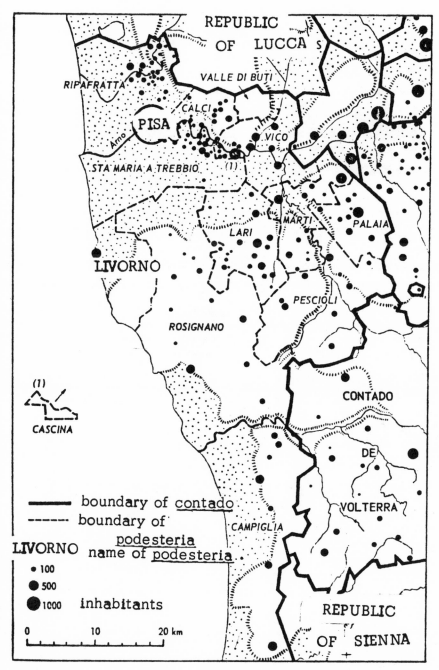

Not shown on the map: CASTIGLIONE DELLA PESCAIA,
an enclave along the coast, thirty kilometers to the south.

Figure 3.5. The Contado of Pisa as Seen in the *Catasto* of 1427–30

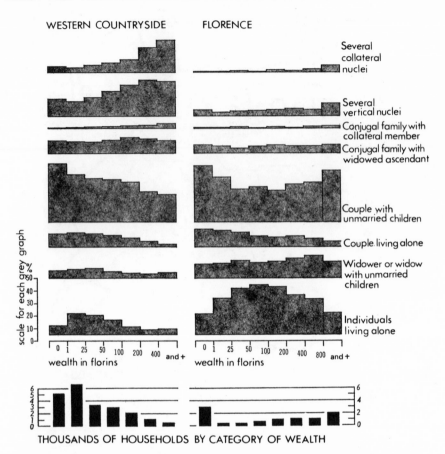

Figure 3.6. Proportion of Types of Households, according to Wealth, in Florence and in the Western Countryside of the Florentine Territory (in % of total for each category of wealth)

4

A System of Customary Law: Family Structures and Inheritance Customs in Sixteenth-Century France

Emmanuel Le Roy Ladurie

A historical anthropology of France is a discipline which, in keeping with the very spirit of this special issue, would constitute one of the pioneering frontiers of the new form of history.[1] Alas, at least for the period 1450–1700, the point of departure for such a discipline cannot be those "elementary structures of kinship" that appeared on the scene twenty years ago to serve as the universal foundation for the ethnography of the savage world. For, despite obvious village endogamy, even among peasants the rules concerning marriage and kinship in old France were too open and too "anomic" to provide the criteria for a regional differentiation comparable to the criteria that

Annales, E.S.C. 27 (July–October 1972): 825–46. Translated by Patricia M. Ranum

[1]The author of this article has tried to propose various ways to develop a historical anthropology of the French people, chiefly on the basis of military archives, in articles which have appeared in *Studi Storici* (1969), *Daedalus* (Spring 1971), and *Annales de démographie historique* (1972), and also in his introduction to A. d'Angeville, *Essai sur la statistique de la population française*, new ed. (Paris, 1969).

Claude Lévi-Strauss proposed for native societies. (In fact, it is Greek to the computer!) However, the strict study of laws relative to the settlement of inheritances as they were set down in provincial customary laws does supply one of the grids that permits us to distinguish the various cultural regions. Such a study, based on selected components, defines the techniques of transformation that permit us to pass logically from one region to another and from one era to another. This detailed and fastidious research into the ethnography of customary laws also gives the historian the opportunity to sense certain differences, or basic fault lines, in the substructure of family life for the various regions of France involved in this study. It was Jean Yver who, in a weighty book accompanied by a series of articles written in technical prose, first proposed a geographical study of old French customary laws, continuing the admirable but outmoded work of Henri Klimrath after a century-long hiatus.[2]

I will summarize here briefly the main points of Yver's analysis. As much as possible I will attempt to incorporate into this analysis the matter-of-fact preoccupations of a historian of the peasant world. First, Yver gave a systematic form to the scattered data piled up in pioneering works. Among these pioneers is Bourdot de Richebourg,[3] whose vast compilation, or *Coutumier général*, published in 1724 grouped together for the first time under a single title the until then disparate body of texts that sixteenth-century jurists had published in separate volumes. We must also mention Klimrath, who in the 1830s drew up a geographical map of the customary regions that long remained the only one of its sort.

Transcribed chiefly at the end of the fifteenth century and during the sixteenth century, regional customary laws are of interest to both the medievalist and the early-modernist. They portray a certain image of the kingdom, at the same time traditional and new, as it was progressively rebuilt and defined after the Hundred Years' War. Indeed, the jurists of the Renaissance, who on this occasion served as local compilers of customary laws, collected elements from several strata of time. Some of these elements represent an archaic layer of rural and landowning laws as they were still more or less actively functioning at the end of the Middle Ages. Other components, juxtaposed with the preceding, indicate that the law was evolving toward more modern urban or municipal forms established during the sixteenth century, or even earlier, as a result of

---

[2]Jean Yver, *Essai de géographie coutumière* (Paris, 1966). And, by the same author, "Les caractères originaux du groupe de coutumes de l'Ouest de la France," *Revue historique de droit français et étranger*, no. 1 (1952), pp. 18–79; and "Les deux groupes de coutumes du Nord," *Revue du Nord*, October 1953 and January 1954; Henri Klimrath, "Etudes sur les coutumes," in his posthumous work *Travaux sur l'histoire du droit français*, 2 vols. (Paris-Strasbourg, 1843), with a customary-law map of France in vol. 2.

[3]C. Bourdot de Richebourg, *Nouveau Coutumier général*, (Paris, 1724).

procedures followed by the population and theories expounded by men of the law. Faced with these sometimes heterogeneous strata, the ethnographer-historian must make up his mind to select a number of pertinent criteria whose presence, absence, or various manifestations are associated with an entire family of cultural traits, which themselves give each customary region its peculiar configuration.

The selected criteria, contradictory but interrelated, are in this case equality among heirs and the exclusion of portioned children. To begin with, in a bird's-eye view of French territory we see that three vast groups of customs stand out distinctly from one another. To simplify, let us call them the Orléans-Paris region; the Normandy-Brittany region; and the regions where the langue d'oc was spoken [roughly, the southern half of France]. To these we must add, as we shall see, sizeable portions of the *pays d'oïl* [the northern half of the country, where the langue d'oïl was spoken], sometimes very northern portions, involving chiefly the Walloons. The principle of this regional differentiation was so admirably described by Yver that I will limit myself to quoting that historian on this point, though I will from time to time clarify his text for those readers who are not familiar with the historiography of customary law.

At a very early date, the Norman jurist wrote,[4] *French customary law showed a tendency toward three major solutions (A, B, and C). The first is the possible preference legacy among children* (the *préciput*, or "preference legacy," is the unilateral advantage given to one of the descendants which permits him to take for his own advantage a specific portion of the total property to be divided before any division with his brothers and sisters); *it is this preferency-legacy solution (A) that we will encounter in the region of the "langue d'oc" and among the Walloons. At the other end of the spectrum are the customary laws involving perfect equality (B) that obliged all children who had received favors* previous to the time of the transfer of the father's and mother's estate *to return these favors and gifts received; the children could not keep these gifts, even by renouncing their inheritance; at the minimum they had to return any excess between the value of the gift received and the equal share that would have been theirs in an "ab intestat" inheritance. The whole main group of customary laws*

---

[4]The passages in italics are those of Jean Yver ("Les deux groupes de coutumes," p. 11). The words in Roman type are my additions. Concerning the various solutions suggested in the paragraph, I should like to refer to Pierre Bourdieu's excellent metaphor, which resembles mine: the goal of customary laws involving inheritances is almost always (but not always, as the atypical case of Brittany shows) to avoid excessive subdividing by heirs; . . . as in a game of chess, the common goal of the two players is to check and mate the opponent's king. But just as certain players prefer to begin their game with the bishop's opening, and others prefer a different opening, so the customary laws of the various provinces each chose very different solutions and means to obtain a goal that was generally identical, the goal of preventing the family plot from being excessively broken up.

of western France belonged to this category of the forced return. Between these two extremes (A and B), customary laws of the Parisian sort always settled for more nuanced systems. In the first of these nuanced systems (C1), chiefly prevalent during the Middle Ages, the child receiving a portion during his father's and mother's lifetime, and as a result of the parents' own actions, was purely and simply excluded from the inheritance to come. Another more flexible system of Parisian customs (C2), which was put into effect after C1 at the end of the Middle Ages and during the sixteenth century, allowed the favored heir to "opt"; he could choose to *keep his advantage and renounce his inheritance or participate in the division of the inheritance by "returning"* to the common property *the gift* that was being questioned. Parisian customary laws from then on *became laws of simple equality or of option.*

These distinctions between three main groups of customary laws are not simply theoretical ones. Indeed, they helped determine the value placed upon the various roles played within the family in each region. We may note, for example, the existence of the right of *mainbournie* ["guardianship"] for fathers and mothers in the old Capetian regions, although it is true that the law tended to become progressively modified in the direction of increased equality. In Normandy we find instead a law favorable to a group of brothers. And lastly, between the two extremes of this decision-making process, the formidable figure of the sovereign father, so dear to jurists influenced by Roman law, dominated the South, where the langue d'oc was spoken.

Intermediate solutions

In the customary laws of Orléans-Paris, that world of "centrist" solutions (C1 and C2), the power of the parents, both father and mother, was promoted in the oldest laws (mentioned in the thirteenth century but destined to survive at least officially until 1510). There was also a certain concern for keeping the property from being divided.[5] *Quanquez fait père et mère est estable* ("whatever the father and mother do remains in force"). At least that was the fundamental concept that was firmly established in customary laws from the Goths on and that subsequently persisted here and there, while gradually disappearing elsewhere. In the rustic law of village people—which also became, perhaps owing to the peasant exodus, the law of the privileged Capetian cities—this *stability* of arrangements among kin had a precise meaning. Indeed, strengthened by

---

[5]For the situation in England, see C. Homans, *English Villagers of the Thirteenth Century* (Cambridge, Mass., 1941; reprinted, New York, 1970).

such an arrangement, the father and mother would give a plow, a cow, a few coins, or on rare occasions a bit of land to the son, or more often to the daughter, who was leaving the home to marry elsewhere and to join or found a household distinct from that of his childhood. The child thus "established" was obliged by customary law to renounce the inheritance that would eventually be transmitted when the ascendants had died.[6] Leaving the family nest to fly elsewhere meant simultaneously receiving a portion and being disinherited. In contrast, the son or daughter (or the several children) who remained firmly rooted upon the family lands—no matter how poor the holding might be—and who remained at home in order devotedly to continue the family farming under the domination of the elders, could expect to inherit the paternal plot when that day finally came. It mattered little whether this heir (a presumptive heir, since he was co-resident) was male or female, elder or younger, only child or one of many. Severe in their dealings with offspring who left to settle elsewhere, the customary laws of the old Capetian *prévôtés* were indulgent and kind to children who remained at home to help parents in their old age. From this point of view, the provisions of customary laws involved no preferences in the form of either primogeniture, male superiority, or in this case, maintaining the family property intact. They permitted both the younger child and the daughter to inherit, and they guaranteed equal division or "simple equality" (in other words, the assurance that one of the heirs would not be given greater advantages than the others) when several children or heirs who had not taken advantage of their opportunity to settle elsewhere and receive a portion upon marrying became candidates to the succession. Thus, these very old and paradoxical customs of the Orléans-Paris region blew both hot and cold simultaneously. On the one hand, they advocated the stability of households and therefore an ever-possible favoritism working to the advantage or detriment of the estab-lished-married-portioned individual; yet, on the other hand, they stipu-lated simple equality among nonestablished children. The exclusion of those receiving portions evidently was intended to make these two rather incompatible assertions fit together as well as possible. Despite these ever-possible contradictions, we can see—using the system of the region of Orléans as an example—that a villein's inheritance as a whole had only a few, generally small fragments taken from it beforehand by the parents in order to create portions for those descendants who left to settle under another roof.

The very nature of this system of inheritance gives rise to a few general thoughts. First of all, it is clear that these customary laws of the Ile-de-

---

[6]"In Paris this practice of excluding established children had to fit in with a principle granting equality to children sharing in the inheritance; from which a well-known system of option and return would issue," Yver, "Les deux groupes de coutumes."

France [the province of which Paris was the capital] or of the region surrounding Orléans were aimed at, or at least resulted in, eliminating superfluous offspring from the inheritance, thus making excessive subdivision of the land more difficult. Although this "goal" was far from always being achieved, it was with a remarkable degree of consistency at least objectively approved, if not consciously sought after. Moreover, the oldest texts stress the often rural character of the disinheritance of portioned children, which was unequivocally presented as being typical of "villeinage."

This very peasantlike concern, which tried to orient the transmission of inheritances in the direction of preserving a substantial bit of land adequate to support a family, also fit in well with the demographic requirement of the times. We know that in the early preindustrial populations that scholars have been quantifying in recent years,[7] the number of siblings that escaped death in infancy or childhood and finally reached a marriageable age rarely averaged more than just over two individuals, year in and year out. Statistically, on the basis of biological probabilities, they would be a brother and a sister. Under these conditions, the inheritance system we have just described was more or less consciously planned to reproduce as much as possible from one generation to the next those structures of the farm or peasant holding that were considered the least undesirable within the static framework of an economy based on the domain or the seigneury. One of the two surviving children, generally the boy, would live with the father and mother and within this family community would learn his trade as a farmer. He was destined, when the time came, to receive the inheritance. The other child in most cases was a girl. (Exclusion of children receiving portions, in fact and even sometimes in the letter of the law, was often synonymous with exclusion of daughters receiving dowries.) Therefore, this daughter "was married off and no more was said about her." She left the paternal home with a more or less meager dowry and with no hope of inheriting, in order, if possible, to become a part of another family group in which, moreover, she would help "reproduce" the structure. Of course, actual situations often did not fit this simple scheme. Yet, even in the very numerous "aberrant" cases, the system was flexible. If necessary, it permitted several children to receive portions in order to become established elsewhere. In the absence of a son it permitted a son-in-law to settle in the parents' house. And lastly, on more than one occasion the old law of the Orléans-Paris region permitted the sharing of the holding among

---

[7]P. Goubert, *Beauvais et le Beauvaisis au XVIIe siècle* (Paris, 1960).

several descendants,[8] an unpleasant but frequent solution, as indicated by the breaking down of the land into little parcels before 1500. However, the descendants had, at least in theory, previously agreed as a contingent plan to collaborate with their father and mother within the framework of a disciplined co-residency.

At the end of the Middle Ages and sometimes even later, these structures, which were so convenient for farmers, seem to have spread over a very wide territory extending far beyond that of the Orléans-Paris region. Indeed, they are found sporadically in the region of Lille and even that of Amiens;[9] to the east and southeast of the northern region speaking the langue d'oïl; and in Germany, Poland, and even Switzerland. The study of German data, for example, gives the French researcher the opportunity to compare, as Dumézil* did, and to reflect upon origins. Beyond the Rhine, the exclusion of the portioned child, followed by the granting of the inheritance to co-residents, is more than a mere juridical trait. It remains closely linked to mental images, to folklore, and even to mythology! Indeed, among certain German peasants, the furnishings of the house remained undivided when the father died. This joint ownership, so advantageous to family continuity, was made possible thanks to the ruse of a fictitious, tripartite—and communal—division. One portion of these furnishings went to the co-resident children; the second, to the likewise co-resident spouse; and the third—to the deceased father's soul! In like manner, in the most traditionalist cantons of French-speaking Switzerland, customary law granted privileges to the "intruncated" children; living at home in the family community, they were destined one day to share the inheritance, while those who had been "detruncated," those who had decided to marry elsewhere, had received portions and were then disinherited.[10]

These customs are equally evident much farther south. In certain parts, both agricultural and urban, of the southern portion of France which spoke the langue d'oc, various customary laws and especially the provisos of wills prove that the exclusion of the portioned child and the monopoly of the inheritance by co-residents was widely practiced until the fifteenth century. Yet this occurred within the framework of the large family so very common in the region of the langue d'oc. And lastly, we find these same customs—which, depending on the specific situation, were either

---

*Georges Dumézil has written numerous comparative studies of Indo-European mythology. See C. Scott Littleton, *The New Comparative Mythology: An Anthropological Assessment of the Theories of Georges Dumézil* (Berkeley, 1973); and a review by Jenny Jochen in *American Historical Review* 79 (1974): 1149–51. —Trans.

[8]This is the so-called simple equality system.

[9]Yver, *Essai de géographie*, chaps. 1 and 4.

[10]Ibid., p. 277.

native or were imported by colonizers—in the Jerusalem of the Crusaders and in the old customary laws of Armenia.[11]

Let us, however, limit ourselves to Western Europe, or simply to France. The vast diffusion of institutions dealing with inheritances that we have just described makes rather tempting the hypotheses claiming that these customary laws derived from a very distant past, from a Ligurian, Celtic, or German substratum. But, Yver asked humorously, must we really "go back to the most distant ethnic origins? Before going all the way back to the Menapii or the Ligurians, could we not save ourselves some energy and stop at some intermediate point?"[12]

Without rejecting paleoethnic investigations, it seems that we ought to make more modest assertions. Let us say, along with Yver, that regardless of the group in which they originated, the exclusion of portioned children and the inheritance preferences shown toward co-resident children were especially well suited to the needs of a very demanding agricultural and seigneurial society. Indeed, anyone using the term "strong seigneury" means, according to the period, a cell-like network of manses or, much later, the constraining bonds of villeinage. Now, these constraints were the bearers of a structure. They gave birth to a law of succession which, in order to be consistent with the lord's demands, had to be based upon exclusion. Indeed, take a lord of the medieval or early-modern type, still armed with exorbitant powers. To the degree that he had anything to say about it, how could he tolerate allowing the land held by rural people, over whom he exercised the right of eminent domain, to be broken down into small bits to benefit the heirs who had already received portions and had left to settle elsewhere? "Elsewhere" could well be outside the generally restricted area over which his manor exerted its power. From the viewpoint of the person controlling the land, the exclusion of the migrating villein was a very appropriate solution. The opinion of the landholders would probably not have been very different from that of their noble master. After all, they had long been merely the uncertain possessors of a bit of land, persons subject to mortmain who held "a scarcely hereditary holding."[13] The very notion of succession was for them reduced to the de facto continuity of one family on a piece of land. Under these circumstances, the previous co-residence of the presumptive heirs, which went hand in hand with the exclusion of those who had received portions, was a wise precaution, a sort of enthronement before the fact, like that which had made the fortune of the Capetians. It guaranteed that once the head of the family had died, the

---

[11]Ibid.
[12]Yver, "Les deux groupes de coutumes," p. 30(50).
[13]Ibid., p. 34.

manse and the holding would routinely be passed on to those descendants who were on the spot, avoiding the unfortunate risk that the plot might be taken back by the lord in the name of some "seigneurial redemption." The customary laws for the Orléans-Paris region therefore represented, if we accept Yver's suggestions, the tough superstructure of a seigneurial and domainal world that had formerly been very powerful and that was still more or less alive at the end of the Middle Ages.

Another sign of archaism is evident. The customary laws based on co-residential succession and exclusion that characterized the former Capetian domain and, at the end of the Middle Ages, certain regions speaking the langue d'oc, were linked to various types of large families. In the Orléans-Paris group, the exclusion of those receiving portions pushed back into the distant shadows *the children who by a distinct establishment were separated from the family house, from their father and mother's household, and from the small domestic group (grown unmarried or sometimes even married children) who lived together in that household.*[14]

In the case of those regions of the Massif Central [the central mountains] speaking the langue d'oc, the exclusion of those receiving portions was specifically derived from the concern for cohesion shown by the most typical extended family. In such a family two or more households of parents and children, or of brothers and sisters with their spouses, lived around the same hearth and used the same kettle under the same roof, reserving the bulk of the inheritance for the co-resident descendants in their concern for continuity.

Since the family institutions in question were in serious decline by the thirteenth century in the North,[15] and the sixteenth century in the South,[16] customary laws involving exclusion were in their turn the object of revisionist attacks during the Renaissance.

Yet, the most stable and perhaps the most striking of the Orléans-Paris structures continued to live on for a very long time. I am referring to the insistence that preference be granted to the father and mother's joint decision and that the "simple and trusting" collaboration of parents and children within the rural setting be advocated. On this point the usages of the old Capetian lands clearly opposed the paternalism of the region of the langue d'oc, as they had opposed the fierce patriarchalism of Norman customary law, which was callous toward women and the wishes of the dead father. The privilege granted the couple and the importance given to

[14]Ibid., p. 38 (I am not dealing with the problem of co-resident servants, who by definition do not share in the succession).

[15]R. Fossier, *La terre et les hommes en Picardie* (Louvain, 1968).

[16]J. Hilaire, *Le régime des biens entre époux dans la région de Montpellier* (Montpellier, 1957).

maternal prerogatives are undoubtedly the one type of data that gives us the least inadequate information about family archetypes and even about the outlook of the landholders in the Paris basin during the formative period of these customary laws.

Favorable to the childbearing couple, the Orléans-Paris customary law also logically placed great emphasis upon the importance of the marriage bed. Even if a man married many times and had children "from several beds," his inheritance would not be divided up according to the total number of his children but into portions corresponding to the number of "beds" or wives the *de cujus* had had during his matrimonial career. This was the so-called division by bed, generally found in an area stretching from the region around Orléans north to that of Beauvais. This distinction was nonexistent in egalitarian Normandy, where equal shares were counted out for each male child, regardless of the "bed" or whether the heir was a co-resident.[17]

Nonetheless, while apparently remaining faithful to the archetypes we have just described, the customs of the Orléans-Paris region evolved from the Renaissance on. This evolution had long been in preparation. As early as the thirteenth to fifteenth centuries, compilations of customary laws for Paris or Amiens had permitted various mitigations that improved the lot—which until then had been a rather hard one—of the migrant child. If, for example, the parents inserted into their daughter's or son's marriage contract a special *recall* clause, the portioned descendant could, despite having settled under another roof, return and request his share of the inheritance after his ascendants' deaths. In all other instances, if this *intentional recall* had not been explicitly provided for, the portioned offspring found himself disinherited once and for all. This recall clause was of capital importance in urban settings. There, by its ingenious flexibility, it guaranteed the old customary law of exclusion a long survival. For this law could henceforth be adapted to the most diverse situations, since it could be declared inapplicable at any time, thanks to the *recall*. On the other hand, such a system of recall could not always easily gain a foothold in the rural areas. In northern France few peasants could have afforded the luxury of a written marriage contract. Their number did, of course, increase, but only much later, when the activity of notaries mushroomed at the end of the Middle Ages, or even later than that. Thus, without a marriage contract, no recall clause was conceivable within the framework of customary law.

This, then, was the old structure: exclusion, with the possibility of recall, although the right to exercise this recall varied considerably. In

[17]Yver, *Essai de géographie*, pp. 273 and passim.

1510, however, new usages in the region around Paris were instituted or simply made official. (Indeed, they had long since existed in the region of Beauvais, where Beaumanoir had made a compilation of customary laws in the late thirteenth century.) These new usages can be expressed in two words: *option* and *return*. On the surface, of course, nothing had changed. The portioned child still theoretically remained excluded from the inheritance. But in reality—as in a game of chess, during the course of which, to use a rather trite metaphor, only one piece need be moved to change the equilibrium of the entire game—the insertion of a new rule resulted in a great modification of the spirit of the customary law. Indeed, beginning with the second decade of the sixteenth century, it was officially conceded that—contrary to previously held principles—a child who had married and settled outside the community formed by its parents and who had been given its portion of the parents' property, could not be excluded from its ascendants' succession. In order to participate, this child merely had to be willing to "return" to the joint property comprising the family inheritance "what he had received in marriage."[18] Having made this sacrifice, he was now entitled to share this property equally with his brothers and sisters, and no one could discriminate against him. Thus, at the end of a long period of development that Yver has traced from the thirteenth to the sixteenth century, we find that the new system was shaped by a simple distortion of the old rules. Indeed, these old rules went hand in hand with the choice between the titles of *almoner, legatee,* or *donee,* on the one hand, and those of *heir, coheir,* or *communist* (that is, holder-in-common) on the other.[19] In the past, once married—or non-married—a child irrevocably took one or the other of these paths. Now, although he could naturally not adopt both of these titles simultaneously, he could at a later date—a date considerably after his marriage—veer toward one or the other when the hour for the parental inheritance arrived. This is the meaning behind the well-known saying, *Aumonier et parchonnier nul ne peut être* ["one cannot be both almoner and coheir"]. At the decisive moment in which the question of the inheritance was settled, the heir could—and was obliged to—*opt.* He must either hold on to the rights he had already acquired, which he had received as a gift, legacy, alms, or portion during the lifetime and from the very hands of the *de cujus,* or else he must share in the succession. To do so he must "return," he must hand back that advantage he had previously received and mingle it with the inheritance as a whole. Then he was entitled to be a coheir or full-fledged member of the family community and to participate in the division and transmission of the property owned jointly by that commun-

---

[18]Compilation of 1510, cited in Yver, ibid., pp. 21–22.
[19]Ibid., pp. 43, 66.

ity which by law went to the heirs. In this new version of the system, option and return were therefore like two sides of the same coin.

These rejuvenated structures involved a more flexible, more permissive law that was much less concerned than previously with preserving the holding intact. In their fashion they express the loosening of seigneurial constraint which had occurred long before. Indeed, although fine remnants of the seigneury still existed, by the sixteenth century it was no longer in a position to oppose the subdivision of the peasant holding into small pieces to benefit heirs who had become established elsewhere. In a more general manner, this final avatar of the customary law expressed and consummated the *coup de grace* dealt to the extended family. Small nuclear families had long dominated among the rural people of the regions where the langue d'oïl was spoken, and it was normal that such families should be able to inherit more easily and not be disinherited in favor of a tacit, or unofficial, joint ownership that increasingly appeared an outdated myth. Thus, the evolution of the superstructure of customary law was belatedly affected by the lessons learned from these changes in seigneurial or family infrastructure.

Did this evolution also momentarily reflect the repercussions of the more relaxed demographic situation of the late Middle Ages? On this point we should ask the specific question that English historians of customary laws have been asking about their own country.[20] Since demographic pressures had lessened for a time, it seems that on both sides of the Channel less stress than in the past—say during the fifteenth century—was laid on the formerly sacrosanct demands that the patrimony be preserved intact. Indeed, what was the good of preserving this hobble, since in any event there was room enough to stretch and enough land to support everyone? At least this was what they believed for a time, and this would help explain the laxity found in the compilations of 1510.

Yet beyond the temporary demographic situation, these compilations reveal on a more general level the lasting thrust of egalitarianism. As we know, the egalitarian trend that spread progressively throughout the rural areas finally toppled all the hierarchies of the societies divided into orders. By 1510 the consequences of the new texts, which of course reflect the prevailing customs, were clearly leveling: children who chose to opt and return started out on an equal footing with their coheirs when the parental property was distributed. But as Yver has emphasized, this egalitarianism was not complete. If the generously portioned descendant, the beloved child, found it more to his advantage to retain the portion granted before his parents' deaths, on the day of the inheritance he merely

[20]R. Faith, "Peasant Families and Inheritance Customs in Medieval England," *Agricultural History Review* 14 (1966).

had to fail to return this gift, at the risk of being eliminated from the succession.[21] Such a choice resulted from a rough calculation indicating that it was better for him to remain an almoner or a legatee than to assume the possibly lesser profits that his position as heir or coheir could give him.

The old customary law of the Orléans-Paris region had *climbed* socially from the obscure strata of the manse and villeinage to the more exalted procedures of the courts. In contrast, the new customary law that was made official in 1510 was a law that moved *downward*, as a decisive reference indicates.[22] It filtered from the legal, clerical, or bourgeois elite and from urban mores (favorable to egalitarianism and to giving each child its chance) down to the rural population. In their turn contaminated, these populations finally gave up the fossilized practices that had long been incarnate in the old form of exclusion.

Despite countless variants and contaminations by neighboring customary laws, the improved option-return system, with its characteristic traits of flexibility, relative equality, and weakened seigneurial and family constraints, can be seen to have spread over rather large areas between 1505 and 1570, the peak period during which customary laws were being compiled. The first of these zones included a great part of the open fields of the central Paris basin. The second zone ran north-south from the region of Beauvais to that of Orléans and on toward Blois. The third zone was limited on the east by the province of Champagne and on the west by the Grand Perche [a region northeast of Le Mans]. In addition, during the same period, enclaves of option-return and less strict equality among heirs also appeared farther to the north and to the northeast. Tiny pockets in Lorraine, such enclaves comprised large areas in coastal Flanders, where they replaced a system of complete equality which seems to have flourished previously in the Flemish regions during the high point of the Middle Ages.[23]

The West of France: the egalitarian and lineage-oriented pole

Despite the egalitarian tendencies I have just pointed out, the Orléans-Paris customary law of option-return, which replaced the law excluding portioned children, still placed considerable stress upon paternal or parental wishes, which might result in an advantage or a disadvantage for one or another of the descendants. Unreliable because subject to option,

[21] Yver, *Essai de géographie*, p. 253; and Yver, "Les deux groupes de coutumes," pp. 9 and 30.

[22] Yver, *Essai de géographie*, p. 21.

[23] Yver, "Les deux groupes de coutumes."

these wishes maintained a certain validity after the death of the person who had formulated them. To the contrary, once one crossed the marshes and entered the western provinces of Normandy and Anjou, the customary laws fiercely proclaimed, in every possible way, the total and definitive death of the father. *After me the equal sharing*, was the cry of the father, whose wishes could be revoked. "If a father," runs the oldest extant Norman customary law, "gives portions to his children during his lifetime and each has held his share a long time and peaceably during the father's lifetime, the portions will not be holdable after his death."[24] In other words, gifts, dowries, and portions given children upon their marriage, during their father's lifetime and with his consent, were not permanent. They were not "firm and in force." Necessarily uncertain and subject to obligatory return, they in no way eliminated that specific child from his right to inherit the patrimony. The father's wish was valid only during his lifetime and was nullified after his death.

From the outset a system of this sort tends to lead to equality. Indeed, by invalidating parental wishes, such a system avoids singling out the beloved or rejected child from among the various offspring. As we have seen, equality among heirs was only affected by the customary laws of Orléans and Paris after an evolution that lasted centuries and after many tortuous ruses such as recall and, later, option-return. On the contrary, such equality was the immediate aim of the very old Norman compilation of customary law,[25] and it was openly confirmed in this province by the new compilation of 1583. Children in Normandy were automatically given equal opportunities; and in many cases, equality of portions leads to individualized behavior.

First let us discuss these automatically equal opportunities. The access of any given child or descendant to a given portion of the inheritance or the consolidated dowry was not the result of the wishes of the couple, as was the case in the region of Paris, or of the father, as in the region speaking the langue d'oc. It resulted simply from the position the child in question occupied in the family's genealogy. Being born meant inheriting, whatever favorable or unfavorable predispositions your parents might have in your case. Of course, this automatic opportunity did not always preclude injustices when the inheritance was divided up into shares. In Normandy where, as we have seen, males reigned supreme, girls were excluded from the succession, which went to sons. They had to find a husband (if need be, their brother was expected to help them in their search); and they had to be satisfied with a scanty portion of the inheritance.[26] On the other hand, in other provinces of western France where automatic inheritance through lineage was also practiced, though

[24]Yver, "Les caractères originaux"; and Yver, *Essai de géographie*, chap. 2.
[25]Yver, "Les caractères originaux."
[26]Ibid., p. 32.

with a very strict sense of equality among heirs, daughters of commoners were equal candidates with their brothers for the estate to be inherited.

In addition, to return to Normandy, certain regions—fortunately they were rare—observed to the maximum all the iniquities of automatic inheritance. Such was the case for the *pays de Caux* [the region of chalk cliffs near the mouth of the Seine], where even among commoners an English sort of primogeniture reigned supreme which ipso facto was extremely detrimental to younger children.

The trees must not, however, be allowed to hide the forest. In Normandy proper (excluding the *pays de Caux*), the "general customary law" for the rights of commoners did not involve primogeniture. Its first and clearest criterion was male equality, a situation which would have been the answer to the prayers of boys from the South, the Walloon regions, or the old Capetian lands, for in many cases they had been disinherited in a cavalier fashion by their father and mother.

This spirit of total equality is most marked when we leave Normandy and move into the provinces of Brittany and Anjou, though we still remain within the great region of western customary laws. There, too, the customary laws, often compiled during the sixteenth century, loudly proclaimed an equality among heirs that was intentional rather than the result of chance and that, this time, involved all children, both male and female. Whether from the thirteenth century or the Renaissance, the texts from the provinces of Touraine and Anjou, for example, are unbending in this respect.[27] The customary laws of the province of Maine are no less clear; they make egalitarianism among commoners inevitable, placing it in marked opposition all along the class barrier to the law of primogeniture observed by the nobility. "For the custom is such that no non-noble person can render the position of any one presumptive heir any worse or any better than that of the others."

The same song was sung in Brittany. Commoners, as contrasted with nobles, did not have the right to show preference for one child. "The children of bourgeois or other persons of low estate must each be as great as the others both in chattels and in inheritances."[28] In addition, the Breton peasants tried to show by their revolts of 1590 and 1675 that they considered egalitarian demands more than a mere legal formula or a vain phrase. However, Breton gentlemen and other well-born persons enjoyed the privilege of being able to favor one heir over another; for example, they might use a preference legacy.[29]

Hostile to this unfairness shown by the nobility, commoners observed equality among heirs throughout western France as far south as Poitou. There, despite influences of the preference legacy coming from the South

[27]Yver, *Essai de géographie*, p. 113.
[28]Ibid., p. 122.
[29]Ibid., p. 123 n.

and the regions of written law, the predominant maxim held that father and mother could not "make one of the heirs better than the others."[30]

These leveling tendencies that were so firmly rooted in western France were not, however, restricted to one geographical area. Indeed, they are found very far from the western lands. Option-return was practiced in Champagne and Brie, to the east of the eastern borders of the Orléans-Paris zone. There a curiously isolated enclave of *complete* equality existed, which Christophle de Thou, a president in the Parlement of Paris, vainly tried to curtail in accordance with Parisian ideas of simple equality and of option. "No more to one than to the other," the jurists of Champagne and Brie unanimously replied to him in 1556.[31]

Hostile to inequality among heirs, these various customary laws tended objectively to devalue parental or paternal roles to the advantage of the group of those "entitled" to inherit—whether it was a question of sons, as in Normandy, or of sons and daughters, as in the western provinces. In a world in which, statistically, adults died before reaching a very advanced age, such procedures could on the average but favor heirs who were still young—adolescents or even small children. In line with a research topic now all the rage, we might say that these customary laws of western France implied a certain idea of childhood and a very positive attitude toward the child. We could not say as much, for example, for the laws of the South.

However valid or invalid this incursion into the realm of psychological history may be, the strict equality observed in the western provinces involved a "return" after the father's death that was not optional, as in the region of Paris, but obligatory. This system of the "forced return," *voulist ou non* ("willing or not"), was especially strict in Normandy. There, in conformity to the rule that invalidated *post mortem* the establishments the father had created during his lifetime to help members of his family, heirs were categorically obliged to return to the mass of common property included in the estate all the liberalities, gifts, portions, and advantages that had been given them prior to the death of the *de cujus*. Under such a system it was not possible for any child to obtain, or in any event maintain, the position of *favored child*.

In the provinces of Maine and Anjou, customary law seems to have been a bit more flexible on this matter than in Normandy, but on the whole it amounted to just about the same thing. In Anjou, the heir who had received advantages during his father's lifetime had to return, after the latter's death, not the entire donation but merely the excess—in other words, the amount over and above the liberality he had received on the

---

[30]Ibid., p. 127.
[31]Ibid., pp. 145–46.

one hand, and the normal share of the inheritance to which he was entitled in a system of complete equality on the other hand. "And if it should happen that someone received too great a portion and he does not wish to return to the division and estate of the father and mother, and the others say to him, 'You have received too great a portion,' his share will be evaluated by wise men; and if he had received too much, he will be obliged to return. . . ."[32] This rule stipulating the return of the excess could be carried to great lengths. In the more rustic local variants, it included both the patrimony and acquests [property gained otherwise than by inheritance], the sole exception being donations made to children and young people for schooling, for equipping themselves for war, or for the costs of a marriage ceremony. Such equality among heirs was so extreme that disinherited children could always return to the succession and demand the excess improperly held by the more pampered brothers and sisters, even when the disinherited were insane, spendthrifts, or girls of loose morals.[33]

Jean Yver has presented an excellent analysis of the philosophy behind these systems in western France. In essence they granted no privileges to the jointly held parental property or to the attempt to consolidate the agricultural holding. In contrast, the archaic system of Paris excluded the portioned child for these ends. The western systems were indifferent to the danger posed by subdivided land and disdainful of the union of the couple with the plot of land. Above all, they favored the long and ramified continuity of the lineage, in other words, the uninterrupted succession of descendants across the generations, during which the possessions were tapped and disappeared, were divided harmoniously and spread about, according to the lineage's divisions into trunks and main branches, and its ultimate bifurcations into branches and twigs. In the customary laws of Normandy and Anjou, these possessions therefore seem to flow like sap which, as the result of some mysterious force, irrigates the pendulous and bushy branches of a great tree. The ultimate goal was to grant each child, and after him the descendants whom he in turn would engender, his equal and just share of the original property, received from the common trunk of the *gens* or kin.

Capetian customary laws were concerned with the stability of the household. Above all else they strengthened the union of the Christian couple who, now one flesh, courageously shared their possessions and tried to organize the lives of their offspring so that they could best perpetuate the property of the household and, if possible, protect it from being dispersed into small pieces. In contrast, the customary laws of

[32]Ibid., pp. 111–12.
[33]Ibid., p. 111.

western France—and also other nonwestern laws found in Brie, Champagne, and old Flanders—preferred to stress the old values of the lineage. Faithful to the rule *paterna paternis, materna maternis*,[34] they granted only slight importance to marriage, which they seemed to feel was only a temporary union of two perishable beings who had each issued from a different lineage, whose permanence was the chief concern. These western customary laws were therefore chiefly concerned with the strict circulation of inheritances along the genealogical network. Archaic, in the case of the Normans these laws seem to have come from the ethnic subsoils of Scandinavia and are perhaps even pre-Christian. Yet, paradoxically, they are nevertheless the bearers of modernity. Indeed, even in the earliest extant editions, most of them are already struggling upward toward the ideals of complete equality and fierce individualism that the jurisprudence of the Orléans-Paris region only discovered at a late date and then only half-discovered, to the detriment of its own structure.

This gave rise to an entire series of "original characteristics" typical of the customary laws of western France. First, there was the predominance of division by head and the absence of shares established as a result of the "marriage bed." There is nothing surprising in this. The bed, that piece of furniture associated with the marriage, formed a temporary link between two lineages and was of little concern to the customary laws of Normandy, so enmeshed in branches, tree forks, and the ultimate sprigs of a family tree and not at all interested in the transitory alliances that were formed by that tree as a result of a marriage with another family tree. In contrast, although the men of the western regions unanimously practiced unlimited representation [the substitution of a child or children to take their share of an estate which would have been inherited by a deceased person], representation was foreign to the logic behind the customary laws of Paris and Orléans, at least to the degree that during their early period of development the latter excluded the portioned child. Indeed, having disinherited his daughter after having given her a dowry, in whose name would the father authorize the son of this girl, who had since died, to claim his rights to the paternal succession and to participate in his inheritance? (However, once the Parisian clause excluding the portioned child weakened in 1510, the compilers of this new text hastened to introduce direct-line representation into their texts.[35])

Now, in all the western regions, the very earliest customary laws, followed by later revisions, unhesitatingly proclaimed the system of direct representation. This was a normal attitude to take. Thus, the law granted

[34]"Paternal possessions to persons of the paternal lineage, and maternal possessions to persons of the maternal lineage."
[35]Yver, *Essai de géographie*, pp. 21 and 266.

privileges to blood relationships and encouraged the most distant buds and sprigs at one extremity of the family tree to participate in the succession within that family. Finally, they did not hesitate, when one of the branches had become sterile and dead and had definitively stopped producing buds, to trace the family back into the past to the closest tree fork—in other words, back to a common ancestor—in order to then distribute these possessions back *down* through the lineage to any green collateral branches that had grown out from this same fork.[36] Thus the rule *propres ne remontent* ("family property does not go backwards") was invalid in the western provinces while, on the contrary, the customary laws of Orléans-Paris rejoiced in this very rule.[37] Such a rule was to be expected to the degree that, when customary laws judged it convenient, they could unashamedly block up the ascendant or descendant channels of the lineage in order to support agreements made by fathers and mothers. To summarize, let us say that the kinship structure was typical of the customary laws of western France, while the joint-property and conjugal models typified the great Capetian open field and its scattering of privileged cities.

In the western portion of the realm, this emphasis upon the kinship structure also gave rise to the strict application of the rule *paterna paternis, materna maternis*. As I have said, it was as if marriage merely formed a precarious link between two branches growing from different lineages, a link that was of little consequence, especially if this marriage remained sterile. Favorable to children, the customary laws of the western regions were scarcely favorable to love. The most extreme among them, those of Brittany and Normandy, carried this rule to the point of absurdity. In the event that no children were born of the union, rather than give the property coming from the paternal lineage to nonlineal members on the mother's side, they preferred to turn these possessions over to the local lord or even to turn them over to the tax agents! (Oh, what a horrible thought for the Norman, who is a born tax-evader.) As late as the eighteenth century a jurist coldly wrote, in a completely humorless text in which he was commenting upon those practices that had come directly from the barbarity of the lineage: "Paternal and maternal relatives are not coheirs. They have nothing in common, and the lord of the place should inherit rather than permit a paternal relative to inherit from a maternal one."[38]

We could discuss almost indefinitely the consequences of this quasi-caricaturized and very Norman concern for protecting the lineage—which

[36] Besnier, in Yver, "Les caractères originaux," p. 34.
[37] Ibid., p. 38; and also, for the interesting problems involved in determining borders of customary laws, p. 61, n. 2.
[38] Ibid., p. 46, n. 3 (a text of Basnage, 1778).

to us seems strange though completely logical. Nevertheless, within the restricted limits imposed by this article, it would be better to discuss briefly the problems of origins. Although fascinated with describing structures, Yver nonetheless did not avoid the difficult question of origins. Why do we find in the old lands of western France this formidable block of customary laws that tend to be lineage-based, egalitarian, inclined to share, and individualist—the latter quality being only an apparent paradox? The explanation proposed by Yver goes back to the eleventh century and even beyond. It cautiously envisages three sorts of causes: the political configuration of this frontier region; the social and domainal, or rather the nondomainal, history of the region; and possible ethnic contributions.

Let us begin with political history. As trivial as it may seem as a means of elucidating the origins of customary laws, political history indubitably did play a role in the crystallization of Norman customs. Indeed, the region of these customary laws coincides very closely with the frontiers of the old Norman duchy. This "very closely" is in itself significant to show what I have in mind, since we are studying frontier "spillovers," especially those found in the curious enclave formed on the eastern limits of the province of Normandy by a group of twenty-four parishes that retained the customary laws of the region of Beauvais, thus enabling Robert Génestal to establish that Norman law was laid down during the reign of William the Conqueror.[39] From a broader perspective, the entire marshy region of the West may have formed an isolated strip on several occasions, during the days of the dukes of Normandy in the northern part and the days of the Plantagenets in the southern part. Does this isolationism go back, as Yver suggests (in one of the very rare moments during which he gives free rein to the game of hypothesis-making) to the formation of the *Tractus armoricanus* [the Breton peninsula] at the end of the Roman Empire?

Whatever the case, and without going back so far, political demarcations certainly contributed to creating a razor-sharp line separating the customary laws of the marshy regions and the other western regions from those that formed the "Capetian" heart of France.

An inquiry into origins could not, however, be based on these assertions which, taken literally, are too similar to the good old history of events. A historian of the law but tainted by social history, Yver does not separate the origins of his groups of customary laws from the conditions within which they were born or even from the specific level of society they found most favorable for their development. The complete antithesis of

[39]Cited in Yver, ibid., p. 5, n. 2.

the customary laws of the Orléans-Paris region, Norman law was not born of the abasement of villeinage but was instead the creation of a superior class of free, independent men who,[40] with the exception of the *pays de Caux*, had not yet been won over by the snobbism of primogeniture, which would become the rage in Great Britain. Sure of their rights and scarcely threatened by the encroachments of their lord as far as their rural property was concerned, these men wanted above all to give equally to their descendants the property that was indisputably theirs. This region already had an efficient political and legal constitution and a more open social structure in which the peasant population, freed from serfdom,[41] was not so deeply enmired as elsewhere in dependence upon the domain. This made it possible—to use Yver's ingenious description—for this law of lineages and of free men to be rapidly diffused or "percolated" from the top of the society to the bottom, from the upper groups that witnessed its birth to the lower classes that accepted it during the great era of the Norman duchy.

Lastly, the author whose research I am summarizing here did not attempt to avoid the spiny question of more distant origins. Indeed, these distant origins provide explanatory elements that are irreplaceable, although by no means exhaustive. In the case of the customary law of Normandy, which provides the most convenient conditions—conditions not always present in other regions—for this pilgrimage back to origins, a perusal of old Scandinavian law permits us to make several major, and rapid, observations during the course of an analysis similar to that made by Dumézil. In the original home of the Vikings we are, of course, far from the customs so dear to the Teutons per se. As we have seen, Teutonic customary law resembled that of the Parisians and provided for the exclusion of portioned children and, later, the option-return system. On the other hand, the laws of Magnus Hakonarson of Norway, the *Jonsbok* of Iceland of 1281, and the customary laws of Scania and of Sjaelland in Denmark provide comparative researchers with rules which to the smallest details were very similar to those of the oldest law of the Normans, and therefore probably of the Vikings. We find a strict equality in the sharing of an inheritance, which involved much hair-splitting and which was certified by the oaths of twelve "oath helpers"; we find the forced return, and so on. Thus, the Nordic contribution played no small role in the formation of at least a part of the customary laws of northwestern France. In this case, as with Dumézil, a structural description provides a good start for an explanation of origins.

---

[40]Yver, *Essai de géographie*, pp. 109 and 120.
[41]Yver, "Les deux groupes de coutumes," p. 4.

The preference-legacy and "household" pole

When compared with the hybrid solutions of the Orléans-Paris law, which lies midstream between total equality and the right to grant advantages to one child, the customary laws of Normandy and, even more, those of western France in general represent the polarization of the lineage in the direction of complete equality among heirs, which was so widely instilled in the old peasant and commoner culture. At the other extreme lies the South, where the langue d'oc was spoken, and beyond it the whole region where preference legacies predominated[42]—some of which were situated far to the north. These regions provide the example of a diametrically opposed trend highly favorable to the right to show preference for one heir. The Normans killed the father. In contrast, the Romans, whose law would be so influential upon the populations of the region speaking the langue d'oc, believed that the father's wishes survived in this world, even when he who had expressed them had already gone to the world beyond.

Between the end of the Middle Ages and the sixteenth century, these patriarchal or paternalist ideas, which were directly implanted in the South by the rebirth of Roman law, easily took root in the rural and mountainous regions of the South, on the old pre-Renaissance subsoil formed by a local unwritten law that has left few traces. Through a few scanty texts,[43] and above all through the procedures of rural notaries,[44] we know simply that the "subsoil" and this unwritten law were strongly inegalitarian and that, like the most archaic customary laws of the Orléans-Paris region, they encouraged the exclusion of portioned children. In this case it was still a matter of keeping the family and the patriarchal peasant holding as intact as possible under the lofty, though very decrepit, authority of the local lord. Thus, in the region speaking the langue d'oc trends granting the right to favor one child—trends so dear to the renascent Roman law—sprouted from a subsoil and a soil that were already fertile. In early-modern times, the father in the region of the langue d'oc was buoyed up by the jurisprudence of local courts and could—thanks to old habits and an easy conscience conferred by juridical

[42]Preference-legacy systems, according to the terminology used by legal historians and especially by Yver, are those permitting a father to grant a lasting advantage, either by donation or by his will, to one or another of his children or heirs (Yver, *Essai de géographie*, pp. 155 and 158).

[43]See the oldest customary law for the city of Montpellier (thirteenth century), which contains both the old customary arrangement excluding portioned children in addition to, at this early date, the very Roman right of the father to show favors for any specific child as he sees fit (ibid., pp. 156 and 25).

[44]Hilaire, *Le régime des biens*; L. de Charrin, *Les testaments dans la région de Montpellier* (Montpellier, 1961), especially *in fine*.

modernity—indulge himself in becoming more Roman than Christian during the years of the Renaissance. On the contrary, the mother, who made her presence so strongly felt in the customary laws of Orléans or Paris, bowed out in the southern regions and became increasingly involved in the insignificance of household tasks.

We have seen how the North, thanks to various methods of safeguarding the holding from excessive subdivisions, formerly practiced exclusion of portioned children or else strict primogeniture among commoners in the specific, localized cases of the *pays de Caux* and the region around Boulogne. The Normans, who were so ready to share equally, practiced automatic disinheritance of girls to benefit the males. In this fight against subdivision, the paterfamilias of the regions speaking the langue d'oc used the right to favor one heir,[45] the preference legacy, the donation inter vivos [a gift made between living persons], and the absolute power granted the last will and testament by Roman written law. His ultimate goal was to give the lion's share to one of his children, not necessarily the eldest. This privileged descendant would thus inherit the bulk of the land or family plot, often after a period of co-residence during his parents' lifetime, while the other children had to be satisfied with more or less scanty portions, tiny crumbs granted by the will, or by a *légitime* [guaranteeing each child one-half of what he or she would have received by intestate succession], that share of the inheritance that was set apart by customary law and that might amount to merely a few sous.[46] From that moment on, these disadvantaged offspring were threatened with becoming a part of the proletariat if they came from the common people or of the clergy if they came from the middle or upper classes.[47]

The "antifather" attitude of western France, which was so egalitarian and such a partisan of automatic succession, was distrustful of the last will and testament.[48] In contrast, the Southerner used it as an effective weapon to spread inequality, to perpetuate paternal arbitrariness, and to preserve the family property intact.

As a result, the characteristic provisions that the customary laws of the Orléans-Paris region had inserted at the end of the Middle Ages and during the sixteenth century in order to promote a tardy and partial equality among heirs declined or did not even exist in the South. Southern jurisprudence was unfamiliar with the option, or voluntary

[45]Among the major customary laws of the South showing the influences of Roman law (Montpellier, Bordeaux, Bayonne, and Agen) which Yver used for this question, we need cite only the old customary law of Agen: "The father can indeed favor any one of his children whom he wishes, and as he wishes" (quoted by Yver, *Essai de géographie*, p. 157, n. 305). For rural observances, see Hilaire, *Le régime des biens*.

[46]Charrin, *Les testaments*.

[47]Robert Forster, *The Nobility of Toulouse in the Eighteenth Century* (Baltimore, 1960).

[48]Yver, *Essai de géographie*, p. 156.

dispensation from making a return,[49] and disregarded the "legatee-or-heir" dilemma that caused such an agonizing decision for those in the Orléans-Paris region.

Another remarkable fact is that, even to the north of the traditional frontier joining the province of Saintonge to Bresse and separating the southern provinces with written, or Roman, law from the northern ones with a customary law, the right to make preference legacies, which is so very hostile to equality among heirs, influenced vast regions. This is undeniably true for the sixteenth century, that great period in which customary laws were being compiled, and many indications lead us to believe that the situation had existed for some time. Thus, the group of "central" provinces (which, according to one's perspective, formed either the northern borders of the region of the langue d'oc or the southern limits of the region of the langue d'oïl) formed a disputed battlefield. Here the preferency-legacy and antiegalitarian influences from the South often won the battle they were waging against the "egalitarianism" of the North—whether it was a question of the "absolute equality" of such western regions as Poitou or the "partial equality" found in Burgundy and in Berry as a result of the new-style set of customary laws from the Orléans-Paris region, which, here and there, were applying the option-return system by the end of the Middle Ages. In the various sectors of this "central" region (Auvergne-Marche, Poitou-Angoumois-Saintonge, Berry-Bourbonnais-Nivernais, and Burgundy) we thus simultaneously find both rash customary laws involving equality among heirs and juridical and cultural traits that smack strongly of the South. Of these I shall discuss briefly—referring the reader to Yver's analysis for the details—(1) the donation inter vivos,[50] which was granted by means of a preference legacy and which the recipient was not obliged to "return" later; (2) the dispensation from the return; (3) preference-legacy donations with the exception of the *légitime*; and (4) the lumping together legally of the positions of legatee and heir.

At the end of the Middle Ages, in the province of Berry for example,[51] the customary law was in certain instances one of option and relative equality among heirs. During the Renaissance the balance tipped in favor of the preference-legacy procedures of the South, which favored the "liberty" of the father of the family. This sort of procedure was therefore called "liberalization," a name that is a bit deceptive for the uninitiated. Indeed, here we are witnessing a veritable "southernization"

[49]Texts of the parlements of Toulouse (1584) and of Bordeaux (1587), ibid., p. 158.

[50]See, for example, in the province of Auvergne, ibid., p. 160. Concerning donations inter vivos, considered a part of the written law rather than of the customary laws of the North, see Molière, *Le malade imaginaire*, act 1, sc. 7, and passim.

[51]Yver, *Essai de géographie*, p. 166.

of the central provinces in the midst of the sixteenth century. In certain regions, for example in Auvergne, phenomena of this sort can be explained by the similarity of the culture within the region speaking the langue d'oc. This common culture made the penetration of the written law, which became the typical form for the regions where the langue d'oc predominated, seem completely natural. We must also take into account the prestige attached to a scholarly law, and Roman law was indeed scholarly. The Renaissance was particularly favorable to its expansion. But in the case of central and southern France, does some relationship exist between the persistence or the triumph, as the case may be, of an antiegalitarian law hostile to subdivisions of property and favorable to the father's authority, and the fact that tacit, or legally unacknowledged, family communities had persisted in the still recent past? The spirit that animated such joint households was in any event very different from that found in the egalitarian, individualist, subdividing, and lineage-centered kinship groups that abounded in Normandy. This is quite clear in the province of the Nivernais, where the analyses of the jurist Guy Coquille, in the mid-sixteenth century, indicate both the strong implantation of such family communities and the unequal influence of the preference-legacy laws.[52] The case is even clearer, or to be exact it is more clearly and more perfectly indicated, in the northeastern and especially in the extreme northern portion of the regions speaking the langue d'oïl. But I must hasten to add that this northern example involves structures that were merely living fossils by the sixteenth century.

A "preference-legacy group," therefore, existed in the Northeast and the North, far from the Mediterranean zones from which Roman law made its successive conquests. It involved to varying degrees Lorraine, the region about Verdun, the Vermandois, and above all Picardy and the region of the Walloons. A systematic comparison of the latter two regions with neighboring Flanders, where customary laws differed markedly, is instructive.

The preference-legacy zone of the Walloon-Picardy region extended roughly from Amiens to Liège.[53] During the sixteenth century, which saw the compilation of customary laws, this region observed on a large scale: (1) the "liberalism" of father and mother, in other words, the liberty to confer an advantage; (2) the absence of or dispensation from the return, notably in the case of donations inter vivos; (3) the lumping together of the positions of legatee and heir; (4) the granting of a preference legacy or

---

[52]Crucial texts and analyses in G. Thuillier, *Aspects de l'économie nivernaise au XIXe siècle* (Paris, 1966), pp. 32–45.

[53]This zone includes the region of Amiens, the province of Artois, and the Cambrésis, Hainaut, French Flanders, and the Walloon regions.

a "fore-part;" (5) the general maxim "to one more, to the other less;" and (6) "the possibility for the father, the mother, and the descendants to use voluntarily a preference-legacy form when giving portions or dowries for a marriage."[54] Nowhere was this "liberalism"—in the worst sense of the term—carried to a greater extreme than in the rural and traditional areas of the *bailliages* of Orchies and of Douai, where the texts proclaim simultaneously a total dispensation from the return and the lumping together of the positions of heir and legatee.

The antiegalitarian and preference-legacy liberalism of the Walloons is all the more evocative and marked since, all along a frontier that is also a rough linguistic boundary, it is diametrically opposed to the customary laws of the Flemish, which exist in several hundred different versions. In complete contrast with those of the Walloons, these compilations specify a system of equality that used the option and that forbade a parent to "create a beloved child," a *chier enffant* or *lief kind*. In Flanders in certain extreme cases, which are perhaps typical of the oldest stratum of Flemish customary laws and which are reminiscent of the Norman structures, we even find localized enclaves of complete equality where forced return was practiced.

Indeed, the comparison between the Walloon regions and Flanders can be carried even farther. The preference legacy and the right to favor one heir, which are characteristic of the French-speaking regions of the extreme North, belong to a general architecture of customary laws and of families which is item by item the opposite of its Flemish counterpart. If Picard-Walloon jurisprudence stressed the easy transfers, large allocations, and massive donations made possible by the right to favor one heir, it did so in order to encourage among the Walloons the household community, which functioned in order to help the married couple and, later, the children who were willing to remain rooted within the family. On the contrary, Flemish laws attempted to pass on an equal and fair portion of the inheritance to even the most distant little branch and bud of the family tree.

Walloon jurisprudence also worked to the disadvantage of the interests of the scattered members of the lineage, the collateral branches, and the "detruncated" children. In contrast, the scattered members of the lineage were the chief concern of the Flemish world. The Walloon commoner provided for, but the Fleming refused, the *ravestissement*, or allocation, in the event of the death of one of the partners in a marriage, of the household's *entire* patrimony to the surviving partner. This *ravestissement* became possible once the couple had definitively proved that they were one flesh by giving birth to a child, even a child that died very soon,

[54]Yver, *Essai de géographie*, pp. 201–21; and Yver, "Les deux groupes de coutumes," pp. 17–213.

providing it had had the time, even for an instant, "to bray and to cry." Contradicting the *paterna paternis* rule and challenging the orientation of the estate about the lineage, in order more effectively to exalt the "household" fusion of the couple's possessions, the Picards and the Walloons could naturally practice only "division on the basis of beds." They could not do as so many Flemish cantons did and divide the inheritance on an individual basis, making no distinction "between the children of all the not clearly defined beds."

In the same spirit that granted preference to things having to do with the family community, the Walloons—once again in contrast to the Flemings—also adopted the practice of devolution [or reversion to a collateral branch for lack of heirs], which had the result of granting the father and mother's property to the children of the first marriage.[55] Lastly, in the Walloon-Picard region, as an analagous result of an imperturbable logic, we find the old measure for exclusion so dear to all customary laws inspired by the earliest Orléans-Paris structures, which placed above everything else, even above the well being of the members of a lineage, the perpetuation of the household community and of its undivided land, which was destined, if possible, to survive beyond the lifetime of the parents. Thus, Picards and Walloons applied various degrees of discrimination against portioned children, reduced the sums given to girls, and excluded bastards; while the Flemings, who were markedly lineage-oriented and to the very end remained faithful to the *materna maternis* rule and to the sovereign rights of the womb, proudly asserted that *een moder maakt geen bastaard* ("a mother cannot have a bastard").[56] In the French-speaking regions of the North, we also sometimes find the law of *maineté*, which granted the *mez*, or family house, intact to the youngest child, that is, to the one who, according to statistical probabilities, would live longest and be the last co-resident with his parents. On all these points, the majority of Flemish customary laws were once again diametrically opposed to their Walloon and Picard counterparts.

In addition to the above, the acid test remains the absence of representation. In all these matters a truly primitive characteristic is evident in the customary laws of the Walloons, for, as Yver expressed it, "there was no reason why a customary law that showed so little concern for equality among children should go to any great lengths to ensure that, if one predeceased the other, in the dead man's stead his children should receive his share."[57]

In contrast, Flanders, which like Normandy was so eager to follow the maxim "to each his due," conscientiously and almost perversely practiced

[55]Yver, "Les deux groupes de coutumes," pp. 13 and 209.
[56]Ibid., pp. 16–36, and n. 3.
[57]Ibid., pp. 21 and 217.

unlimited representation, "even to the hundredth degree and beyond," as the Customary Law of Antwerp of 1545 stated in all seriousness.[58] One of the inevitable consequences of this divergence of attitudes was the absence in Picardy and in the Walloon region of that curious institution, the *Fente*, or "split," which was also missing from the old customary laws of the Orléans-Paris region. Indeed, should the collateral branches become heirs when a childless branch became extinct, the Picards and the Walloons would give to the closest relative the chattels and the acquests that were a part of the estate of those dead descendants. In contrast, the Flemish customary law remained faithful to the distinction between lineages and to unlimited representation and literally *fended*, or split like a log, the estate in escheat, dividing it fifty-fifty between the members of the father's and the mother's lineages, or even in quarters or eighths among the members of the lineages of the four grandparents or the eight great-grandparents!

This polarization of the Walloon regions in the direction of a jurisprudence oriented about the household or the manse and quite unfavorable to the lineage undoubtedly reflects the existence of a well-defined political territory and a cultural zone that stressed linguistic individuality to the point of rivalry. Must we also view this polarization as the clear result of a social structure? On the basis of an evocative text,[59] Yver cautiously formulated the hypothesis that the law of the Walloons, which was oriented about the family, was initially that of a population of dependent peasants or *meisenedien*, who were obliged to pay prudent heed to the fragile and barely hereditary nature of their holding or manse and who therefore stressed what seemed their only recourse: the unity of the couple and the perpetuation of the plot of ground. By contrast, within another ethnic group and a different culture, Flemish law, like the customary laws of Normandy, represented the practices of a stratum of free men with more elbowroom. These men were capable of carrying out the egalitarian solution "to each his due" as far as the individuals in their respective blood lines were concerned, precisely because they did not feel penned up in the iron cage of the domainal organization.

The important point, of course, is not this hypothesis, which the author himself realized was merely exploratory. It is rather the grid Yver established, introducing a Cartesian logic and a rigor into the apparent hodgepodge of French customary laws, whose diversity at times evokes a naively eclectic building. About the two opposing poles, that of genealogical *consanguinity* and that of the conjugal *alliance*, contradictory solutions took form at the two extremes of the possible arc. Thus, equality

[58]Ibid., pp. 8 and 28.
[59]Ibid.

among heirs and the self-centeredness of the lineage are contrasted with the right to show preferences in order to serve the household and the family community. Each in its own way, Normandy and Flanders were in this respect located at the antipode from the Walloon regions or those speaking the langue d'oc. Between the two we find the hybrid or centrist constructions which, moreover, were in constant disequilibrium and evolution, as evidenced in the Orléans-Paris region. Whether important or merely quaint, isolated traits such as unlimited representation or the *Fente* appeared in their logical places within one or another regional configuration. Even if questioned because of its inflexible completeness, this grid can indicate not only actual customary practices, but the range of possible customs in the territory under consideration.

The highly deductive nature of the model I have thus proposed by no means implies that in this instance Clio, the muse of history, broke with empirical reality as it had existed in the past. By digging out the geography of customary laws from the rut of a purely factual description and by directing it toward a logical and comparative study of these laws, Jean Yver in the end returned to the most proven ways used by the historian. Indeed, his revelation of a group of northern regions—Normandy and Flanders—which for ethnic and lineage-centered reasons observed equality among heirs at an early date or which tried to achieve equality through a partial but vigorous evolution—as in the Orléans-Paris region—is consistent with the observations made long ago by those interested in the earliest revolts of the rural world. Those early rebels were also seeking equality, whether in the rebellion of the Norman peasants described by Wace, that of the Flemings so dear to Henri Pirenne, or the jacqueries in the Ile-de-France and the region of Beauvais. Formidable egalitarian traditions often abounded, though not everywhere, among commoners in the northern half of France. These traditions are of interest to historians of development, who are aware of the precocious modernity of northern France. They should also fascinate specialists of the French Revolution, who are concerned with the eternal problem of its causes. Although Yver's incredibly minute and careful research must, of course, not be considered complete but must continually be augmented, strengthened, or rectified through on-the-spot research in notarial records and legal documents, the end result of his work is a new approach to family history. The extended families of the Nivernais and of the mountains of the Massif Central, the household communities of the old Ile-de-France or of Picardy and the Walloon region, and the Flemish and Norman lineages that paradoxically nourished individualism and egoism, are revealed, more or less clearly, as having been more than mere intimate or collective images. We see that, during the sixteenth century and even before, they made a lasting impression upon the compilation of customary laws.

5

The Scattered Family: Another Aspect of Seventeenth-Century Demography

Micheline Baulant

The favorite quarry in demographic hunts has long been the so-called complete family, the family that lasted long enough for the couple to give birth to all the children they were physiologically able to have. Let us, instead, ponder for a moment what happened to incomplete families and ask ourselves successively what happened to the surviving spouse, to the children, and to the household's property when one of the partners died prematurely.

In the sixteenth, seventeenth, and early eighteenth centuries, in the majority of cases in the Parisian region (more specifically around Meaux) the spouse remarried very rapidly. As a general rule, the men—sometimes saddled with children—remarried after several months or even after several weeks. Etienne Becheret and Jean Becheret of Mareuil in 1691,[1]

Annales, E.S.C. 27 (July–October 1972): 959–68. Translated by Patricia M. Ranum.

[1] Etienne Becheret lost his first wife, Marie Hébert, on 27 February and married Simone Caster on 2 July; he had two young daughters. Jean Becheret lost his wife, Nicole Pagot, on 9 April and married Denise Loyson on 2 July; he also had two children, a third, Jean, age two, having died shortly after his mother's death. Both of the young mothers had died as a result of childbirth and each left a surviving newborn infant (Archives départementales, Seine-et-Marne, R.P. [*registres paroissiaux,* or parish registers for the town of] Mareuil, 1691. Archives départementales, Seine-et-Marne, will be cited hereafter as A.D., S-et-M).

Louis Choslin in 1709,[2] and Jean Guillemot in 1729[3] showed no abnormal haste in contracting a new marriage at the end of two or three months. Even women (although they remarried somewhat less frequently than men) would find a new husband within a period ranging from a few months to a year or two. At Varreddes, Adam Denis died on 28 April 1715, and his widow, Marie Piètre, married Henry Piètre in July.[4] Nicolas Lhoste and Nicolas le Riche drowned in the Marne in January 1720;[5] their respective widows remarried in April and June of the same year. At Chauconin, miller Louis Hervault died on 19 November 1731; Véronique Despost, his wife, remarried on 18 February 1732.[6] In the event of a second widowhood or widowerhood, the surviving partner did not hesitate to marry again. In 1700 Germain Chiboust, an innkeeper at Germigny, took as his fourth wife Jeanne le Jeune, who had already been married twice;[7] Nicole Picard of Chambry married Isaac le Blanc on 20 January 1727, Nicolas Oudot on 26 September 1740, and Charles Patron on 15 July 1743;[8] Françoise Choslin married Jean François Becheret on 18 June 1743, Louis Denis on 7 January 1754, and Pierre Tussin on 11 June 1754, all three of whom were already widowers. These women were by no means exceptions. The documents available do not permit us to calculate the percentage of persons marrying more than once, but we know that at the beginning of the eighteenth century at least 30 percent of all marriages were second weddings for one of the partners.[9]

[2]Louise Blot died on 28 March or 28 April 1709, and her husband married Marie Turpin on 8 June (A.D., S-et-M, R.P. Mareuil, 1709).

[3]Jean Guillemot lost his wife, Jeanne Neveu, on April 27. He had had nine children by her, at least four of whom had died. He then married Marie Marguerite Degrain on June 20 (A.D., S-et-M, R.P. Mareuil, 1729).

[4]A.D., S-et-M, R.P. Varreddes, 1715. At Saint-Soupplet, of 86 widows and widowers who remarried at the beginning of the eighteenth century, there were 53 men and 33 women (62 percent and 38 percent); at Neufmontiers, 38 men and 28 women; at Mareuil, 70 men and 50 women (in both cases, 58 percent and 42 percent). F. Lebrun (*Les hommes et la mort en Anjou au XVIIe et XVIIIe siècles* [Paris, 1971], p. 429), who has also mentioned the speedy remarriages, has found that in Mouliherne, in the parish of Baugeois, the percentage of women remarrying was markedly lower: 181 widowers and 61 widows (75 percent and 25 percent) (based on R. Plessix, *Etude de Mouliherne, paroisse angevine au XVIIIe siècle*, Doctorat ès sciences, Rennes, 1966).

[5]Marie Lhoste, widow of Nicolas Lhoste, married Pierre le Riche on 22 April; another Marie Lhoste, widow of Nicolas le Riche, married Jean Moreau on 10 June (A.D., S-et-M, R.P. Varreddes, 1720).

[6]A.D., S-et-M, R.P. Chauconin, 1731 and 1732; Véronique Despost married Louis Moisy of Reez and gave birth to a son on 3 November.

[7]A.D., S-et-M, B 389, pieces 24, 25, and 83.

[8]A.D., S-et-M, R.P. Chambry, 2d and 3rd registers, passim. Isaac le Blanc had died on 7 June 1740, and Nicolas Oudot on 3 January 1742. Nicole Picard bore eight children during her first marriage, one during her second, and six during her third—fifteen children in all, including two sets of twins.

[9]During the seventeenth century the title "widow" or "widower" was almost never used, especially for men. It might at times still be omitted until about 1720, but much less

This persistence and precipitation can perhaps be explained by the climate of insecurity that made solitude difficult to bear. Solid economic reasons also played their part. Jean Plicque, vine-grower at Villenoy, and Catherine Girardin, his wife, who had obtained both a physical separation and a separation of property on the grounds of incompatibility in September 1694, appeared seven months later before the tribunal of the chapter of Meaux and explained that for them it would be "not only more praiseworthy but much more advantageous and useful to be united in marriage again than to remain separated."[10] Indeed, in a household of small peasants—the vine-growers and hired men typical of the region —not only did the wife cook, keep house, mend, and raise her own children and those of previous marriages, but she also spun and cared for the livestock, both poultry and cows. Without a wife, there was no cow and therefore no milk and no cheese; nor were there hens, chicks, and eggs. In addition, inventories made after death for bachelors or men who had been widowers for a number of years are always characterized by an almost total lack of linens—shirts, sheets, tablecloths, napkins. On the other hand, although the wife, always as busy as a bee, could care for the vineyard or "saw" the grain almost as well as a man, the male was irreplaceable for certain types of heavy work, especially for the vintage. (Indeed, women living alone would sell their harvest on the vine rather than pay the salary of vintners and basket carriers.) In addition, only the man was capable of bringing a sufficient amount of money into the household. Not only was the woman less well paid for a similar amount of work—about half as much as a man—but many fewer opportunities for work were available to women.

In principle, the children were given a guardian and an administrator[11] by a family council,[12] which was theoretically composed of four relatives

---

frequently after that date, at least in the villages I have studied. Therefore, the figures I have drawn up represent a minimum. At Mareuil, of 182 marriages performed between 1707 and 1739, there were 42 in which one of the partners had been widowed and 12 in which both had been widowed, i.e., 30 percent of the total. At Neufmontiers between 1702 and 1739, of 152 marriages 34 involved one widow and 8 involved two widowed partners (28 percent). At Saint-Soupplest between 1700 and 1735 there were 231 marriages, 57 of them involving one widowed partner and 15 involving two widowed partners (31 percent). Of course, we encounter extreme variations in numbers depending upon the year. At Saint-Soupplest, for example, no widowed person was involved in any of the 12 marriages performed in 1719, but of the 6 marriages performed in 1712, 4 had involved one widowed partner and 2 had involved two widowed partners.

[10]A.D., S-et-M, B 387, piece 12.

[11]The administrator does not seem to have been considered indispensable at the beginning of the seventeenth century.

[12]The term is never found in texts, which instead refer to the "assembly of relatives" or, more broadly, to the "relatives."

on the maternal side and four on the paternal side. In practice, there was no immediate obligation to give the children a guardian. This legal step only became necessary at the moment of the father's or the mother's remarriage,[13] or when the minor's interests had to be represented—for example, if he inherited from a grandmother or an uncle. Although this family council was not absolutely closed to women—since, if need be, the mother or more rarely the grandmother was included in it—the relatives were in principle males. No aunt or feminine cousin was to be found there. If a sufficient number of relatives could not be found in the village or in neighboring villages, the council had to be completed by neighbors or friends; but sometimes five or six relatives would have to do.[14]

The guardianship was almost always entrusted to a surviving parent;[15] but when the mother remarried, it was often transferred to the stepfather. To compensate, the administrator had to be selected from the deceased parent's family.

Should the children be completely orphaned, the family council would meet again and give them a new guardian. In certain cases the administrator became the guardian and a new administrator was chosen, but there seems to have been no general rule on this matter. Of course, the

[13]Widows or widowers who were neglectful or too poor sometimes avoided this obligation or only partially fulfilled it. In 1732, for example, the *procureur fiscal* of the *bailliage* of the bishopric received "word" that Antoine Lefranc, vine-grower of Crégy, and Marie Barthellemy, both widowed and both parents of a minor child, had married without having had a guardian and administrator chosen for each minor child and without having had an inventory of possessions drawn up (A.D., S-et-M, B 400, pieces 4, 5, and 6). In 1694, the inventory made of the joint property of the late Claude Hebuterne had neither been completed nor certified. The record shows that Catherine Girardin, his widow, had however been in "widowhood" for more than four years and that she had borne a child by her second husband (ibid., B 387, piece 12).

[14]In practice, the composition of family councils was extremely varied. Here are a few examples. For the Merlan children in 1682, on the paternal side there were two second cousins and three second cousins once removed; on the maternal side, three uncles and two cousins, making a total of ten relatives (A.D., S-et-M, B 68, piece 17). For the Boitel family in 1706, which had two children from two different marriages, on the paternal side the council included two uncles and one second cousin, and on the first maternal side were one uncle and two second cousins, while the second maternal side included the mother, one second cousin, and one neighbor (ibid., B 389, piece 110). For the Flocq children in 1707, on the paternal side were the father and two uncles, while the maternal side included two uncles and one great-uncle; for the Fayot child in 1709 the paternal side consisted of three uncles and one cousin, and the maternal side included the mother and one uncle, but one of the uncles was an uncle on both sides by marriage (ibid., B 390, pieces 1, 2, and 46). For Marie-Louise Salomon in 1711, the paternal side included the father and the grandmother, and the maternal side included the grandmother's second husband and one uncle (ibid., B 69, piece 26).

[15]Beginning in December 1657 an attempt was made to name a guardian for the children of Didier Régnier and the late Marie Moreau. In the meeting of relatives held on 23 August 1658, the father was selected. The *procureur fiscal* replied that Didier Régnier had "already formerly been guardian," without specifying why he no longer held that position, and an uncle was appointed instead (A.D., S-et-M, B 380, piece 119).

stepfather disappeared from the family council, since he had to care for his own minor children, whose interests could conflict with those of the first marriage. In addition, the family council had the task of solving the problem of the minor children's support until they were of an age to earn a living—on the average at about fifteen years of age[16]—and of establishing the conditions for that support. The guardian might care for the minor children, but this was not obligatory. Children were most frequently divided up among various relatives who would choose one or the other because it was a godchild, because of the "fond affection" they bore the child, or because they thought they might obtain some work from the child. Thus, when François Merlan, a plowman at Puisieux, died in 1682, he left five minor children who had already lost their mother.[17] No arrangements were made to assure the support of the two oldest, Nicole, aged sixteen, and François, aged fifteen. Sébastien, aged thirteen, was placed in the care of a cousin, who would ask nothing for his food and upkeep "in consideration of the small tasks" he would render until his eighteenth birthday;[18] in return, Sébastien could ask for no wages. Marie, aged ten, went to her uncle. He was to send her to school for two more years and would receive thirty livres in all for those two years; then he would support her at his own expense and only receive in return any services that Marie could give him until she was eighteen. Jeanne, aged seven, went to live with another uncle; she would also attend school and pay twenty livres a year (a very modest sum) until she was fifteen. Between the ages of fifteen and eighteen, her uncle would ask nothing of her, but she could make no claims upon him either. Earlier, Barthélémy Hebuterne and Etienne Fayot, the uncles, had offered to take Marie and Jeanne free until their fifteenth birthdays on condition that Barthélémy Hebuterne not be made guardian, a burden he was eventually forced to accept.

Indeed, during this period, relatives agreeing to care for a young child frequently proposed as a condition that they be relieved of the obligation of guardianship.[19] In the seventeenth century this function seemed an

---

[16]Until age fifteen: A.D., S-et-M, B 384, piece 15; B 387, piece 38; B 386, pieces 74–76; B 387, pieces 83–84. Until age sixteen or seventeen: B 389, piece 25; B 384, pieces 16–105; B 387, piece 2. No arrangements were made for Etienne Régnier, age fourteen, or for Laurence Villeré, between fifteen and sixteen years of age. Children could also be made wards until they were eighteen, but in such an event it was often a matter of their performing services in order to make up for the scantiness of the maintenance allowance they had been able to pay or for the free food they had been given.

[17]A.D., S-et-M, B 68, pieces 17 and 19.

[18]This cousin was a plowman, as were the two uncles who cared for Marie and Jeanne. All three referred to the "affection" they bore one or the other of the children.

[19]Jeanne Régnier (A.D., S-et-M, B 384, piece 15), Marguerite Trouët (B 384, piece 105), and Marie Tavernier (B 386, pieces 74–76) were accepted upon this condition.

unbearable burden to many. In certain cases uncles, great-uncles, and cousins avoided the task on various pretexts: age, family obligation, offices,[20] etc., and after several months of meetings and discussions,[21] the *procureur fiscal* was finally forced to initiate legal proceedings to oblige one of them to accept the position.

In 1698 this is exactly what happened to the five children of Jean Philippes, blacksmith at Barcy, and Anne Vigneron. Excuses were made one after the other by Michel Philippes, their great-uncle, who was recording clerk at Marcilly and was then sixty-nine years old; by Denis Picou, their uncle, recording clerk at Barcy (although he only obtained this position after Jean Philippes' death); by Jean Pasquier, another great-uncle, who was a sixty-year-old *procureur fiscal* with five minor children and a pregnant wife of his own; and by Jacques le Roy, on the grounds that he was only their uncle by marriage. The position finally was forced upon another cousin, Antoine Philippes, who in vain pleaded poverty, four children, and the fact that he could neither read nor write, to which the other relatives retorted rather cruelly that his ignorance was "of no consideration in view of the poverty of the minor children, whose incomes were inadequate for their food and upkeep."[22]

A very common practice during the seventeenth century was "giving minors to the lowest bidder," that is, entrusting them to the person—not necessarily a member of the family council—who agreed to accept the smallest allowance for their upkeep. If there was not enough money to pay these support allowances, a child might be placed with someone at no cost for a time, on condition that the relatives agree to leave the child with this foster parent for several years without pay. The most difficult minors to place were always the youngest children. They were, however, not usually very numerous, for a great number did not long survive their mother's death.

The joint estate shared by the married couple—in reality a joint estate reduced to acquests [property acquired other than through inheritance] was the most frequent type of marriage settlement in the region. It could be continued by the surviving partner and the children born of that marriage. In order to break this arrangement, an inventory of possessions was required, with their evaluation by a sworn appraiser and a declara-

---

[20]For example, their work as parish priest, schoolmaster, recording clerk for the tax offices, or *procureur fiscal*.

[21]François Merlan, plowman at Puisieux, died in early August 1682, and Barthélémy Hebuterne accepted the guardianship of his children on 1 February 1683. Jean Philippes, blacksmith at Barcy, died in March 1698, and Antoine Philippes accepted the guardianship in July.

[22]A.D., S-et-M, B 387, pieces 91, 93, and 94.

tion before a judicial official.[23] This procedure was obligatory before any remarriage.[24]

Contracts for the second (or third) marriage generally made provisions for the maintenance of minor children in return for the income from their property and a dower for the second wife if she preferred not to hold property jointly with her husband. (Such jointly held property would be decreased by half of the initial joint property due the children of the first marriage.[25])

If, at the time of the death of one of the partners, the household had no surviving child, the inherited family property of the deceased and his share of the couple's acquests and personal property went to his heirs: brothers, sisters, parents, and cousins. This half-share of the personal property could be claimed immediately. Thus, a tenant farmer could be obliged to turn over to distant cousins of his wife not only half his furniture, linens, and dishes, but also half his flocks, horses, plows, grain, and fodder. In such a manner Denis Jourdain, a tenant farmer on property belonging to the chapter of Varreddes,[26] who had no surviving child, was almost ruined financially by the unreasonable demands of heirs after his wife's death and could only continue his lease after Pierre Denis Adam, a plowman and notary at Varreddes, stood bond for him.[27] Geneviève Thévenard, who had lost her husband, Pierre Bledmortier, turned things to her advantage by making an arrangement with her late husband's heirs, who had come to claim a share in the inn that she had been directing alone for twelve years.[28]

---

[23]Claudine Aubry, tenant-farmer at Champfleury, wanted to make a settlement with her children of the personal property left by Pierre Rain, her husband. Her son-in-law, Toussaint Théronde, and Pierre Merlan, her grandson's guardian, objected on the grounds that the inventory made after Pierre Rain's death in 1681 had never been completed or certified and was not valid (A.D., S-et-M, B 68, piece 34).

[24]See above, n. 13.

[25]For example, take the contract between Claude-Etienne Martin, plowman at Boutigny and widower of Marguerite Pinguet, and his second wife, Marie Nicolle Martin. The fiancée would receive either the customary jointure or the sum of 300 livres, as she chose. In addition a reciprocal preference legacy of 300 livres, plus the clothing and linens used by the surviving partner and a bed complete with bedding were also stipulated. The child born of the first marriage was to be fed, sheltered, and clothed until the age of eighteen by funds coming from half of the chattels inherited from its mother and from the income of its real property (A.D., S-et-M, B 413, piece 29).

[26]A farm, 167 *arpents* [an *arpent* is roughly equal to an acre], and various tithes.

[27]A.D., S-et-M, B 413, pieces 37–38 and 132–33. Marie Piettre died at the end of April 1755, the seals were affixed on the 30th, and the inventory was drawn up on 13 May and in the days that followed. The surety bond of P. D. Adam was dated 4 June. Denis Jourdain died on 27 July 1757.

[28]A.D., S-et-M, B 414, pieces 56–57. Geneviève Thévenard was relatively well protected by her marriage contract, which limited to 800 livres the amount the collateral heirs could claim in the event of Bledmortier's death. The contract also assured her the use during her lifetime of all real property included in the estate.

Indeed, customary law permitted a married couple to assure the survivor the use until his or her death of all their possessions (both property inherited from his family and joint property) through a donation inter vivos, either as a part of the marriage contract or after the marriage ceremony.[29] This practice seems not to have been very common. Thus, the chief bit of good fortune for a husband who had lost his wife lay in having children,[30] for he could become the heir of a baby who survived his mother for a few hours,[31] he could have the joint estate continued temporarily with his children, or as guardian, he could delay making an accounting of the administration of his children's property until their majority.

These customary laws and usages had undoubtedly existed since an early period and continued during the entire course of the eighteenth century. However, they assumed a special importance during this period, when the early death of young adults, both men and women, and high mortality rates shattered many homes that had been together only a few years.

This high mortality rate does not even take into account the epidemics that decimated populations in the sixteenth century and during the first half of the seventeenth century. Since a series of parish records for those years has not been preserved for the region of Meaux and since the priest sometimes specified that he was only recording the deaths of those dying of "contagion," it is impossible to analyze which age groups were affected.[32] After 1668, despite gaps and imperfections in regional records, we can, however, take a brief but conclusive sampling. First we find, by village and by periods of twenty or thirty years, the number of deaths for persons over ten years of age. To this we add for the same villages and periods of years the number of deaths for males between the ages of eighteen and fifty,[33] and for women between the ages of eighteen and forty-five—in other words, roughly the number of men and women who theoretically could father or give birth to children. In every instance the

[29]A.D., S-et-M, B 390, piece 38.

[30]Or occasionally of a woman losing her husband, especially if it was a question of a woman holding a tenant farm.

[31]For example, A.D., S-et-M, B 386, piece 99, the inheritance of Geneviève Lucy, wife of Jean Touron.

[32]In addition, until 1668 the age of death was only indicated in an irregular manner. Since many persons in a village bore the same surname and the same first name, it is always risky to identify any one dead person as the child born 20, 40, or 60 years earlier.

[33]Fifty years is a rather low limit for men, with such examples available as Jean Pasquier (see above, p. 109). But he was actually a rather rare case. This Jean Pasquier, a *procureur fiscal*, must in addition have been a plowman, and the demographic behavior of plowmen was rather different from that of other peasants.

ratio between these two figures, which varies according to the village, either reaches or is greater than 40 percent for the late seventeenth century and the period of transition between the seventeenth and eighteenth centuries: at Neufmontiers it is 43 percent for 1668–90 and 46 percent for 1691–1720; at Varreddes, 44 percent for 1672–94 and 39 percent for 1696–1724; at Monthyon, 40 percent for 1681–1711; and at Crégy for the period 1680–1719 it even reaches the enormous figure of 64 percent. Likewise, this percentage decreases everywhere during the eighteenth century: at Marcilly to 34 percent for 1710–31, at Monthyon to 37 percent for 1712–34, and at Neufmontiers to 33 percent for 1721–55, while remarriages become less speedy and less frequent. For the seventeenth century we have been unable to calculate the percentage of marriages performed in which one of the partners was a widow or a widower, but in the eighteenth century we find that this percentage went from 30 percent before 1739 to 27 percent after that date at Mareuil, and from 27 percent to 23 percent at Neufmontiers. Thus, the ratio tended to decrease between the beginning and the middle of the century.[34]

Even during the worst periods, quite a number of households undoubtedly managed to spend thirty or forty years or even more together. Certain couples survived periods of scarcity and epidemics and died in old age at a few years' or even a few months' interval. Take, for example, Etienne Piettre of Varreddes, who died at age seventy-five in May 1678 and whose wife, Jeanne Notin, was nearing eighty at the time of her death in February 1684; or Marie Bourgoing of Mareuil, who died in March 1732 at seventy-three and whose husband, Roland Cholin, died at eighty-four in 1740; or Etienne Vicquet of Neufmontiers, who died at eighty-seven and a half in 1752, followed by his wife, Louise le Beufve, aged eighty-one, in May 1753,[35] an extreme but not an isolated case. Also, there is no doubt that not all the "possible parents" whom we have located were married and that not all those who were married had children.

Yet during these years we see the following trends developing: (1) with the increase in deaths among young married couples, a greater number of children were left without either father or mother; (2) because few persons wanted to take charge of a swarm of children, even in return for a maintenance allowance, orphans were scattered among the homes of various uncles and cousins, the oldest being put out to service at an early age; and (3) with the number of remarriages increasing, an increasing number of complex families of different sorts developed. Marie Noël, for example, died in 1683 leaving three daughters—Marie, Marguerite, and Nicole—by her three successive husbands, Laurent Oudot, Pierre Trouët,

---

[34]At the moment we have no data available after 1767. See above, n. 9.
[35]Parish registers of Varreddes, Mareuil, and Neufmontiers for the indicated dates.

and Nicolas Cochois.[36] Clémence Lucas died in 1679, having borne Etienne and Jeanne by her first husband, Jacques Régnier; she remarried Michel Charlot, a widower with three children, and gave birth to an additional daughter before dying in 1679. Before Michel Charlot died in 1680 he had had time for a third marriage, with Magdelaine Tavernier.[37]

Or take another example, Catherine Clémence: she first married Michel Deligny and had two sons by the time of his death in 1683; she then married Pierre Nonclerc and upon her death in 1691 left a third son, Pierre. When Pierre Nonclerc, the father, married Anne Sombert and in his turn died in 1693, little Pierre was "given to the lowest bidder," his uterine brother, Pierre Deligny.[38] Or take the case of Pierre le Duc, widower of Marguerite Moreau, by whom he had two living children when he married Jeanne Dumont, who had also been widowed and who was the mother of two children (a third had died at an early age). The marriage of Pierre le Duc and Jeanne Dumont produced at least two more daughters.[39]

The existence of children from several marriages did not necessarily imply that they all lived under one roof. When Jean Plicque and Catherine Girardin of Villenoy resumed their life together in 1695 after their attempted separation, it was decided that the children born of Catherine's first marriage, who had been the cause of the quarrels within the household, would be put out to service.[40]

By the chance workings of deaths and remarriages, children were shifted from family to family, and the family cell (at least a certain number of family cells) formed, and then dissolved and became indefinitely unstable.

From this collected data we can draw a number of conclusions. First, the couple lost its stability. It seemed as if husband and wife no longer knew one another, no longer felt united for eternity but merely destined to spend a few years together.[41] Contemporaries were aware of the precariousness of marriage and sometimes expressed this concern. Thus, in 1679 Michel Messager, who had been selected as guardian for the Régnier children, protested that he was only their half-uncle through his wife,

[36]A.D., S-et-M, B 384, pieces 104–6.

[37]A.D., S-et-M, B 384, pieces 14–15, and 62–70.

[38]A.D., S-et-M, B 384, pieces 94–95; and B 386, pieces 63–69, and 118–21.

[39]A.D., S-et-M, R.P. Varreddes. Charles Butel married Jeanne Dumont on 5 July 1708; he died on 10 June 1715. Pierre le Duc's first marriage was to Marguerite Moreau on 4 June 1707; she died on 9 March 1716, and he then married Jeanne Dumont on 11 May 1716.

[40]A.D., S-et-M, B 387, piece 12.

[41]Lebrun, who has observed the same phenomenon, interprets it in a slightly different manner. He sees what he calls a "primacy granted to the family over the individual" (*Les hommes et la mort en Anjou*, p. 429).

"who having just died, he was no longer anything to them."[42] We believe that it is to this weakening of the marital bond that we must attribute the scarcity of donations inter vivos made by the partners in a marriage. This seems all the more probable since, in those donations we have encountered, no provisions were made for limiting the effects of the act to a period during which the surviving partner refrained from remarrying.

As a corollary, if the man-woman couple seems to have become less firmly united, the bond between brothers and sisters seems to have been strengthened. An analysis of acts naming guardians certainly would indicate the predominant role played by uncles and on occasion by brothers. The brothers' role was, moreover, not limited to raising their younger brothers and sisters. If the sister became pregnant or if her "honor" merely suffered as a result of slander, it was the brother who, in the father's absence, began legal proceedings.[43]

The second conclusion is that, for both sexes, remarriage often occurred so rapidly that the rhythm of births within the family was scarcely altered by the change in marriage partner. Nicole Picard had her eighth, ninth, and tenth children in June 1739, August 1741, and May 1744 respectively, in other words, at intervals between births of two years and two months and two years and nine months, during which period she managed to be twice widowed and twice remarried.[44] Three and a half years passed between the birth of Jeanne Dumont's third child (born of her first husband) and that of her fourth (born of her second husband); but there had been three years between the births of her second and third children, and three years and three months between the births of her fourth and fifth.[45]

These are, however, only secondary aspects of a more important phenomenon: the existence of a third type of family between the nuclear family and the extended family, a family whose form is blurred, a family that is by nature extremely unstable and that includes father, mother, and their children, plus a certain number of orphans—half-orphans from a previous marriage or complete orphans who are nephews, cousins, and sometimes even younger brothers.

[42]A.D., S-et-M, B 384, piece 15.

[43]We even encounter an older sister who takes her younger sister to the midwife to have her pregnancy verified (A.D., S-et-M, B 377, pieces 55–56).

[44]A.D., S-et-M, R.P. Chambry. Isaac le Blanc, her first husband, died in June 1740. In September of the same year Nicole Picard married Nicolas Oudot, who died in January 1742. She married Charles Patron in July 1743.

[45]A.D., S-et-M, R.P. Varreddes. Jeanne Butel, the second child of Charles and Jeanne Dumont, was born in December 1710; Jean was born on 31 December 1713. Charles Butel died on 10 June 1715, and Jeanne Dumont married Pierre le Duc on 11 May 1716. Geneviève was born in July 1717, and another daughter in October 1720.

Assigning dates limiting the existence of this sort of complex family is a delicate task. Very common during the seventeenth century, this type of family certainly existed during the sixteenth century, when remarriages were frequent.[46] As for the eighteenth century, we might say that after about 1730, since the number of early deaths tended to decrease and since remarriages therefore became less frequent, this type of family became less common, although it did not completely disappear. It is also possible that the epidemics which darkened the last years of the *Ancien Régime* once again prompted people to piece together the scattered bits of their families as best they could.

It is even more difficult to fit this phenomenon within specific time limits, since adult deaths occurred in waves that do not necessarily coincide with years of scarcity or high mortality. At Monthyon, for example, of nineteen adult deaths in 1709, only nine adults were between eighteen and forty-five or fifty years of age, while in 1702, of seventeen adult deaths, sixteen were between eighteen and forty-five years old. In addition, the curve for remarriages does not necessarily follow closely that for deaths; the number of widowers and widows was far from remaining constantly in equilibrium. For example, in 1724—again in Monthyon—of twenty adult deaths (sixteen men and four women), fifteen occurred in the twenty-four to forty year-old group (fourteen of them occurred in March), and of those fifteen dead, twelve were men.

In the region about Meaux, the archives of the seigneurial jurisdiction of the cathedral chapter contain an impressive number of records concerning "complex families." But normal families do not appear in these records, since there was no reason to draw up an act providing guardians unless parents left minor children upon their death or unless another marriage appeared probable, an even more frequent occurrence. We are therefore unable to compile any statistics on the basis of these documents. Thus, in the absence of precise listings showing the composition of families, we must use the evidence provided by a study of reconstituted families, on condition that a part of the sample be selected so that we can trace the various marriages of the members of a single family. In addition, the study should focus upon a cluster of neighboring villages, for experience has shown that widowers often remarried outside their own parish.

While awaiting such detailed information, we can nevertheless try to make a rough evaluation of the proportion of "complex families" found

[46]Lacking a coherent series of parish records for this period, we can find these remarriages in account books. For example, the tenant farm of les Touches, which belonged to the Hôtel-Dieu of Meaux, was held successively by a woman and her two husbands, then by the daughter of one of the latter, and by her three successive husbands.

at the end of the seventeenth century. We know that thirty percent of all marriages at the beginning of the eighteenth century involved at least one partner who had been married before. Assuming that in one out of three cases no child was born of the first marriage—which seems to be a maximal estimate—twenty percent of all households would have children from several marriages, to say nothing of families that accepted into their home a young half-brother, a nephew, or a small cousin. During the seventeenth century, when death rates were high among young adults, we can therefore assume that at least a quarter of all families were of this hybrid sort. This figure is, of course, only an estimate and may vary in one direction or the other.

6
Marriage Strategies as Strategies of Social Reproduction

Pierre Bourdieu

"The beneficiary of the entail, the eldest son, belongs to the land. The land inherits him." K. Marx, *A Contribution to the Critique of Political Economy.*

The strategies by which the peasants of Béarn, a remote area in the Pyrenees, tended to ensure the reproduction of their lineage and their rights to the means of production appear with marked statistical *regularity*. But one must be very careful not to see this regularity as the result of obedience to fixed *rules*. Indeed, we must break away from the legalistic kind of thinking which, to this day, haunts the entire anthropological tradition and tends to treat every practice as an act of *execution*. Adherents to straightforward legalism regard practices as the execution of an order or a plan, as if practices could be directly deduced from expressly constituted or legally sanctioned rules or from customary prescriptions coupled with moral or religious sanctions.[1]

Annales, E. S. C. 27 (July–October, 1972): 1105–25. Translated by Elborg Forster.

[1] It could be proven over and over again that ethnology has borrowed not only concepts, tools, and problems but also an entire theory of practices from the legalistic tradition. This theory is most obvious in the way ethnologists see the relationship between the "names of kinship" and the "attitudes of kinship." As one example, I would cite Radcliffe-Brown's *euphemistic* use of the term *jural* (and recall that Radcliffe-Brown still said *father-right* and *mother-right* for *patriarchy* and *matriarchy*). "This term," observes Louis Dumont, "is difficult to translate. We shall see that its meaning is more than only legal or juridical. It applies to relationships that can be defined in terms of rights and duties—customary rights and duties, regardless of whether they involved legal or only moral sanction, possibly in conjunction with religious sanctions. In short, it applies to relationships subject to precise and strict prescriptions, involving persons as well as things" (L. Dumont, *Introduction à deux théories d'anthropologie sociale* [Paris: Mouton, 1971], p. 40). Obviously, such a theory of practices could only survive in an ethnological tradition that

117

Structuralists regard practices as the execution of subconscious models, for structuralism revives the theory underlying straightforward legalism under the guise of the subconscious and treats the relationship between structure and practice, like that between language and speech, according to the model of the relationship between the musical score and the execution of the music.[2]

In reality, the generating and unifying principle of practices is constituted by a whole system of predispositions inculcated by the material circumstances of life and by family upbringing, i.e., by *habitus*. This system is the end product of structures which practices tend to reproduce in such a way that the individuals involved are bound to reproduce them, either by consciously reinventing or by subconsciously imitating already proven strategies as the accepted, most respectable, or even simplest course to follow. Those strategies that have always governed such practices finally come to be seen as inherent in the nature of things. However, the various strategies either for the transmittal of the undiminished patrimony and the maintaining of the family's social and economic position or for the biological continuity of the lineage and the reproduc-

---

speaks the language of the *rule* rather than that of the *strategy*, as long as it was in tune with certain assumptions that are inherent in the relationship between the observer and his object and that are part of the process of defining the object, unless they themselves are explicitly under investigation. Unlike the observer who cannot personally master the rules he is trying to discern in practices and words, the informant perceives the system of objective relationships—of which his words or his practices are so many partial indications—only as *profiles*, that is, in the form of relationships arising one by one or successively in emergency situations of daily life. Thus, when asked by the ethnologist to reflect in a quasi-theoretical manner on his practices, the best-informed source will, even with the ethnologist's help, produce a discourse belonging to two opposing systems, both of which are incomplete. Inasmuch as it is a *discourse of familiarity*, it will not mention those things that are "understood" because they are self-evident; inasmuch as it is a *discourse for an outsider*, it can only be intelligible if it excludes all references to particulars (and this means roughly all information directly related to proper names that evoke and summarize an entire system of preexisting information). It is a fact that the informant is willing to use his natural language of familiarity freely only if he feels that the observer is familiar with the world of reference of his discourse (a familiarity that is revealed by the form of the questions asked, either detailed or general, informed or ignorant). This explains why ethnologists are usually virtually unaware of the distance between the scholarly reconstruction of the world of their subjects and the actual experience of it. For the latter can only be inferred from silences, elliptic statements, and gaps in the discourse of familiarity, which is fully understood only in a restricted universe where the same knowledge is shared by practically everyone, so that individuals simply become proper names and situations simply "commonplaces." The very conditions leading the ethnologist to an objectivating perception of the social world (in particular his situation as an outsider) tend to prevent him from reaching the objective truth of his objectivating perception itself: access to that third kind of knowledge is possible only if one makes a conscious effort to reconstruct the truth of all the experiences the informants *virtually* could have, and if it is understood that an objective knowledge of their social world must not be limited to an understanding of their *actual* experiences.

[2]To cite only Saussure: "Nor is all of the psychic component always totally involved: the *ability to execute* plays no part, for *execution* is never performed by a collectivity; execution is always an individual act, controlled by the individual. This we will call *la parole*" (F. de Saussure, *Cours de linguistique générale* [Paris: Payot, 1960] pp. 37–38).

tion of its work force are by no means necessarily compatible, even though they have the same function. For this reason, only *habitus*, a system of schemes structuring every decision without ever becoming completely and systematically explicit, can furnish the basis for the casuistic thinking required to safeguard the essential at all times, even if it should become necessary to violate the "norms," which, to be sure, exist only in the legalistic thinking of the ethnologists anyway.

Thus, a transgression against the principle of male predominance such as the act of conferring upon women not only part of the inheritance but the status of heiress (*hereté*, m., *heretère*, f.) is bound to puzzle, even deceive, an observer who is aware, that is, forewarned, of all the strategies deployed to defend the (socially defined) interests of the lineage or—and this amounts to the same thing—the integrity of the patrimony. Just as the ethnologists have reduced the marriage patterns of Berber and Arab societies to marriage with a parallel cousin, because this type of marriage, which only represents one among a number of marriage strategies and not even the most frequent, appeared to them as the distinctive trait of that pattern by reference to the classificatory system of the ethnological tradition, so most of those who have analyzed the system of inheritance of Béarn have characterized it as "integral right of the eldest," likely to favor an eldest daughter as well as an eldest son, because the legalistic bias induced them to see a mere transgression against principles as the distinctive feature of the entire system, even though these very principles were still operating in such cases.

In reality, only the *absolute* necessity of keeping the patrimony in the lineage can bring about the desperate solution of entrusting a woman with the task of transmitting the patrimony, which is the very basis for the continuity of the lineage. Such a solution can only be produced by a single, extraordinary circumstance, namely, the absence of any male descendant. For we know that the status of heir does not fall to the first-born child, but to the first-born son, even if he is last in the order of birth. This revision of the traditionally held view becomes incontrovertible as soon as one ceases to treat the rules of inheritance and marriage as legal norms, after the manner of the historians of law who, even and especially when they base their work on the study of notarial documents, which provide them with no more than the actual or potential failures of the system, are still very far from showing how these practices really worked, or of the anthropologists who, by means of their classificatory systems usually derived from Roman law, produce spurious problems, such as those involving a canonic distinction between unilineal systems of succession and bilateral or cognatic systems.[3]

---

[3]The errors inherent in legalistic thinking are most clearly evident in the works of historians of law and custom. On the basis of their entire training and also because of the

And yet there are very strong reasons for postulating that marriage was not based on obedience to any ideal rule but came about as the end result of a *strategy* which, availing itself of strongly interiorized principles of a particular tradition, was able to reproduce in a manner more subconscious than conscious any one of the typical solutions explicitly contained in that tradition. The marriage of each one of its children—older or younger, boy or girl—presented every family with a specific problem it could solve only by weighing all the possibilities for perpetuating the patrimony offered by the tradition of succession and marriage. Acting as if this supreme function justified any means, the family could avail itself of strategies which the classificatory system of anthropological legalism would consider totally incompatible. It could, for example, disregard the "principle of the predominance of the lineage," so dear to Meyer Fortes, and entrust women with perpetuating the lineage. It could also minimize or even entirely nullify—if need be, by means of legal artifices—the consequences of inevitable concessions to a bilateral succession that would normally be fatal to the patrimony. In a more general sense, it could even manipulate the relationships objectively present in the genealogical tree in such a way that they would, *ex ante* or *ex post*, justify such kinship relations and alliances as were necessary to safeguard and augment the interests of the lineage, in other words, its material or symbolic capital. "They have discovered that they are close kin to the X's," said one of the informants, "ever since the latter have become important through the marriage of their daughter to the son of the Y's."

It is too often forgotten that, especially in illiterate societies, genealogical trees exist as such only when they are put together by the ethnologist, who is the only person capable of calling forth this complete network of relationships over several generations *tota simul*, i.e., all of it at the same time, in the form of a spatial schema that can be perceived *uno intuitu* and followed in every direction, starting at any one of its points. The network of relationships between contemporaneous relatives is a *system of relationships that may or may not be used* and represents only one part of the entire network.[4] The kinship relations that are actually and presently

---

nature of the documents they are studying (particularly the notarial documents representing a combination of the legal precautions produced by the repositories of a learned tradition, the lawyers, and the procedures actually envisaged by those who availed themselves of their services), such historians feel compelled to elevate inheritance and marriage strategies to the status of strict rules. (Cf. the bibliographical notes at the end of this article, particularly numbers 9, 10, 12, and 14.)

[4]The Kabyles make an explicit distinction between the two points of view under which kinship relations can be considered, depending on the circumstances, i.e., depending on the *function* imparted to these relations. They distinguish between *thaymath*, the group of brothers, and *thadjadith*, the group of descendants of one real or mythical ancestor. *Thaymath* is invoked when it becomes necessary to oppose another group, for example, if

known, recognized, practiced and, as the saying goes, "kept up," are to the genealogical *construct* what the network of roads that are presently built, traveled, kept up and therefore easy to use—or, better, the hodological space of actual comings and goings—is to the geometric space of a map furnishing an imaginary representation of all the theoretically possible paths and itineraries.

To carry this metaphor even further, all genealogical relationships would soon disappear, just as abandoned paths disappear, if they were not constantly kept up, even if they are used only intermittently. One often realizes how difficult it is to reestablish a relationship that has not been kept up by visits, letters, gifts, and so forth. ("You don't want it to look as if you only went there to ask a favor.") Just as the exchange of gifts dissimulates its objective purpose as long as it is spread out over time, although its reversible nature as an act of "give so that you may be given" becomes cynically evident when gifts are exchanged simultaneously, so the fact that kinship relations are continually kept up as if for their own sake dissimulates their objective function, which would be unmasked by the discontinuous use of the assurances that are always involved in them. It is a fact that the upkeep of kinship relations is clearly incumbent on those who, standing to profit most from them, can keep them in working order and at the same time camouflage their true function only by continuously "cultivating" them. For this reason, the proportion of "working relationships" among the "theoretical" relatives figuring in the genealogy almost automatically grows ever larger as one comes closer to the top of the hierarchy recognized by the group. In short, nepotism is created by nephews. Indeed, we only have to ask ourselves how and why the powerful have so many nephews, great-nephews and great-great-nephews to realize that if the great have the greatest number of relatives and if "poor relatives" are also poor in relatives, it is because, here as elsewhere, wealth attracts wealth. After all, the awareness of cousinship and the desire to maintain it are a function of the material or symbolic advantages to be obtained from "cousining."[5]

---

the clan is attacked. It is an actual and active bond of solidarity between individuals united by real bonds of kinship spreading over two or three generations. On the other hand, the group united by *thaymath* only represents one section, larger or smaller depending on the circumstances, of the total unit of theoretical solidarity that is referred to as *thadjadith*, the totality of theoretically founded kinship relations. "*Thaymath* is of today," they say, "*thadjadith* is of yesterday." This clearly indicates that the role played by the "brotherhood" (*thaymath*) is infinitely more real than the reference to a common origin, for the latter attempts an ideological justification of a threatened unity while the former expresses feelings of a living solidarity.

[5]This means that the use of genealogy for the ideological purpose of justifying existing political structures (as in the case of the Arab tribe) is only one specific, though not particularly significant, example of the functions that can be imparted to kinship structures.

Let us imagine that in the society under consideration here the marriage of every one of its children represented the equivalent of a round in a card game for a family. In this way we can see that the value of this round (measured according to the criteria of the system) depended on the quality of the game in its double sense, that is, on the nature of the hand the family had been dealt, whose strength was defined by the rules of the game, and on the greater or lesser degree of skill with which this hand was played. In other words, given the fact that marriage strategies (at least in well-situated families) were always designed to bring about a "good marriage" rather than just a marriage, that is, to maximize the advantages or to minimize the economic and symbolic cost of the marriage as a transaction of a very special kind, these strategies were in every case governed by the value of the material and symbolic patrimony committed to that transaction and by the mode in which the patrimony was transmitted. The latter established the systems of interests of the claimants by assigning differential claims to the property to each one of them according to sex and order of birth. In short, the matrimonial opportunities generically open to the descendants of the same family by virtue of that family's position in the social hierarchy—a position that was mainly, though not exclusively, based on the economic value of its patrimony —were specified by the mode of succession that introduced such criteria as order of birth.

While it was the first and most direct function of the marriage strategy to reproduce the lineage and thereby its work force, it also had to assure the safeguarding of the patrimony, and that in an economic environment dominated by the scarcity of money.[6] Since the share of the property to which a descendant was entitled by tradition and the compensation paid at the time of marriage were one and the same, the value of the property determined the amount of the *adot* (from *adoutà* = to make a donation, to give a dowry) which, in turn, determined the matrimonial ambitions of its holder. By the same token, the size of the dowry demanded by the family of the future husband depended on the size of its own property. It follows that, through the mediation of the adot, marriage exchanges were a matter of economics and that marriages took place between families on the same economic level.

It is true, of course, that extensive property was not enough to make a "great" family: letters of nobility, as it were, were never accorded houses that owed their elevation and their wealth only to stinginess, hard work, or lack of scruples and were otherwise unable to exhibit such virtues as

---

[6]The investigation on which these analyses are based was conducted in 1959 and 1960 and again in 1970 and 1971 in a village of Béarn we shall call Lesquire. It is situated in the center of the hill country, between the two Gave rivers.

could rightfully be expected from the "great," particularly a dignified bearing, a sense of honor, generosity, and hospitality; conversely, a "great" family could very well survive impoverishment.[7] There definitely was a cleavage between the mass of the peasantry and an "aristocracy" distinguished not only by its material capital but also by its symbolic capital, which was measured by the value of its entire kin on both sides of the lineage and over several generations;[8] by its style of life, which respected the values of honor (*aunou*); and by the social respect it commanded.

This cleavage made certain marriages, considered to be misalliances, impossible under the law. However, these status groups were neither

[7]The consciousness of a social hierarchy was most clearly expressed in the relations between the sexes and in the reactions to marriages: "At the dance a younger son of a modest family (*u caddet de petite garbure*) was careful not to pay too much attention to the younger daughter of the Gu.'s (rich farmers). The others would have said, 'He is pretentious. He wants to dance with one of the rich ones [*la grande aînée*].' Some of the servants, if they were good-looking, sometimes asked heiresses to dance, but that was rare" (J. P. A., an informant who was eighty-five years old in 1960). Does this very strongly felt distinction between "important houses" and "small farmers" (*lou paysantots*) correspond to a clear-cut economic difference? In fact, even though the histogram showing the distribution of landed property permits us to distinguish between three kinds of property, namely, properties under 15 hectares [the hectare equals about 2.5 acres] (175), properties between 15 and 30 hectares (96) and properties of more than 30 hectares (31), the cleavages between these three kinds of property were never too pronounced. There were very few *métayers* ("sharecroppers"), and *fermiers* ("tenant farmers"); furthermore, very small plots (less than 5 hectares) and large domains (over 30 hectares) also represented a small percentage of the total landholding, namely 12.3 and 10.9 percent respectively. It follows that economic criteria alone were not of a nature to account for marked cleavages. Yet there was a keen awareness of difference in status between two groups of families. An "important" family was recognized not only by the extent of its landholdings but also by a whole set of signs, among them the external appearance of its house: there was a distinction between two-story houses (*maysou à dus soulés*) or "masters' houses" (*maysous de meste*) and the one-story houses in which the *fermiers, métayers*, and small farmers lived. Another mark of the "big house" was the monumental entrance-gate leading into the courtyard. "Girls," one bachelor said, "look to the entrance-gate rather than to the man."

[8]Here are the *calculations* of an informant who was asked to explain why he considered a recently concluded marriage to be a "good match": "The father of the girl who came [to marry] one of the Po.'s was a younger son of the La.'s of Abos, who had come to Saint-Faust to marry into a good property. The oldest of that family, brother of the girl's father, had kept the "*case*" (homestead) in Abos. He was a schoolteacher and then went to work for the railroad in Paris. He married the daughter of La.-Si., a big shopkeeper in Pardies. My mother told me all this. One of his sons became a doctor in Paris (intern at one of the hospitals), the other a railroad inspector. The father of the girl who married one of the Po.'s is the brother of that fellow." We have been able to verify in many other instances that the local inhabitants had complete recall of the genealogical information at the level of marriage possibilities (a fact that calls for a permanent mobilization of their competence). For this reason, bluff is practically impossible ("Ba. is very grand, but at his family's home everything is very small"), since every individual can be reduced at any moment to his objective truth, that is, the social value (as measured by the standards of a particular society) of his entire kin over several generations. This is not true in the case of an outside marriage. "He who marries outside," the proverb says, "either cheats or is cheated" (on the value of what he is getting).

totally dependent on nor totally independent of their economic foundations, and while considerations of economic interest were always involved
in a family's refusal to accept a misalliance, it was possible for a "modest
house" to bleed itself white in order to marry one of its daughters to the
eldest son of an important family (*"un grand aîné"*) ("The things I had to
do to put her there! I couldn't do it for the others."). Conversely, the eldest
son of an "important house" might also forego an economically more
advantageous match in order to marry according to his rank. But the
margin of acceptable disparity was rather narrow, and beyond a certain
threshold, economic differences effectively ruled out an alliance. In short,
differences in wealth tended to determine the cutoff points within the field
of possible, that is, legitimate, marriage partners that was assigned to each
individual by virtue of his or her family's position in the hierarchy of
status groups. ("Madeleine, a younger daughter of the P's, should have
married one of the M's, L's, or F's.")

Marriage strategies were determined by a combination of the principles of male supremacy and primogeniture and those principles which,
through the adot, tended to rule out marriages between overly unequal
families on the basis of an implicit "cost analysis" aimed at maximizing
the material and symbolic profit to be derived from the matrimonial
transaction within the limits of the family's economic means. We shall see
that the privilege accorded to the eldest son, a simple genealogical
retranslation of the absolute primacy conferred upon the continued
integrity of the patrimony, together with the recognized precedence of the
male members of the lineage, amounted to favoring a strict homogamy
since it did not permit males to marry "upward," despite the fact that such
marriages would maximize their material and symbolic advantages. An
eldest son must not marry too high, not only because he might some day
have to return the adot, but also and especially because such a marriage
would threaten his position in the domestic power structure. Nor must he
marry too low, because a misalliance was apt to dishonor him and also
would make it difficult for him to dower his younger brothers and sisters.
And a younger son, for whom the risks and the material and symbolic
costs of a misalliance were even greater than for an eldest son, could not
yield to the temptation of marrying too obviously above his condition
without incurring the risk of finding himself in a dominated and humiliating position. To the extent that it afforded peasant families one of the
most important opportunities for monetary and also symbolic exchanges
that asserted the family's position in the social hierarchy and thereby
confirmed that hierarchy itself, marriage, an institution that had a direct
bearing on the improvement, conservation, or dissipation of a family's
material and symbolic capital, was no doubt one of the mainstays of both
the dynamic and the static elements of the entire social system. All of this,

to be sure, pertains only within the limits of the traditional mode of production.

The legalistic vocabulary often used by scholars to describe the ideal norm or to analyze a particular case as treated or reinterpreted by notaries reduces the complex and subtle strategies by which families —who alone are competent (in the double sense of that word) in these matters—attempt to steer a course between these two opposing risks to formal rules which, in turn, can be reduced to quasi-mathematical formulas. Each of the younger sons and daughters was entitled to a specified share of the patrimony,[9] the adot; since this share was usually given at the time of marriage, almost always in money in order to avoid fragmentation of the property and only exceptionally in the form of a piece of land (which, however, constituted no more than a security redeemable at any time through the payment of a sum agreed upon in advance), it is often mistakenly identified with a dowry. In fact, however, it was only a compensation accorded younger children in exchange for their renouncing any claim to the land. Here again we must caution against a legalistic approach which, by treating patterns of landholding in the same manner it treats genealogy, would interpret measures taken only as a *last resort* by the head of a family determined to keep the property intact as universally applied norms of inheritance law which are as unreal as a mechanical model of marriage agreements.[10] The extreme scarcity of liquid capital (related, at least in part, to the fact that wealth was measured first and foremost by the size of the landed property) sometimes made it impossible to pay the compensation, even though custom

---

[9] Given a family with two children, the share of the younger son is one-third or $\dfrac{P - \frac{P}{4}}{n}$ while the share of the eldest is $\dfrac{\frac{P}{4} + P\frac{P}{4}}{n}$, where P designates the value of the property and n the total number of children. It was customary to evaluate the property as precisely as possible; in cases of litigation local experts chosen by the different parties were consulted. The price of the *journée* [literally, "day's work"] of fields, woods, and fernland was arrived at on the basis of the sale price of a property in the same or a neighboring village. These calculations were fairly accurate and were therefore accepted by all. "The Tr. property, for example, was estimated at 30,000 francs (this was about 1900). The family consisted of the father, the mother, and six children, one boy and five girls. The eldest son was given one fourth, or 7,500 francs. The remaining 22,500 francs had to be divided into six parts. The share of the younger daughters was 3,750 francs each, or 3,000 francs to be paid in money and 750 francs in linen and clothes, sheets, towels, napkins, shirts, featherbeds and *lou cabinet*, the armoire that was always brought to the marriage by the bride" (J. P. A.).

[10] It seems rather likely that a change in economic values and the advent of new attitudes, which made a mere compensation appear as a right to the patrimony, increasingly induced the peasants of Béarn to avail themselves of the weapons offered by the legal system and its practitioners. These jurists then, consciously or not, tended to create a need for their own services since they were able to formulate strategies for marriage and succession conforming to the language and the logic of the law, with the result that these strategies were often used contrary to their principles.

afforded the possibility of echeloning payments over several years or even deferring them until the death of the parents. In such cases the division had to take place when one of the younger children married or when the parents died. This meant that the family had to pay the adots in the form of land, hoping to be able some day to restore the patrimony to its full size by somehow raising the money needed to repurchase the land sold in order to pay the adots or given away as adots.[11]

But the family property would have been very ill-protected indeed if the adot, and hence marriage itself, had always depended only on the value of the patrimony and on the number of legitimate heirs, and if there had been no other means of dealing with the threat of division that was unanimously considered to be a catastrophe.[12] In fact, the parents themselves "made the eldest," as the saying went, and a number of informants have stated that in earlier times the father was completely free to decide the amount of compensation to be paid to younger children, since the proportions were not fixed by any rule. In any case, we know that in many families the young couple was totally without information, let alone control, concerning the family finances until the death of the "old folks." (Any income from important transactions, such as the sale of livestock, was entrusted to the old mother and locked up in the armoire [*lou cabinet*].) Under these circumstances it is unlikely that legal rules were ever very strictly applied, except in the pathological cases that came before the law and its practitioners, or in the cases produced in advance by the pessimism of the law which were invariably foreseen in the

[11]Applying the principle under which property belongs less to the individual than to the lineage, the *retrait lignager* ["right of repurchase"] afforded every member of the lineage the possibility of regaining possession of any land that might have been alienated. "The *maysou mère* ("original family") always kept its "rights of return" (*lous drets de retour*) over lands that had been sold or given away." Therefore, "when such lands were for sale, one knew that certain families had rights over them, and one offered them to these families first" (J.-P. A.).

[12]Even though, at the time of the investigation, we failed to ask systematic questions concerning the incidence of division over a specific period of time, it appears that it was a rare, even exceptional occurrence and therefore faithfully recorded in the collective memory. Thus we are told that about 1830 the Bo. property and house (a big two-story house) were divided among the heirs who had been unable to settle matters amicably. As a result, the property is now "crisscrossed with ditches and hedges" (*toute croutzade de barats y de plechs*). (There were even specialists, called *barades*, who came from the Landes, the flat areas around Bordeaux, to dig the ditches dividing such properties.) "After these divisions, there were sometimes two or three families living in the house, each in its own section and each with its share of the land. In such cases the room with the big chimney always went to the eldest son. This is what happened on the Hi., Qu., and Di. properties. At the An.'s there are some pieces of land that have never come back. They were able to buy back some after a while, but not all. The division created terrible difficulties. In the case of the Qu. property, which was divided among three children, one of the younger sons had to take his horses all the way around the neighborhood to reach a far-away field that had fallen to him" (P. L.). "In order to retain sole possession, eldest sons sometimes put the property up for sale (with the aim of buying it themselves), but it also happened that they were unable to buy back the house" (J.-P. A.).

contracts but which were statistically exceptional.[13] In reality, the head of the family was always at liberty to manipulate the "rules" (even those of the Civil Code) if he wished to favor one of his children more or less secretly by means of cash gifts or fictitious sales (*ha bente* = "to make a sale"). It would be extremely naive to be taken in by the word "distribution" (*partage*), which is sometimes used to designate family "arrangements" intended to avoid the division of the property. These "arrangements" were made at the occasion of the "institution of the heir", which usually took place with the consent of all concerned (though duly sealed in a notarial document) when one of the children married or else was stipulated in a will. Many men "instituted the heir" in this manner before they went to war in 1914. Following an evaluation of the property, the head of the family proceeded to define the claims of everyone concerned; those of the heir, who was not necessarily the eldest,[14] and of the other children, who often willingly endorsed provisions that were more advantageous to the heir than those of the Civil Code and even the customary law. If the arrangement was made at the time of the marriage of one of the younger children, he or she would receive a portion whose equivalent was to be given to the others either at the time of their own marriage or upon the death of the parents.

We would continue to be taken in by the fallacies of legalistic thinking if we continued to cite examples of anomic or regulated transgressions against the supposed rules of succession. If it is not certain that, as the old grammarians would have us believe, "the exception proves the rule," it does at least tend to confirm *the existence* of the rule. The only evidence that counts is the practices, and they indicate that all means were justified when it came to protecting the integrity of the patrimony by

[13]There are strong reasons to believe that the innumerable protective clauses surrounding the adot in the marriage contract in order to ensure its "inalienability, imprescriptibility and unseizability" (guarantees, "*collocations*" [establishing the order of creditors], etc.) are products of the legalistic imagination. Thus, separation of the spouses, one of the instances of dissolution of the marriage which, under the terms of the contract, calls for the restitution of the dowry, is unknown in peasant society.

[14]The head of the family was in a position to place the interest of the patrimony above the customary rule under which the title of heir normally went to the first-born boy. He might decide upon such a course, for example, if the eldest son was unworthy of his rank, or if there was a real advantage in having another child inherit (e.g., in the case where a younger son, by his marriage, could easily bring about the unification of two neighboring properties). The moral authority of the head of the family was so great and so strongly approved by the entire group that the customary heir had no choice but to submit to a decision that was dictated by considerations involving the continuity of the house and adopted the course best suited to that end. Also, the eldest son automatically lost his claim if he should leave the household, since the heir is always the one who stays on the land, as we still see clearly today. And even today, there are elderly heads of families who do not have children and are looking—not always successfully—for a true heir, that is, some relative, even distant, such as a nephew, who will stay on the land and cultivate it.

forestalling the potential division of both the property and the family as a network of competing claims to the ownership of the patrimony, for this threat arose with every marriage. It is as if all the strategies were rooted in a small number of implicit principles. The first of these, the primacy of men over women, implied that, even though claims to the property could sometimes be transmitted through the female line, and even though the family (or "house"), a monopolistic group defined by the ownership of a specific set of assets, could be identified with all those who had claims to these assets, regardless of their sex, the status of heiress could fall to a woman only in the last resort, namely in the absence of any male descendant; for we know that girls were relegated to the status of younger child, regardless of their place in the order of birth, as soon as there was a single boy, even if he was younger. And this is only logical, once we understand that the status of "master of the house" (*capmaysouè*), repository and guarantor of the name, the reputation, and the interests of the group, gave him not only rights to the property, but also the quasi-political right to exercise authority within the group and, especially, the right to represent and involve the group in relationships with other groups.[15]

Under the logic of the system, this right could be conferred (after the death of the parents) only upon a man, either the eldest of the agnates [males of the lineage] or, in his absence, the husband of the heiress. When the latter, an heir through the female line, became the representative of the lineage, he was in some cases obliged to sacrifice his very family name to the house that had appropriated him by entrusting him with its property.[16] The second principle, the primacy of the eldest over younger siblings, tends to show the patrimony as the true basis of the economic and political decisions made by the family.[17] Identifying the interests of

---

[15]The head of the "house" had the monopoly of outside contacts, particularly the important transactions negotiated in the market place. He thus had authority over the financial resources of the family and, hence, over its entire economic life. The younger son who was usually confined to the homestead (a situation that further reduced his chances for marriage) could acquire a modicum of economic independence only if he were able to put away a small nest egg of his own (for example, the income from a war pension), for which he was respected and envied.

[16]The *relative* autonomy of political rights in relation to property rights is convincingly demonstrated by the ways in which the adot was used. Even though it theoretically belonged to the wife even after the marriage (since the obligation to return its equivalent in quantity and value could take effect at any time), the husband was entitled to the income and, as soon as offspring was assured, he could use it to give portions to his younger brothers and sisters. (Of course, this right to the income was rather more restricted when the adot was in the form of real estate, particularly land.) For her part, the wife had the same rights to her husband's dotal property as he had over her dowry, so that her parents enjoyed the income from the assets their son-in-law had brought into the marriage and managed it as long as they lived.

[17]Whenever the subject of a sentence is a *collective noun*, such as society, the family, etc., one should try to ascertain whether the group in question really constitutes a *unity*

the designated head of the family with those of the patrimony is a more effective way of establishing his identification with the patrimony than the application of any expressly stated and explicit norm. To assert that power over the land is indivisible and to place it in the hands of the eldest son amounts to asserting the indivisibility of the land and to making the eldest son responsible for its perpetuation.[18] In short, as soon as we postulate the basic equation that the land belongs to the eldest son and that the eldest son belongs to the land, in other words, that the land inherits its heir, we have established a structure that generates such practices as conform to the basic imperative of the group, namely, the integral perpetuation of the patrimony.

It would, of course, be naive to assume that this identification always took place, or that it took place without conflict or tragedy, despite the efforts at indoctrination by the family and its continuous reinforcement by the entire group to make the eldest son, especially in an "important house," aware of the duties and privileges of his rank. The fact that there were occasional failures in this concerted effort at indoctrination and cultural reproduction shows that the system never functioned in a mechanical fashion and that it was not always free of contradictions between dispositions and structures, in which case the contradiction might be experienced as a conflict between sentiment and duty. Nor was it always free of subterfuges intended to satisfy individual wishes within the limits of what was socially acceptable. In this manner the same parents who, on other occasions, felt free to bend the custom in order to satisfy their own inclinations (for example, by permitting a favorite child to accumulate a little nest egg),[19] felt duty-bound to prohibit a misalliance and to force their children, regardless of feeling, into unions that were best suited to safeguard the social system by safeguarding the position of the lineage within that system. In short, they made their eldest son pay the

---

conforming to a rigorous usage of this category of concept, at least from its own point of view. If the answer is positive, one should further ask by what means this unity of viewpoints, practices, or interests has been achieved. This question is particularly important here, since the very survival of the house and its patrimony depended upon its ability to maintain the integration of the group.

[18]Proof that the "right of the eldest" is but the transfiguration of the rights of the patrimony over the eldest lies in the fact that the distinction between older and younger children pertains only in property-owning families. It has no meaning at all for the poor—small proprietors, farm hands, or servants. ("There is no such thing as youngest or eldest," one of the informants said, "when there is nothing to chew.")

[19]One of the most widely used subterfuges for favoring one of the children consisted of handing over to him, long before his marriage, one or several heads of livestock which, held under a *gasalhès* arrangement, brought good profits. (*Gasalhès* is an informal contract by which one entrusts a reliable friend with the care of one or several heads of livestock, having first estimated their value. Proceeds from the products, as well as gains and losses from the sale of the meat, are shared by both partners.)

price of his privileges by subordinating his own interest to those of the lineage: "I have seen people give up a marriage because of 100 francs. The son wanted to marry. 'How are you going to pay the younger children? If you want to marry [that girl] you can leave!' The Tr.'s had five younger daughters. The parents were always favoring the eldest son. He was always given the best piece of salt meat and all the rest. The eldest son is often spoiled by the mother, until he talks of marriage. The younger daughters did not get meat, nor anything. When the time came for the eldest son to marry, three of the girls were already married. The boy was in love with one of the La. girls, who did not have a sou. The father told him: 'So you want to get married? I have paid for the three girls, now you must bring in the money for the other two. A wife isn't made for being put in the china cupboard (*lou bachère*) [i.e., for being shown off]. This one has nothing; what is she going to bring? What she has between her legs?' The boy married one of the E. daughters and received a dowry of 5,000 francs. The marriage did not go well. He took to drink and went to pieces. He died childless."[20]

Those who wanted to marry against the wishes of their parents had no choice but to leave the house at the risk of being disinherited in favor of a brother or sister. But for the eldest son of an important house the obligation to maintain his rank was so compelling that he could choose this extreme solution which went against all the norms of the group even less than anyone else. "The eldest son of the Ba.'s, the richest family of Lesquire, could not leave. He had been the first one in the hamlet to wear a jacket. He was an important man, a municipal councillor. He could not leave. And besides, he would not have known how to make a living elsewhere. He had become too much of a gentleman (*Il était trop 'enmonsieuré'*)" (J.-A. P.). Furthermore, so long as the parents were living, the heir only had potential rights to the property, so that he did not always have the means to uphold his rank. He often had less freedom than some younger sons or eldest sons of lesser families. "The father 'doled out' the money pretty slowly. . . . Quite often they could not even go out. The young folks would work and the old folks would hold on to the money. Some [of the younger sons] would make a little spending money elsewhere; they would hire themselves out for a while as coachmen or day laborers. In that way, they had a little money they could spend as they

[20]The end of the story is no less edifying: "After a lot of quarreling, they had to return the entire dowry to the widow, who went back to her family. Shortly after the marriage of the eldest son, about 1910, one of the daughters had been married to La., also with a dowry of 2,000 francs. When the war came, the family brought back the daughter who had married into the S. family (on one of the neighboring properties) to take the place of the son. The other daughters who lived further away were very upset about this decision. But the father had chosen the daughter who was married to a neighbor because this was the way to increase the patrimony" (J.-A. P.).

wished. Sometimes the younger son was given a little property of his own before he left for military service, maybe a little piece of woodland that he could exploit, or a couple of sheep, or a cow that permitted him to make a little money for himself. To me, for example, they gave a cow and I let a friend keep it as a *gaselhès*. But the eldest sons, most of the time, didn't have anything, and they couldn't even go out. 'You will get everything' (*qu'at aberas tout*), the parents would say, but in the meantime they wouldn't let go of anything."[21] Thus parental authority, the principal means of perpetuating the lineage as long as the interests of the parents coincided with those of the lineage—and this was usually the case—could also be counterproductive of its legitimate function and deter an eldest son, who could neither revolt against the authority of his parents nor renounce his own feelings, from marrying at all, for this was the only way he could protest if he was not permitted to make his own choice.[22]

[21]This phrase, often used ironically because it appears to symbolize the arbitrariness and tyranny of the "old folks," is at the very core of the specific tensions that are created *whenever privilege and power are transmitted* in such a way that there is no intermediate status between the class of resourceless claimants and that of *legitimate* proprietors. Indeed, it is the very purpose of this system to teach future heirs to tolerate the lack of freedom and the sacrifice of a prolonged minority in the name of the future gratifications attendant upon their coming of age.

[22]The full cruelty of this *teratological* situation—and it is cruel even from the standpoint of the very norms of a system that considered the continuity of the lineage to be the supreme value—can be seen in the testimony (taken in the dialect of Béarn) of an old bachelor artisan (I. A.), born in 1885, who lives in the center of the village: "Right after school, I began working in the shop with my father. I was drafted in 1905 and served with the 13th Alpine chasseurs at Chambéry. . . . After my two years of military service I again lived at home. I went with a girl from Ré—— We had decided to get married in 1909. She had a dowry of 10,000 francs plus her trousseau. It would have been a good match (*u bou partit*). But my father was strictly against it. At the time parental consent was necessary (both "legally" and materially since only the family could provide the household equipment (*lou menadje garnit*): the "buffet," the armoire, the featherbed, the mattress, etc.). 'No, I don't want you to get married.' He did not give any reasons, but he hinted at them. 'We don't need a woman here.' We were not rich. It would have meant another mouth to feed, for my mother and my sister were already living with us. My sister had left the household only for six months after she was married. When her husband died, she came back and she is still living with me. Of course, I could have left. But in those days an eldest son who took his own house with his wife brought disgrace to the family (*u escarni*, i.e., an affront that made both the perpetrator and the victim look ridiculous). It would have looked as if we couldn't get along at all. It would not do to let people know about one's family troubles . . . I was very much upset. I no longer went to dances. The girls of my age were all married. I was no longer interested in anyone else. When I went out on Sundays, I played cards; sometimes I would watch the dancing for a while. I spent the evenings with the boys; we played cards, and then I would go home about midnight." This testimony is similar to that of another informant: "P. L. M. (an artisan of the center of the village, aged 86 in 1960) never had any money to go out, so he didn't go out. Others would have stood up to their father; they would have tried to earn a little money elsewhere, but he buckled under. He had a sister and a mother who knew everything that went on in the village, whether it was true or not, even though they never left the house. These two ruled the household. When he talked of getting married, they allied themselves with the father: What good will a woman do? We already have two in the house!" (J.-P. A.).

But these pathological cases in which it was necessary to assert parental authority expressly in order to repress individual feelings are the exception and should not make us forget the many cases in which the norm could remain unspoken because the dispositions of the individuals involved were objectively in conformity with the objective structures. But how could younger sons who, after all, were sacrificed to the imperatives of the land, be made to consent to that which not even the heir, the privileged of the system, was always willing to do? We should certainly not forget—as we might if we considered marriage strategies as autonomous—that fertility strategies could also contribute to solving the problem, simply by eliminating it. This would be the case if, due to a biological chance by which the first child happened to be a boy, the succession could be entrusted to an only child. And indeed, parents could manipulate their "hand" by limiting the number of cards, if they were satisfied with those they had been dealt. Hence the capital importance of the order in which these cards were dealt, that is, the biological chance that made a first-born child either a boy or a girl. Given the close interrelation between these two reproductive strategies, marriage and fertility, a family could limit the number of its children to one in the first instance but not in the second. If the birth of a girl was never greeted with enthusiasm ("When a girl is born in a house," the proverb says, "one of the main beams comes falling down"), it was because she invariably represented a bad card. This was true even though she could move upward and, unhindered by the social strictures a boy had to respect, could marry legally and in fact above her station. If she was an heiress, i.e., an only child (and this was very rare, since families kept hoping for an "heir"), or if she was the eldest of one or several sisters, she could only ensure the preservation and continuity of the patrimony at great risk to the lineage. For if she married an eldest son, her "house" was in a sense annexed by another, and if she married a younger son, domestic power fell to a stranger—at least after the death of her parents. If she was a younger daughter, the only thing to do was to marry her off and, therefore, dower her, since, unlike a boy, she could not very well be sent away or kept, unmarried, at home; the reason being that the labor she could furnish would not be commensurate with the cost of her upkeep.[23]

Now let us consider the situation if the progeny included at least one boy, whatever his position in the order of birth. The heir may or may not

[23]Occasionally, one of the important families who could afford such an additional burden might keep one of the daughters at home. "Marie, the eldest daughter of the L.'s of D., might have married. She was treated like a younger daughter and, like all younger daughters, she became an unpaid servant for life. They made her stupid. Very little was done to find her a husband. In this way they kept the dowry, they kept everything. Now she takes care of the parents."

be an only child. In the latter case, he may have one or several brothers, one or several sisters, a brother and a sister, or several brothers and sisters in varying proportions. In themselves, these combinations offered very unequal chances for success when dealt with under the same strategy. Each one of them therefore called for a different strategy, but some of them were easier to apply and more profitable than others.

When the heir was an only son,[24] one would assume that the marriage strategy would stake everything on obtaining as high an adot as possible through a marriage with a wealthy younger daughter, thus bringing in money without giving up anything. However, these efforts at maximizing the material and symbolic advantages to be derived from a marriage, if need be by bluff (although this was a difficult and risky business in an environment where people knew practically everything about each other), were limited by the economic and political risks inherent in an unequal or, as it was called, upward marriage. The economic risk was the *tournadot*, the return of the dowry, which could be demanded should the husband or the wife die before the birth of a child, an eventuality that aroused fears not justified by its probability. "Suppose a man marries a girl from an important family. She brings him a dowry of 20,000 francs. His parents tell him: 'You take the 20,000 francs and you think you have done well. But you are really taking a chance. You have received a dowry by contract. You are going to spend part of it. What if something goes wrong? How are you going to give it back, if you have to? You can't!' After all, a marriage is expensive, the groom must pay for the celebration, he must get things for the house, etc." (P. L.). Most people did not touch the dowry for fear that one of the spouses might die before children were born.[25]

The risk that can properly be called political was undoubtedly more directly considered in these strategies, since it involved one of the fundamental principles of all marriage practices. Due to the bias in favor of the male in the cultural tradition, which judged every marriage from the male point of view ("upward" thus always implicitly meant between a man of lower and a woman of higher status), there was no reason, aside

---

[24]The chances of seeing the extinction of the lineage due to the celibacy of the son were practically nil in the heyday of the system.

[25]The adot, normally paid to the father or the mother of the young husband and only exceptionally (that is, if his parents were deceased) to the heir himself, was meant to become part of the patrimony of the family issued from the marriage. If the alliance was dissolved or if one of the spouses died, it went to the children, if there were any, although the surviving spouse continued to have the use of the income. If there were no children, it reverted to the family of the spouse who had brought it into the marriage. Certain marriage contracts stipulated that in the case of separation, the father-in-law only had to pay the interest on the adot brought by his son-in-law, thus giving the younger man the possibility of returning to his [wife's] family after a reconciliation.

from economic considerations, why the eldest daughter of a modest family should not marry a younger son of an important family, while the eldest son of a modest family was prevented from marrying the younger daughter of an important family. More generally, among all the marriages made for economic reasons, only one kind was fully acceptable, namely, an alliance in which the arbitrary cultural bias in favor of the male was confirmed by a corresponding discrepancy in the social and economic status of the spouses. The size of the adot thus definitely reinforced the position of the spouse who brought it into the marriage.

Although we have seen that power within the household had relatively little to do with economic power, the size of the adot did represent one of the factors in the balance of authority, particularly in the structural conflict opposing mother-in-law and daughter-in-law.[26] A mother who, as mistress of the household, would normally use every means at her disposal to prevent a "downward" marriage for her son, would be the first to oppose his marriage with a woman of relatively higher status, being very well aware that it would be much easier to exert her authority over a girl from a modest background than over one of those girls from an important family who, as the saying went, "take over (*qu'ey entrade daune*) the moment they come into their new families."[27] An "upward" marriage threatened the principle of male preeminence, which the group recognized not only in a social context but also in the context of work and domestic affairs. By defending her own authority, that is, her interests as the mistress of her household, the mother therefore only defended the interests of her lineage against outside usurpation.[28]

The risk of imbalance was greatest when an eldest son married a younger daughter of a large family. Given the approximate equivalence

[26]Of an authoritarian woman it was said, "She does not want to give up the ladle," the symbol of authority over the household. Wielding the ladle was the prerogative of the mistress of the house. When the meal was ready and the pot was boiling, she would place the "soups" of bread into the tureen, pouring the soup and the vegetables over them. Then, when everyone was seated, she would bring the tureen to the table, stir the soup with the ladle in order to soak the bread, then turn the handle toward the head of the family (grandfather, father, or uncle) who would serve himself first. Meanwhile the daughter-in-law was occupied elsewhere. To remind the daughter-in-law of her rank, the mother would say, "I have not yet given you the ladle."

[27]To evoke the marriage settlement was the supreme argument in the struggle for domestic power: "One who has brought what you have brought" (*dap ço qui as pourtat*). At times the initial imbalance was such that only after the death of her mother-in-law it could be said of the young wife: "Now the young woman is the mistress of the household (*daune*)."

[28]The influence wielded by each of the spouses in the domestic power structure is, in fact, a very important factor in the family's marriage strategies. Obviously, the mother is in a much better position to profit from the opening made by her own marriage and to marry her son in her native village or neighborhood, thereby enhancing her own position in the family, if she has brought an important dowry. This means—and we shall prove this point further—that the entire matrimonial history of the lineage had a bearing on every marriage.

between the adot and a share of the patrimony (which is attested by the double meaning of the word *adot*), the adot brought by a girl from a very rich but very large family might well not be higher than that of a younger daughter of a modest family who had only one brother. Despite the apparent balance between the value of the dowry and the new family's patrimony, this situation could disguise a discrepancy that could lead to conflict, for authority and claims to authority were based as much on the material and symbolic capital of a spouse's original family as on the size of the actual adot.

The question of political authority within the family became most acute, however, when an eldest son married an eldest daughter, especially if the heiress was the wealthier of the spouses. Except in cases where it united two properties because the spouses were neighbors, this type of marriage tended to create a permanent back-and-forth between the two homes or even led the spouses to maintain their separate residences. What was at stake in this open or hidden conflict over the place of residence was, again, the predominance of one or the other lineage and the extinction of a "house" and its name.[29]

Possibly because it approached the question of the economic basis of domestic power more realistically than other societies and therefore came closer to the objective truth in its statements and strategies,[30] the society of Béarn suggests that the sociology of the family, which is so often depicted as based on sentiment, might be nothing but a specific aspect of political sociology. The position of the spouses in the domestic power structure or, to use Max Weber's vocabulary, their chances of success in the competition for authority over the family, that is, for the monopoly of legitimately exercising power in domestic affairs, are definitely related to the material and symbolic capital they bring into the marriage (although the nature of that capital may vary according to time and society).

[29]It is significant that in all the attested cases, properties united in this manner were eventually separated, often in the very next generation when each of the children received one of them as their inheritance. Thus, two of the most important families of Lesquire had become united through the marriage of two heirs who continued to live on their separate properties. ("One wonders when they ever got together to produce these children.") The eldest son of that marriage (born about 1890) received his father's property, his younger brother that of his mother, the eldest daughters a farm inherited from an uncle who had been a priest, and the two youngest daughters a house in the center of the village. Questions concerning marriages between heirs always call forth the same negative reaction, always for the same reason: "That is the case of Tr. who married the Da. girl. He keeps going back and forth between the two places. He is always on the road, he is everywhere, he is never at home. The master should be there" (P. L.).

[30]It is said that in order to assert his authority within the marriage the groom should step on the bride's dress, if possible during the religious ceremony; while the bride should bend her ring finger in such a way that the groom is unable to push the ring all the way down.

However, one male heir without siblings was a relatively rare phenomenon. In all other cases, the marriage of the heir largely determined the
size of the adot that could be given to younger siblings, hence the kind of
marriage they could make and even their chances of marrying at all. The
best strategy, therefore, consisted of obtaining from the parents of the
bride an adot sufficiently large to pay the adots of younger sons and
daughters without having to divide or mortgage the property, yet not so
large as to threaten the patrimony with the restitution of a dowry beyond
the means of the family. This, incidentally—contrary to the anthropological view that every marriage is an autonomous unit—means that every
marriage transaction can only be understood as one element in a series of
material and symbolic exchanges, since the economic and symbolic
capital a family is able to commit to the marriage of one of its children is
largely determined by the position this particular exchange occupies in
the entire *matrimonial history* of the family.[31] Although it is not readily
apparent, the case of an eldest son who had a sister (or sisters) was quite
different from that of one who had a brother (or brothers). All our
informants have indicated that the adot of girls was almost always higher
than that of boys, so that their chances of marriage were greater. The
reason, as we have seen, was that families had no choice but to marry off
these useless mouths, and as quickly as possible.

In the case of younger sons the strategies could be more complex, the
first reason being that an abundant, even superabundant, supply of labor
will create a great desire for land that can only be beneficial to the
patrimony. It follows that families were less anxious to marry off a
younger son (except, perhaps, the first of the younger sons in an
important family) than a younger daughter or even an eldest son. One
way would be to marry him to an heiress, a course that was very normal
and best suited to his own interests, though not necessarily to the interest
of the lineage: If he married into a family of the same rank (and this was
usually the case), brought a good adot, and made his mark in terms of
fertility and work, he was honored and treated as the true master.[32] If, on
the other hand, he married "upward," he was made to sacrifice everything
to the new house where his parents-in-law were determined to "remain in
charge"; "everything" meaning his adot, his work, and sometimes his very
family name ("Jean Cazenave," for example, could become "Jean dou

---

[31]The order in which the children of the same family marry can also be a determining
factor. This is the case when the marriage of the first boy absorbs all of the family's
resources or when a younger daughter marries before her older sister, who is thereafter
more difficult to "place" in the marriage market because she is suspected of having some
hidden flaw. In this situation it was said of the father: "He has placed the one-year heifer
(*l'anouille*) to the yoke before the two-year old (*la bime*)."

[32]The situation of such a younger son is very realistically described in a proverb: "If he is
a capon, we'll eat him, if he is a cock, we'll keep him."

Tinou": "Jean of the Tinou family").[33] There were very few younger sons willing to face the prospect of a marriage with a younger daughter, one of those "marriages between hunger and thirst," sometimes also called *esterlou* ("sterile"), which the very poorest among them could only avoid by hiring themselves and their wives out as "pensioned servants" (*baylets à pensiou*). On the other hand, the possibility of founding a family while staying in the paternal home was a privilege for eldest sons only. For these reasons, those who were unable to marry an heiress, thanks to their adot, possibly supplemented by a small, laboriously accumulated nest egg (*lou cabau*), had only two options: they could either emigrate to the city or to America in the hope of establishing themselves in some craft or else they could forego marriage and become servants either to their own family or (in the case of the very poorest) to others.[34] It is therefore understandable

[33]Although it was as effective for assuring the continuity of the lineage and the transmittal of the patrimony as a marriage between an eldest son and a younger daughter, a marriage between a younger son and an eldest daughter was completely respectable only if the economic situation of the "son-in-law" was such that it gave him the authority to take his place as the head of his new family. In all other circumstances—of which the marriage of a servant to his *patronne* [boss] was only the extreme case—the most fundamental cultural imperatives were violated. "When the son of a modest family moves in with a great heiress, she will always be the boss" (J.-P. A.). "The daughter of one of the important families married one of her servants. She played the piano and was in charge of the harmonium at church. Her mother had many acquaintances and entertained people from town. After a number of marriage plans had come to nothing, the girl picked her servant Pa. The man was never anything but a Pa. His friends told him, 'You should have taken a good little peasant girl, she would have been much more helpful to you.' He was always uncomfortable. He was considered the fifth wheel on the wagon. He could not frequent his wife's former acquaintances. He just did not belong to that world. He did the work, she gave the orders and had herself a good time. He was always embarrassed and he was also an embarrassment for the family. Why, he didn't even have enough authority to keep his wife from being unfaithful" (J.-P. A.). "H. loved the land of the family where he worked. He would suffer when there was no rain! And when there was a hailstorm! And all the rest! He ended up marrying the *patronne*. All these fellows who marry upward are marked for life" (P. L.).

[34]Day laborers found "days" (*journaus*) only in summer, were often out of work all winter and on rainy days, and were often obliged to take on piecework (*à près heyt*) in order to make ends meet. A day laborer spent almost everything he earned ("until 1914 a sou a day and meals") for bread or flour. By contrast, domestic servants (*baylets*) were hired for the year and received free room, board, and laundry service. A very good domestic servant earned 250–300 francs per annum before 1914. If he was very careful, he could hope to buy a house with ten to twelve years' wages and a farm and some land with the dowry of a girl and some borrowed money. But he was often condemned to bachelorhood: "As the youngest, I was placed as a domestic servant at Es. when I was very young, at the age of ten. I knew a girl down there. If we had gotten married, it would have been, as they say, a marriage between hunger and thirst. Both of us were equally poor. My older brother, of course, he got the 'full household (*lou menadje garnit*)' of our parents, that is, the livestock, the fowl, the house, the farm tools, etc., so that it was easier for him to go before the mayor. The girl I went with left for the city; it is often like that, girls don't wait. It is easier for them to leave and to work in town as a maid, especially if they have a girl friend who is already there. In the meantime I amused myself as well as I could with the other fellows who were in the same situation" (N., a farmhand, born in 1898. He spoke in the dialect of Béarn). The condition of the day laborer, which used to be worse than that of the domestic servant, has improved, at

that for the family it was much better to have younger sons than younger daughters, since it was rather less costly to marry them off and even more advantageous for them to remain unmarried. And, of course, the advantage of having boys rather than girls became increasingly great with the size of the family. Indeed, the burden of providing for the marriages of three or four younger daughters created almost insurmountable difficulties even for the wealthiest houses and could even lead to breaking up the property. This amounts to saying that in the last analysis the entire system was based on fertility strategies.[35] A negative proof for this contention can be found in the fact that the very poorest—the smallest holders, domestic servants, day laborers—who could not play at this game anyway, excluded themselves by the excessive size of their families.

In short, it is not enough to say that families were not anxious to have younger sons marry; we should say that they did not press the matter. In a world where marriages were arranged, such a "hands-off" policy was enough to lessen their chances of marriage considerably. Some families went so far as to make the payment of the adot conditional upon the younger son's working for his brother for a certain number of years, some signed veritable work contracts with him, and some families even deferred payment by making him hope for a higher sum. No doubt there were other ways in which a younger son could become a confirmed bachelor, from the marriage that did not materialize to a gradual process of getting used to the situation until it was "too late to marry," all of this taking place with the complicity of families who were, consciously or unconsciously, glad to keep such an "unpaid servant" in their service, at least temporarily.[36]

---

least in relative terms. This is due to the increasing practice of payment in money and an improvement in the bargaining position of agricultural labor resulting from the flight to the city and the emergence of a few nonagricultural occupations. By the same token, the position of the domestic servant and the dependent relationship it implies is increasingly felt to be unbearable.

[35]Among other things, belated marriage, which tends to limit fertility. Thus, the average age at marriage between 1871 and 1884 was 31.5 years for men and 25 years for women compared to 29 years and 24 years respectively for the period 1941-60.

[36]One rather typical example should suffice to make this point: "I was the youngest in a family of five children. Before the war of 1914 (born in 1894) I was a servant with the M. family, later with the L.'s. I remember this as a very good time. Then I was in the war. When I came back, my family had been hard hit. One of my brothers, the eldest, had been killed, the third one had lost a leg, the fourth was not quite right in the head because of the war. . . . My brothers were very good to me; all three had pensions as war casualties. They gave me money. The one who had a bad chest could not stay by himself, so I helped him and went to the fairs and markets with him. After he died in 1929 I went to live with the oldest of my brothers and his family. And that is when I realized how isolated I was in that family, having lost my brother and my mother who had been so good to me. For example, one day when I had taken the liberty of going to Pau, my brother blamed me for the loss of a couple

In opposite ways both the younger son who left home to make his living in the city or to seek his fortune in America, and the younger son who stayed at home supplying his labor without adding to the expenses of the household or detracting from the property, made a contribution to the preservation of the patrimony.[37] Younger sons had learned since childhood to embrace the traditional values and the customary distribution of tasks and powers among brothers. They had a deep attachment to the family patrimony, to the house, the land, the family, and perhaps especially, the children of the eldest son. Many of them might therefore be willing to accept this kind of life which, to use the frankly functionalist formulation of Le Play, "gave [them] the peace and quiet of bachelorhood as well as the joys of family life."[38] Being inclined, for all these reasons, to give himself totally to a family and a patrimony he had every reason to consider his own, a younger son who stayed at home represented (to the family—that is, to the system) the "ideal" outer limit of a servant. For the servant, too, was often treated as a "member of the family," his private life invaded and virtually taken over by the family life of his employer. He too was consciously or unconsciously encouraged to give a large part of his time and affection to his borrowed family and usually paid for the economic and affective security afforded by this inclusion in family life by foregoing marriage.[39] Thus the younger son was, if you will permit this expression, the *structural victim*, that is, the socially primed and therefore willing victim of a system that lavished a panoply of protective devices

---

of cartloads of hay. They had been rained on in a thunderstorm and would have been brought in if I had been there. I had simply become too old to get married. The girls of my age had left or were married. I was often depressed and spent what free time I had drinking with the fellows, most of whom were in the same situation. I can tell you, if I had to do it over again, I would leave the family right away, take a job someplace else and perhaps get married. It would be a much better life for me. First of all, I would have a separate family that was all my own. And besides, when a younger son works for the family, he never works hard enough. He must always be on hand. And he is talked to in a way that no master would dare talk to his servants."

[37]In principle, the younger son was entitled to the income from his portion for his lifetime. If he had not married, his share reverted to the heir after his death.

[38]"There were some old bachelors living at the Sa.'s, and the Ch.'s in the Le. neighborhood, a two-hour walk (7–8 km) from the village center. They came to mass only on religious holidays and in all their seventy years had never once been to Pau or Oloron. The less they go out, the less they feel like going out. . . . Only the eldest went out. These fellows kept the family going. A few of them are still around" (J.-P. A.).

[39]We are told that sometimes, in cases where the eldest son had no children, an old bachelor brother was asked to marry in order to ensure the continuity of the lineage. Marriage between a younger brother and the widow of the eldest (*levirate*), although not really an institution, was relatively common. After the war of 1914–18 marriages of this type were rather numerous. "These things were worked out. The parents usually pushed in that direction in the interest of the family and because of the children. And the young people went along. Sentiment had nothing to do with it" (A. B.).

upon the "house," a collective entity and also an economic unit or, better, a collective entity based upon its economic unity.

It was as if marriage strategies attempted to correct the failures of fertility strategies. There were, however, hands that defied the skill of even the best player—for example, a family with too many children, including too many daughters. A really well-designed marriage strategy had no need to become explicit in order to operate, for *if it worked*, it tended to avoid conflicts between duty and feeling, between reason and passion, between collective interest and individual interest. Like the norm intended to resolve and overcome them, these conflicts arose from a "breakdown" of that socially induced instinct which was the end product of a certain *habitus* inculcated by a particular way of life; a way of life that was itself perpetuated and glorified in the injunctions and precepts of morality and education. For this reason it is artificial or quite simply beside the point to ask questions concerning the relationship between the structure and individual feelings. While individuals and even families may not have admitted to an interest in anything but the outwardly respectable criteria such as the virtue, the beauty, and the good health of a girl or the dignity and zest for work of a young man, they were quite aware of the criteria that were truly pertinent to the system, namely, the value of the patrimony and the size of the adot.

There are several reasons why in the great majority of cases the system functioned ostensibly on the basis of the least pertinent criteria relative to the true principles of that system. First, family upbringing tended to ensure a very close correlation between the basic criteria demanded by the system and the primordial characteristics in the eyes of the individuals involved: just as the eldest son of an important family was called upon to embody the virtues of a "man of honor" (*homi d'aunou*) or "good peasant" more than anyone else, so it would not do for a "great heiress" or "younger daughter of a good house" to settle for the conventional virtue that might be good enough for a girl from an ordinary family. Furthermore, the earliest learning experiences of children, reinforced as they were by all of their social experiences, tended to model their schemes of perception and appreciation, in a word, their *tastes*, which, since they played as large a role in their selection of a sexual partner as in other areas, led them to avoid improper alliances, even aside from considerations of a properly economic or social nature. Here as elsewhere, a happy love, that is, a socially approved and therefore success-bound love, was the same thing as that *amor fati*, love of one's own social destiny, which brings together socially compatible partners by way of a free choice that is unpredictable and arbitrary in appearance only. And it is as if only the most patent discrepancies—the scandal created when a poor man marries a rich but ugly, or much older, heiress—represented a situation precarious enough to bring about the misrecognition of such preestablished harmony and the transfiguration of fate into free choice.

The constraints surrounding every matrimonial choice are so numerous and appear in such complex combinations that the individuals involved cannot possibly deal with all of them consciously, even if they have mastered them on a different level. They can therefore not be expressed by a set of mechanical rules; and if practices are implicitly represented as the execution of explicit or express norms or of subconscious models, an infinite number of rules would have to be invented in order to account for the infinite variety of practices, especially for all the strategies that enable families to reconcile, counterbalance, or even cancel out these constraints. Faced with the constant danger that the compensation accorded younger children might necessitate the breaking up of the patrimony—precisely the eventuality the privilege accorded the eldest son was designed to avert at all costs—families can always counter the potential threats every marriage poses to the property and, by implication, to the family that is perpetuated by its ownership, by deploying a whole array of "parries" and "moves" similar to those of fencing and chess. Far from being simple procedures, analogous to those invented by the legalistic imagination in its efforts to bend the law, far also from being reducible to formal and explicit rules, these strategies are the product of *habitus*, meaning the practical mastery of a small number of implicit principles that have spawned an infinite number of practices and follow their own pattern, although they are not based on obedience to any formal rules. Hence, since these patterns emerge "spontaneously," it is unnecessary to make them explicit or to invoke or impose any rules. *Habitus* is thus the product of the very structures it tends to reproduce. Predicated upon a "spontaneous" compliance with the established order and with the will of the guardians of that order, namely, the elders, *habitus* is the principle that will generate the different solutions (such as the limitation of family size or the emigration or enforced celibacy of younger sons) which individuals, depending on their position in the social hierarchy, their place in the family's order of birth, their sex, and so forth, can bring to the practical dilemmas created by the various systems of exigencies that are not necessarily mutually compatible. Marriage strategies as such must therefore not be seen in the abstract, unrelated to inheritance strategies, fertility strategies, and even pedagogical strategies. In other words, they must be seen as one element in the entire system of biological, cultural, and social reproduction by which every group endeavors to pass on to the next generation the full measure of power and privilege it has itself inherited.

Bibliographical List

1. De Maria, *Mémoires sur les dots de Béarn*, with appendix entitled "Mémoires sur les coutumes et observances non écrites de Béarn." Manuscript, Archives départementales of Basses-Pyrénées.

2. De Maria, *Mémoires et éclaircissements sur le for et coutume de Béarn.* Manuscript, Archives départementales of Basses-Pyrénées.

3. Laurent Labourt, *Les fors et coutumes de Béarn.* Manuscript, Bibliothèque municipale of Pau.

4. J.-F. Mourot, *Traité des dots suivant les principes du droit romain, conféré avec les coutumes de Béarn, de Navarre, de Soule et la jurisprudence du Parlement* (cited by Laurent Laborde, *La dot dans les fors et coutumes du Béarn*, p. 15).

5. J.-F. Mourot, *Traité des biens paraphernaux, des augments et des institutions contractuelles, avec celui de l'avitinage* (cited by Laurent Laborde, *La dot*).

6. A. Mazure and J. Hatoulet, *Fors de Béarn, législation inédite du XIᵉ au XIIIᵉ siècle.* Latin texts with French translations, notes, and introduction. Pau and Paris, n.d. [1841–43].

7. P. Rogé, *Les anciens fors de Béarn.* Toulouse and Paris, 1908.

8. J. Brissaud and P. Rogé, Textes additionels aux anciens fors de Béarn. *Bulletin de l'Université de Toulouse, mémoires originaux des facultés de droit et des lettres*, Series B, no. 3. Toulouse, 1905.

9. Laurent Laborde, *La dot dans les fors et coutumes du Béarn.* Bordeaux, 1909.

10. G. Dupont, *Du régime successoral dans les coutumes de Béarn.* Thesis, University of Paris, 1914.

11. A. Fougères, *Les droits de famille et les successions au Pays basque et en Béarn, d'après les anciens textes.* Thesis, University of Paris, 1938.

12. Pierre Luc, *Vie rurale et pratique juridique en Béarn aux XIVᵉ et XVᵉ siècles.* University of Toulouse, Thesis, 1943.

13. Frédéric Le Play, *L'organisation de la famille selon le vrai modèle signalé par l'histoire de toutes les races et de tous les temps.* With epilogue and three appendixes by E. Cheysson, F. Le Play, and C. Jannet. 3d ed., containing new documents, edited by A. Focillon, A. Le Play, and M. Delaire. Paris, 1884.

14. J. Saint-Macary, *Les régimes matrimoniaux en Béarn avant et après le Code civil.* Thesis, University of Bordeaux, 1942; *La désertion de la terre en Béarn et dans le Pays basque.* Thesis, University of Bordeaux, 1942.

15. J. Bonnecaze, *La philosophie du Code Napoléon appliquée au droit de la famille. Ses destinées dans le droit civil contemporain.* 2d ed. Paris, 1928.

Bibliographical Notes*

Unlike most of the other provinces of southern France, the provinces of the Pyrenees, Bigorre, Lavedan, Béarn, and the Basque country had preserved an original customary law that was virtually untouched by Roman law. This fact has not failed to attract the attention of historians and legal scholars. "The law of Béarn," wrote Pierre Luc, "appears to be essentially a customary law and shows very little influence of the Roman law. It therefore offers us an extremely interesting model. Such things, for example, as the swearing of oaths of innocence with oath-helpers, the

*Compiled in collaboration with Marie-Claire Bourdieu. Numbers within parentheses refer to numbered items on the Bibliographical List that precedes these notes.

designating of hostages to guarantee contracts, mortgages and the possibility of acquitting monetary obligations in kind were still currently practiced there in the fourteenth and fifteenth centuries, while in certain other regions they had fallen into disuse more than two centuries earlier" (12, pp. 3–4). In the past, juridical and historical studies were exclusively based on collections of customary laws, in other words, on the *Fors de Béarn*. Thus, as early as the eighteenth century, some local jurists, De Maria (1 and 2), Labourt (3) and Mourot (4 and 5), wrote commentaries on the *Fors de Béarn*, particularly on the subject of the dowry and on the customs of succession. Unfortunately, there is only one rather mediocre edition of the *Fors*, which brings together often very corrupted readings dating from various periods and therefore needs a great deal of critical editing (as was already observed by Roget [7 and 8]) before it can serve as the basis for an analysis. Since such an edition does not yet exist, modern scholars have concentrated on the *For reformé* of 1551, on the wide variety of legal treatises available since the sixteenth century and, above all, on the commentaries on these texts by the legal scholars of the seventeenth and eighteenth centuries. Even though two of these modern studies, Laborde's work on the dowry in Béarn (9) and Dupont's book on the practices of succession in Béarn (10), are based on the *For reformé* and on the jurisprudence of the last two centuries of the monarchy, they are extremely valuable. As for A. Fougère's voluminous thesis (11), it repeats, at least for Béarn, what has already been said in earlier works.

The historians of law have come to the conclusion that the treatises on customary law should be used with caution, since they are concerned with a relatively theoretical law and deal in outmoded rules while neglecting the arrangements that were actually made. They have found that notarized documents are the one source that can furnish information on the actual practices. The model for this type of research is the work of Pierre Luc (12). On the basis of notarial registers this author first studied the living conditions of the rural population and the system of landownership, the structure of the family of Béarn, and the rules under which its patrimony was preserved and passed on to the next generation. In the second part, he examined the technical and legal procedures involved in working the land in the framework of the family and of the community, as well as a number of problems concerning the rural economy, such as credit and practices of exchange.

The mountains of Béarn are the place where Frédéric Le Play, the most outspoken critic of the Napoleonic Code, has situated the extended family, which he considered the ideal family organization, especially by contrast with the "unstable" family resulting from the application of the Napoleonic Code. (13). Having first defined three types of families, namely, the patriarchal family, the unstable family—which is characteristic of modern society—and the extended family, Le Play proceeds to describe the latter (pp. 29 ff) and enumerates the advantages each one of its members derives from it: "On the eldest, who carries a heavy burden of obligations, it (this regime of inheritance) confers the respect attached to the ancestral home or shop; to those members who marry outside the family, it gives the support of the extended house along with the satisfactions of independence; to those who prefer to remain in the paternal home it gives the peace and quiet of bachelorhood as well as the joys of the family; and to all it afford the happiness of reliving in their paternal home the joys of early childhood, even in advanced old age" (pp. 36–37). "By instituting one heir at every generation, the landowning extended family does not sacrifice the interests of the younger children to those of the eldest. On the contrary, it obliges the latter to renounce the net profit of his work throughout his life, first in favor of his siblings, then in favor of his children. The family can only obtain this material sacrifice by granting him a compensation of a moral order, namely the respect attached to the possession of the ancestral home" (p. 114). The second part of Le Play's book is a monograph on the Melouga family, an example of the extended family of the Lavedan in 1856. An epilogue by E. Cheysson describes the end of that family under the impact of the law and the new mores: "Until very recently, the Melouga family had continued to exist; it was like a living remnant of a once powerful and fruitful social organization. But it, too, finally succumbed to the influence of the law and of the new mores that had spared it owing to an exceptional combination of favorable circumstances. The Code is doing its work; the leveling process continues; the extended family is dying; the extended family is dead" (p. 298). The claims of the theoreticians of the Le Play school are not borne out by the results of ethnographical studies. They are also contradicted by the work of Saint-Macary (14) who, on the basis of the notarized documents of the eighteenth and nineteenth centuries, has shown the persistence of inheritance and marriage patterns that do not conform to the Civil Code.

7

Illicit Sexual Activity and Society in Eighteenth-Century Nantes

Jacques Depauw

The available information concerning illicit sexual activity in early modern French society must be sought in a number of places. Most of it comes from monographs in historical demography that have used the baptismal records of illegitimate children. These indicate that the number of illegitimate children was very small in the second half of the seventeenth and the first half of the following century and that it slowly increased in the countryside beginning sometime in the second half of the eighteenth century.[1] What we know about the cities is even scantier. So far, it has not been possible to measure either the incidence of illegitimacy in the cities or the extent to which unwed mothers from the countryside migrated to the cities.

Historians have recently become interested in the declarations of illegitimate pregnancies. More detailed than the entries in the parish registers, these declarations enable us to know more about the nature of the illegitimacy. Moreover, they are also a source for urban history.

Annales, E. S. C. 27 (July–October 1972): 1155–82. Translated by Elborg Forster. The translator gratefully acknowledges the help of Doris Lidtke in the paragraphs concerning the computer treatment of the data.

[1]It is impossible to cite all the studies from which information can be gleaned. A general evaluation of the findings can be found in P. Chaunu, *La civilisation de l'Europe classique* (Paris, 1966), p. 196, and in P. Guillaume and J. P. Poussou, *La Démographie historique* (Paris, 1970), p. 173.

Grenoble has given us a small contingent,[2] and Lille has a magnificent series, although the latter does not permit us to make a distinction between girls from the countryside who conceived their child in the city and those who only came to the city to be delivered.[3] The present article is based on a series of declarations of pregnancy from the municipal archives of Nantes.[4]

There are several types of these declarations. The oldest represent the first step in the judicial proceedings instigated by the girl against the author of her pregnancy; for this reason, they are obviously voluntary. Allusions to them can be found in very old ordinances,[5] and they were received throughout the *Ancien Régime*. These declarations were particularly effective when made while the woman was in the throes of labor, at which time they were sufficient to condemn the father she named to paying for the delivery and the initial outlays for the child,[6] although this was a provisional decision that did not prejudice the final judgment. Other declarations were made in compliance with the edict of Henri II, which, except in a certain number of circumstances, considered the failure to make a declaration a presumption of infanticide.[7] A third type of declaration was that demanded by the municipalities in an effort to stop the influx of pregnant girls and to charge the cost of receiving them at the Hôtel-Dieu to the designated father. The declarations of Lille and Nantes were of this type.

In 1725, the municipality of Nantes decided to demand such declarations of pregnancy, but this policy was not easy to implement.[8] Hospital matrons were not interested in collaborating, many deliveries took place in secret, and masters or landlords were apt to be discreet. Given the presence of a large floating population in an active port such as Nantes, it

---

[2]J. Solé, *Passion charnelle et société urbaine d'Ancien Régime.* Annales de la faculté des lettres et des sciences humaines de Nice, no. 9–10 (Nice, 1969).

[3]A. Lottin, "Naissances illégitimes et filles-mères à Lille," *Revue d'histoire moderne et contemporaine* 17 (1970): 278–332.

[4]The call numbers and dates of the registers consulted are as follows:

GG 747, 96 pp., from 27 viii 25 to 15 ix 33; GG. 748, 94 pp., from 18 ix 33 to 21 vii 42; GG. 749, 103 pp., 26 vii 42 to 16 viii 47; GG. 750, 100 pp., from 21 viii 47 to 25 iv 51; GG. 751, 98 pp., from 28 iv 51 to 4 vi 54; GG. 752, 152 pp., from 4 vi 54 to 11 iii 58; GG. 753, 198 pp., from 11 iii 58 to 6 xii 62; GG. 754, 150 pp., from 9 xii 62 to 22 xii 66; GG. 755, 144 pp., from 23 v 71 to 18 iv 74; GG. 756, 202 pp., from 25 iv 74 to 4 x 77; GG. 757, 190 pp., from 4 x 77 to 12 xi 82; and GG. 758, 173 pp., from 5 xi 82 to 24 xii 88.

[5]A. Favre, *Codex definitionum* (Geneva, 1628): "Virgini creditur iuranti se ab aliquo cognitam non etiam meretrici," bk. 4, Tit. 14, def. 18, p. 312.

[6]P. Baret, *Histoire et critique des règles sur la preuve de filiation naturelle en droit français et étranger* (Paris, 1872).

[7]F. A. Isambert, *Recueil des anciennes lois françaises*, 29 vols. (Paris, 1822–33; reprinted, Ridgewood, N.J., 1964–66), 12: 471.

[8]Archives municipales, Nantes, series GG no. 746. Extract from the register of the Parlement of 4 August 1725.

is easy to see that many obstacles arose. A different kind of resistance to this policy also developed in the course of the century. It was voiced by enlightened opinion, especially by the physicians, who objected to subjecting girls to such a humiliating procedure. By 1780, many felt that all children presented to the authorities should be received without formalities. This attitude is clearly reflected in the quality of the declarations, for many girls asked third parties to make the declaration for them, and we hear of frequent incidents with the registering clerk. Nonetheless, Nantes was not as advanced as Paris, so that the law remained on the books until the Revolution. Figure 7.1 shows the evolution of the number of declarations of illegitimate pregnancies in comparison with a sampling of data from parish registers. By 1740 the correlation between the number of baptisms of illegitimate children and the number of declarations is very close.

How reliable is such a series of documents? Some of the declarations are demonstrably false, since they were subsequently either corrected by the registering clerk or superseded by a second declaration of the girl. This suggests bargaining with the father of the child. Some kind of compromise, or conversely, a broken promise, often produced a new name on the declaration. To be sure, the document does not provide absolute certainty—how would we know more than the registering clerk?—but many of its features make a strong case for its usefulness to the historian. Declarations that were repeated during subsequent judicial procedures shed light on the legal system and on the way a girl was treated when she appeared before an inquisitorial registering clerk, and the quality and the keeping of the registers, particularly the massive size of the series, are of great historical interest. After all, we have 8,000 cases, distributed over the years 1725–88, although, unfortunately, there is a gap between 1767 and 1771.

METHODOLOGY: CODING AND COMPUTER TREATMENT

Each declaration was first transcribed on a card that provided a space for many qualitative details. The coded card was developed only after we had gone through all the registers, for it was not possible to determine earlier what information could be coded and how it should be coded, especially since the document had evolved over a period of sixty years (see figs. 7.2 and 7.3).

The continuity of the coding was assured by five columns that show not only the year in two columns (the tens and the units, since all declarations date from the same century) but also the consecutive number of the declaration in that year in three columns. It would have been insufficient to use only the date of the day or the number of the sheet in

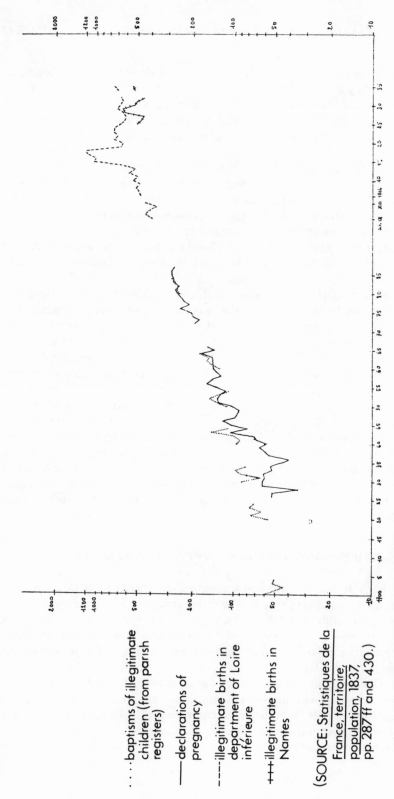

Figure 7.1. Numerical Development of Illegitimacy, 1700–1835

····· baptisms of illegitimate
children (from parish
registers)

—— declarations of
pregnancy

- - - illegitimate births in
department of Loire
inférieure

+++ illegitimate births in
Nantes

(SOURCE: Statistiques de la
France, territoire,
population, 1837,
pp. 287 ff and 430.)

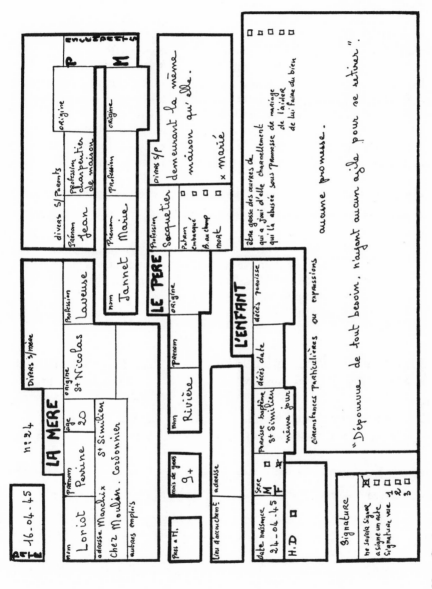

Figure 7.2. Note Card

the register, since several declarations were sometimes made on the same day or on the same sheet. There is no problem with the age of the girl, which was placed in two columns. For the place of origin, we used the I.N.S.E.E. code in five columns, two for the department and three for the consecutive number of the commune in that department. For Nantes itself, however, a special number was given to each parish.

Nor was there any problem with the sex of the child or the date of its baptism—two columns each for the years and months. Finally, in order to enable us to retrieve those girls and those fathers who appear in the registers more than once, we used the first four letters of the girl's name and the first four letters of her mother's name—thus eliminating any homonyms—and the first six letters of the child's father's name; six because we had no double-check, such as the mother's name for the girl.

Columns 25–29 of the computer card contain the following information:

Column 25 gives a general indication of the social position of the fathers of the children:

1. *The upper classes.* This is a strictly qualitative category that was empirically arrived at on the basis of various indications given in the documents, such as "Monsieur" before the name, "gentilhomme," "maître des comptes," etc.
2. "Sieur" before the name

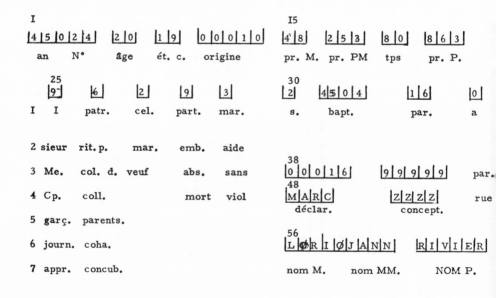

Figure 7.3. Computer Card

3. "Master"
4. "Journeyman"
5. "*Garçon*," which at Nantes means "apprentice"
6. "Day laborer"
7. "Apprentice," which appears later than "*garçon*"

Column 26 gives details concerning the relationship between the girl and her lover:

1. He is her master
2. He is a relative of her master
3. He is a domestic servant in the same household
4. He is also employed in the same household, but not as a domestic servant
5. He lives in the same house
6. She is living with him

Column 27 gives the marital status of the lover

1. Unmarried
2. Married
3. Widower

Column 28 gives details on a number of special situations concerning the lover at the time of the declaration:

1. Has left
2. Has gone to sea
3. Is not present
4. Is dead

Column 29 gives details on the promises against which the girl claims to have yielded:

1. Promise of marriage
2. Promise of help
3. No promise
4. Case of rape

Some of the columns serve particular purposes. Columns 20–21 give certain details for the girls: those who were born in Nantes are coded "80," those who only came to Nantes for the delivery are coded "70," underage immigrants are coded "60," and immigrants who had come to Nantes for an indetermined period of time are coded "50". Code numbers lower than 50 show the number of years spent in Nantes: "08," for example, indicates that a girl claimed to have spent eight years there. Code number 99, in this matter as in others, indicates that there is no information.

Column 37 enabled us to sort out, for elimination or use in other operations, false declarations, double declarations, and a certain number of special cases.

Columns 25–29 are self-explanatory. It should be noted that each of them admits of eight different possibilities, so that one must be very careful to distribute the information in such a way that the data entered in the same column are mutually exclusive.

Difficulties arose when it came to the occupations. In a first phase we chose to establish a detailed code, that is, to assign a particular code to each occupation or trade we encountered. Thus we have two columns for female occupations, giving us 99 occupations, including "no information," and three columns, or 999 possible male occupations. We then had to assign a code number to each occupation, keeping them in alphabetical order for the sake of convenience. We established this list by using every tenth register as a sample, noting every occupation we encountered. This gave us about 200, to which we assigned every fourth number, so that three out of every four numbers were left free for occupations that might turn up later. Code numbers still left free at the end were used to take care of certain categories too numerous to be placed in their proper place, such as the various kinds of shopkeepers [*marchands*]. Altogether, 407 codes were used for male and 57 for female occupations. Such a classification later permits any number of manipulations, from the most detailed list to grouping by type of activity, degree of skill necessary, or any other criteria one might wish to apply, since the composition of each one of these groups is known.

Assigning a code to the addresses was another thorny problem. Since there is no table listing the streets of Nantes in the eighteenth century, we have used the first four letters of the street. We now realize that a numerical code, based on the same principles as the code of occupations, would have been preferable because it would have been more flexible and more adaptable to the great toponymical variety and to the descriptive character of the addresses. It also would have permitted various groupings.

The entire coding operation was performed by two persons, one dictating to the other, at the rate of sixty declarations per hour. This slowness was largely due to the coding of the communes, which are too numerous to be learned by heart as the work progressed.

The data were processed by the Laboratoire de mathématiques appliquées of the University of Caen.[9] We have used the sorting program of that institution, although we also added a number of program modifications of our own. One of these, for example, enabled us to determine the age of the girls and the date of their arrival at Nantes on the basis of the number of years spent at Nantes.

[9] I would like to thank Professor Pierre Chaunu of the Sorbonne, who encouraged me to apply for a grant from the Centre national de la recherche scientifique. I also thank professor Pham of the University of Caen, who permitted me to use his laboratory, and M. Dubois, a technical expert of the CNRS, who devoted a great deal of time to this project.

As for the results, there is no comparison between the time required for these preparations and the time it would have taken to sort these data by hand, especially since the data had to be extracted in any case. The computer allows ready access to the desired information in the codified data. Furthermore, the massive nature of the data allows for increasing refinement through repeated analysis of subgroups. These, in turn, open up a wide variety of possibilities for differentiation. On the other hand, the more or less rigid classification of the data also influences our way of looking at them and, hence, the very conclusions we draw from them.

Just one word on the question of cost, which is related to the dilemma of coding versus simple alphabetic punching. For a small study, involving a file of manageable dimensions for which no extensive program is indicated, the punching operation represents an important part of the total cost, about a third in the present case. To have foregone coding would have meant to go from one card to two cards per case, particularly because of the three series of occupations. This would have raised the cost of the operation considerably, even if we did not count the computer-time required by alpha-processing and the higher price of a computer with greater storage capacity.

Here, then, are our results—pages upon pages of numbers. It is the weakness of the computer that it yields its data in this rather unprepossessing form. The only thing that can be done with these data is to present a graph or, rather, a whole series of graphs assembling all the information that, through its various correlations, has led to the present interpretation.

General Evolution of Illegitimacy in the Region of Nantes

THE NUMBER OF CASES

The graph showing the general evolution of illegitimacy between 1700 and 1835 immediately gives us a clear picture of the situation in the eighteenth century. We see a rising trend between two plateaus. The first plateau is that of low illegitimacy. The parish registers yield an average of fifty illegitimate births per year [for the region] in the beginning of the century. Given the fact that girls from the countryside who came to the city to conceal their pregnancy may account for as many as one-fifth of all illegitimate pregnancies as indicated by later percentages, only about 2.5 percent of all the births in Nantes itself were illegitimate. It must be added that foundlings were included in the number of illegitimate children. Almost all of these appear in rich parishes such as Saint-Laurent or Saint-

Vincent, and all of them were probably not conceived outside of marriage. Later we see a rising phase, which reaches a second plateau in 1820, after a sharp rise during the years 1815–20. This plateau spans a period of fifteen years, and the situation changes again in the subsequent years.

The rise of illegitimacy during the eighteenth and the beginning of the nineteenth centuries shows two phases of deceleration, one being the rather brief slowdown during the years 1747–49. This was followed by a steep rise, which was in turn arrested between 1757 and 1763. These two phases correspond exactly to the two recessions experienced by the port of Nantes during the War of the Austrian Succession and the Seven Years' War. This correlation became visible when we established separate categories for the girls born at Nantes, those who worked and conceived their child there, and those who only came there for the delivery of their child (see fig. 7.4).

The percentage of girls who could not be placed into one of these three groups is a good indicator of the precision of our data. This percentage is very high at the beginning and the end of our period. The percentage of girls who came to Nantes only for the delivery of their child shows a steady decline. During the Seven Years' War the percentage of girls from the country diminished so much that it fell below that of girls from Nantes, while during the subsequent rising phase it again became significantly higher. Unless I am mistaken, the proportion of clandestine illegitimate births in a city has been isolated here for the first time, and it appears to be rather small. At Nantes, at least, it is not true that the influx of girls from the country for the purpose of giving birth accounted for the rise in illegitimate births. Within the urban population, there was a constant rise in illegitimacy which, however, began to level off after about thirty years. As for the major fluctuations, they must have been related to the general rise in female mobility.[10]

REGION-WIDE ILLEGITIMACY[11]

Altogether, 879 cases are recorded. Girls from villages and small towns account for 90 percent of them. Chronologically, there is a higher incidence of illegitimacy after 1778, which is somewhat earlier than in western France as a whole.[12]

---

[10]On this point, see the forthcoming article "Mouvement migratoire féminin, métiers féminins et structures urbaines," to be published in the next issue of *Cahiers du Centre de recherches d'histoire de la France-Atlantique*, University of Nantes. Twelve maps and plates will be included.

[11]Figure 7.5.

[12]Y. Blayo and L. Henry, "Données démographiques sur la Bretagne et l'Anjou de 1740 à 1835," *Annales de démographie historique*, 1967, p. 107.

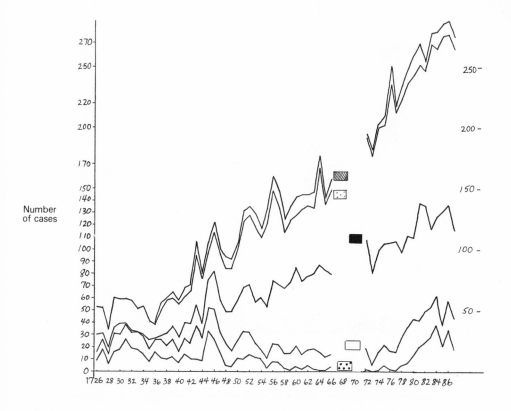

Number of cases

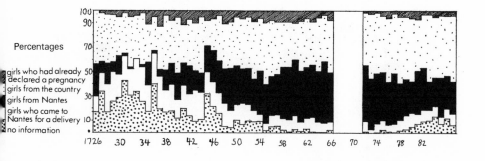

Percentages

girls who had already declared a pregnancy
girls from the country
girls from Nantes
girls who came to Nantes for a delivery
no information

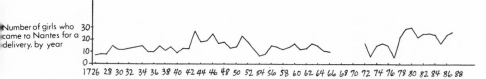

Number of girls who came to Nantes for a delivery, by year

Figure 7.4. The Different Types of Declarations

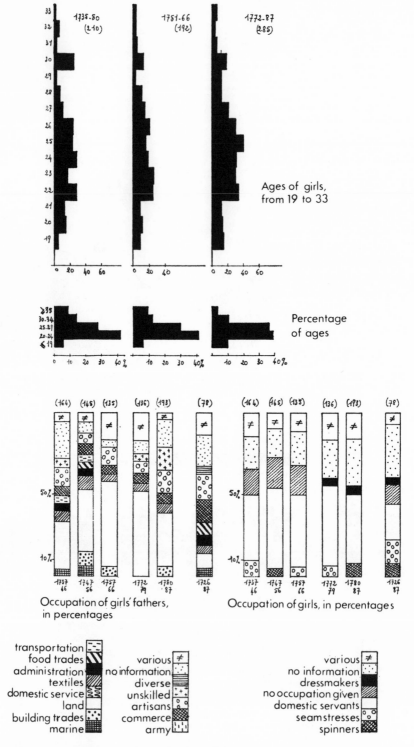

Figure 7.5. Illegitimacy in the Region of Nantes

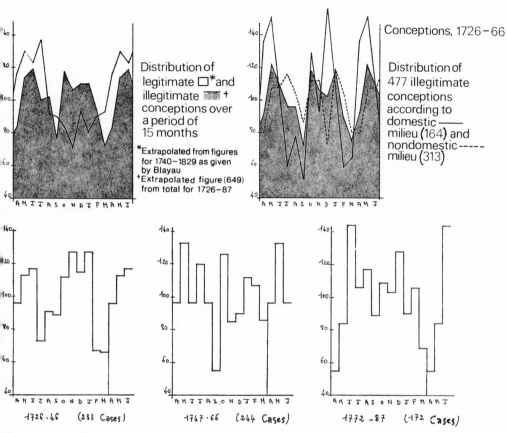

Conceptions, 1726–66

Distribution of legitimate □* and illegitimate ▨ † conceptions over a period of 15 months

*Extrapolated from figures for 1740–1829 as given by Blayau
†Extrapolated figure (649) from total for 1726–87

Distribution of 477 illegitimate conceptions according to domestic ——— milieu (164) and nondomestic ----- milieu (313)

1726-46 (233 Cases)

1747-66 (244 Cases)

1772-87 (172 Cases)

Distribution of illegitimate conceptions over a period of 15 months

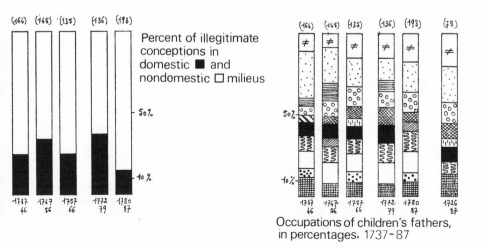

(164) (145) (135) (136) (193)

Percent of illegitimate conceptions in domestic ■ and nondomestic □ milieus

50%

40%

1737 1767 1757 1772 1780
46   86   66   79   87

(164) (145) (135) (136) (193) (78)

50%

10%

1737 1747 1757 1772 1780 1726
46   86   66   79   87   87

Occupations of children's fathers, in percentages, 1737-87

The age of the girl is given in practically every case, except for widows. However, the girls had only an approximate notion of their age. They said, for example, that they were thirty, rather than twenty-nine or thirty-one, and they usually gave an even rather than an odd number. Round numbers seemed to be more important than the precise decimal system. The greatest clustering occurs in the age group twenty-two to twenty-six. Thus, we are not dealing with very young girls. But most of them had not reached the age of marriage, either: 47–48 percent were minors, which is a higher percentage than that of newlywed minors.[13]

The daughter of a peasant is the daughter of a ploughman [*laboureur*] or market gardener [*jardinier*], very rarely of a tenant farmer [*fermier*] or a sharecropper [*métayer*].* Three hundred and seventy-five, or almost 40 percent, can be traced to this agricultural milieu, but this is less than the proportion of people who worked the land. In the first phases, the document even shows a relatively high proportion of girls whose fathers we have placed in the tertiary or administrative sector, a heterogeneous grouping of all those who did not work with their hands, such as barristers and physicians or, more simply, attorneys, clerks, and employees of the tax farms and artisans guilds. This probable overrepresentation of the middle levels of the population eventually disappears and even drops below the 4 percent minimum we have set for ourselves. It is higher in the more restricted sample of the city.

Among the fathers of the children, we find many sailors and domestic servants, which is not surprising. There are very few peasants. The social pyramid for these men is rather top-heavy. The tertiary administrative sector is becoming increasingly involved, and if we add the men who exercise no professional activity, being referred to as *"bourgeois,"* *"hommes de condition,"* or *"gentilshommes"*—and these are small groups that we have placed in the category "diverse"—these lovers who enjoy a certain modicum of wealth, power, and respectability account for 10.7 percent of the total, a proportion roughly equivalent to that of the peasants.

The last phase marks a different situation. Between 1772 and 1779 the lower classes, i.e., construction workers, textile workers, artisans, and unskilled laborers, still appear in only 22 of 136 declarations; between 1780 and 1787 they are involved in 53 of 193 cases. This represents a rise from 16.2 to 27.5 percent. This marked increase around 1780 indicates

---

[13]Ibid., p. 115.

*Given the present concern with the social categories of the *Ancien Régime*, it is important to be as precise as possible on this point. Hence, the various occupational terms have been given the closest possible English equivalent; the French term is shown in brackets whenever no exact equivalent is available. —Trans.

that illicit sexual activity was becoming more prevalent in these classes of the population.

Forty percent of all the girls are explicitly characterized as domestic servants. The actual percentage was undoubtedly higher, for many of them gave no information as to their occupation. Aside from these 40 percent of known domestic servants, only 18 percent of the girls gave other occupations. Girls who became involved in illicit sexual activity, then, were for the most part domestic servants.

MENIAL AND OTHER ILLICIT RELATIONSHIPS

The curve showing illegitimate conceptions, like the curve of legitimate conceptions, shows a high in the spring, although the former is somewhat less marked and shorter. This is not surprising. In the winter, however, there is a marked difference between the two curves. Over the entire year, the curve of legitimate conceptions shows a two-phase rhythm with reduced activity in autumn and winter; that of illegitimate conceptions shows a four-phase rhythm because of the renewed activity in winter. Should we say that these patterns show nothing more than the classic uneven distribution of legitimate conceptions and that the greater regularity of illegitimate conceptions is due to the fact that they involve more varied and less conformist types of couples? In principle, this is true, but it must be pointed out that the most prevalent illicit relationship is between the servant and her master.* Let us now isolate, within the group of girls who came to Nantes to have their child, those who conceived it in a domestic situation. This operation will immediately yield a more even curve for conceptions due to "nonmenial" relationships and will strongly accentuate the rhythm of menial relationships. It is therefore very interesting to compare the two.

Conceptions by servant girls start early in the spring, very much like the legitimate conceptions, and show a sharp decline by July. The other illegitimate conceptions start somewhat later, reaching their high point only by June-July. The menial and, hence, quasi-legitimate relationships have been prepared by the long intimacy of winter and come to fruition early in the spring; while the other, less defined relationships lead to conceptions later in the spring, even in summer, when conceptions by servant-girls have become relatively rare. From then on, until about October, the curves of conceptions due to menial and nonmenial relationships run roughly parallel. October marks the beginning of a great

---

*For want of a better equivalent for the French "*amours ancillaires*" we must call this a "menial relationship." —Trans.

increase in conceptions involving menial relationships; it reaches its highest point in December, when it eclipses all other kinds of illegitimate conceptions in absolute terms. Both kinds, finally, show a low phase at the end of winter, particularly in March; this trend is also present in the curve of legitimate conceptions.

The interpretation of these curves is a rather delicate matter. Sexual activity in winter and very early spring was related to staying in the house. But why do we not see the influence of this factor on marital activity? One hypothesis is that all conceptions, legitimate or not, were a sign of the upsurge in vitality that took place in the spring but that the pool of legitimate couples whose relation might lead to a conception did not increase, except by the return to fertility of women who had been sterile due to pregnancy or breastfeeding and by the addition of newly married couples. Return to fertility, however, could take place at any time. As for the addition of newly married couples, it was rather strictly circumscribed in time, since western France was very faithful to the tradition of January and February marriages.[14] These would lead to conception sometime between February and July, but not in winter. The pool of legitimate fertile couples thus remained fairly stable. This was not true for illicit couples within the household. Their very instability renewed the pool, particularly during the frequently cited hiring turnover on Saint John's day (21 June). This turnover also accounted for the low level of illegitimate conceptions during the summer, for the hiring of a new servant did not necessarily lead to a seduction, while a new marriage usually led to its consummation. All of these things may have accounted for increased erotic activity during winter.

This still leaves the low level of illegitimate conceptions in February-March, a phenomenon that has often been noted for legitimate conceptions as well, although no absolutely convincing explanation has yet been advanced. Abstinence or sterility? Cultural conditioning or physiological reasons? But then, what about the illegitimate conceptions due to menial relationships? Further shrinking of the always restricted pool of couples? But the upsurge in these conceptions during April and May cannot be explained by a replenished pool—there was no great turnover in March. Sterility? It would have to be of a very sudden and very temporary nature. Lent? It is difficult to imagine that abstinence of an ascetic kind was involved. However, it is possible that Lent was indeed the period when the sense of sin was strongest, especially for the girl, who faced the prospect of confession before her Easter communion, with all the questions the priest would ask; for every confessor's manual told him that this was the great danger to which servant girls were exposed. Like all other writers on

[14]Ibid.

the subject, I must admit that these suppositions are none too satisfactory, but they do point to a hitherto rather unexplored area, that of the cultural conditioning of sexual behavior in early modern French society.

While not exactly legitimate, these menial relationships at least conformed to a certain pattern. Thus Marie Toutescôtes yielded to M. de Kernoël "during the three days when he came to stay at Sieur de Poulpiquet's (her master) who was his friend but happened to be away on a military campaign at the time; and she felt that she should not refuse him, being afraid that her master would be angry with her" (30 iii 48).*

Aside from menial relationships, we find a great variety of circumstances. There were a few cases of violence, of girls taken by surprise while watching the flocks, of traveling women raped on the highways or victimized by their traveling companions. We also find a number of habitués who regularly brought in their mistresses for a delivery. More numerous are illegitimate conceptions in marginal milieus, in the world of petty commerce and transportation, involving servant girls in inns or sailors' daughters, like one Marguerite Gisno, who made two declarations, designating a sailor both times (7 iv 79 and 29 viii 81). In addition to this variety there is a host of scattered categories.

PERSPECTIVES

Even at the end of the eighteenth century, there was no high tide of illicit sexual activity in Brittany. Nonetheless, a slight change occurred about 1780. During the eight years 1772–79, avowed menial relationships accounted for 50 of 136 cases, while for the following eight years, they accounted for 22 of 193 cases, or 36.4 and 11.4 percent, respectively. The last figure represents the lowest percentage of the century. A new social milieu had become involved, as we have already noted. But we must not be misled by percentages. In absolute terms, the figures remain low. The cost of raising illegitimate children was no great problem, except in the cities. It is true that the communities, which, according to the customary law of Brittany, were responsible for such children, engaged in costly lawsuits in an effort to shift this burden to other communities. But the cost of supporting the children of the poor was a much more troublesome problem.[15]

---

*The dates are written throughout in the European fashion, i.e., day-month-year, since they appear in this fashion on the computer card. —Trans.

[15]Archives départementales 35 (Loire-Maritime) series C, *liasses* 1286 and 1287, "Evaluation of the number of illegitimate children." See, among other things, the reply of the subdelegate of Dinan: "This case [failure to declare the pregnancy] is so rare because young women sit away from the men in church, so that none of them can escape the searching eyes

By the beginning of the nineteenth century, the situation was essentially unchanged. On the maps drawn up by Comte d'Angeville, the department of Ille-et-Vilaine shows the lowest level of illegitimacy in all of France, followed by the department of Côtes-du-Nord. Vendée, Morbihan, and Finistère are in fifth, sixth, and eighth lowest place, respectively. Loire-Inférieure, which, it should be noted, includes Nantes, is in twenty-eighth place. Comparable departments, such as Seine-Inférieure or Gironde, are in seventy-ninth and eighty-second place.[16] Can we establish a correlation between this rigorous morality and the solid sociological structure of religious life that is evidenced in religious observance? A comparison of the map of illegitimate children with Gabriel Le Bras's map of religious observance shows that the two coincide in many cases.[17] A low level of illegitimacy and a high level of religious observance coincide in Brittany and also on the eastern slope of the Massif Central; weak religious observance and a high level of illegitimacy coincide in the South-West.[18] This coincidence, however, does not explain everything, for we also find clear-cut exceptions: strong religious observance and a high level of illegitimacy go together in the department of the Nord, in Pas-de-Calais, and in the two Alsatian departments.

Illicit Sexual Activity in the City and Social Inequality

Domestic servants, prostitutes, and kept women were in an obviously inferior position vis-à-vis the men who made them pregnant. Before we study these three groups of women separately, we should examine this social inequality in its general setting, regardless of categories.

PROMISES AND POVERTY

In their declarations the girls usually mention the promises that caused them to yield. The promises concerned, first of all, the cost of the delivery

---

of their knowledgeable elders. When the latter are no longer in doubt, they inform the suitable authorities, who then make sure that the person declares her pregnancy and designates the father of her child."

[16]Comte d'Angeville, *Essai sur la statistique de la population française considérée sous quelques-uns de ses rapports physiques et moraux* (Paris, 1836).

[17]Gabriel Le Bras, *Etudes de sociologie religieuse*, 2 vols. (Paris 1969), 1: map in appendix.

[18]One of the indications that western France continued to uphold traditional religious observances can be seen in the fact that, even in the middle of the nineteenth century, marriages did not take place during Advent and Lent. The new requirement for a certificate of marriage from the secular authorities did not change this pattern. (Cf. Blayo and Henry, "Données démographiques.") Nothing comparable can be found for the center of the Paris Basin. See M. Lachiver, *La population de Meulan* (Paris, 1969), p. 88.

and the upkeep of the child. They were promises "to take the child from her," "unburden her of her child," "that she would not have to take care of the child." There are only two clear-cut allusions to abortive intentions: "If she were to become pregnant, there are ways to take care of this," Jean de la Ville, a merchant [*négotiant*], said to Jeanne Rousseau (8 iii 37). And Jean Le Ray, a widowed stocking-maker, "asked Marie Laneau to do away with her child" (13 vi 40). But the most important promises were those that provided for the girl's future or elaborated on the terms of her work contract. We have grouped these promises together under three rubrics: "promise of marriage," "promise of help" (and, for the sake of convenience we have included in this frequently used expression all analogous formulations of promises, which we shall study in greater detail later), and finally, "no promise." The results are as follows:

	1726–36		1757–66		1780–87	
Promise of marriage	108	63%	386	73%	1230	89%
Promise of help	63	37%	43	8%	122	9%
No promise	—	—	102	19%	28	2%
Total	171		531		1380	
	of 265 cases		of 1190 cases		of 1706 cases	

This table yields more than just factual information. The number of promises of marriage is obviously excessive, but one thing is rather unexpected. The number of promises of marriage is proportionately lower at the beginning of the century than at the end. Even though we cannot have much faith in these supposed promises of marriage, they still give the measure of the aspirations of these girls or, rather, the measure of their *possible* aspirations. Our table indicates that at the beginning of the century, when their number was smaller and, hence, the scandal created by their adventure was greater, fewer of them claimed that there was any prospect of marriage. The reason is that such a prospect could only be claimed if marriage were plausible. There was no chance of marriage when the social distance was too great. Furthermore, one might also say that this very distance constituted the most persuasive excuse.

This, then, was the time when the benefactors made grandiose promises. "Promise to make her fortune" (24 iii 27 and 14 vii 27). Some promised considerable sums of money to protect a girl from want: a pension of 125 livres per year or a lifetime annuity (17 xi 56 and 7 iii 30), a sum of 1,000 livres in three installments (29 iii 60).

We find many promises to provide for a girl's future. "Promise to buy her a place in Bièce where she can live comfortably" (21 xii 30), "promise to take her with him to Saint-Malô and to set her up in a good business dealing in muslin and other Indian dry-goods" (8 iv 62), "promise to give her money for opening a shop" (24 iv 53). Finally, there are a great many more vague but similar "promises to set her up" (4 i 29, 13 ii 29, 16 ii 29, etc.).

The strangest of these promises to take care of a girl is the "promise to marry her if his wife should die."

Many girls had to settle for less, but even the more modest prospects envisaged some kind of permanent installation: "Promise to have her learn a trade" (22 iii 36), "promise to dress her properly and to pay for her learning a good trade" (24 ix 30).

These girls lived close to poverty. Others really were poor. They were poor, first of all, because they did not have work. Biret, an employee of the judicial administration, promised Marie Cadieu "to give her work and to recommend her to others" (21 xi 30). Thérèse Raymond, a seamstress, had "long been out of work" (11 vi 48). Françoise Pellerin, another seamstress, often [could not] find a day's work" (18 x 58). Sieur Coubert, a dealer in clay pots, took "Marie Hubron to his country house, claiming that he would give her work" (21 xi 46 and, for an identical case, 2 iv 55).

Then there were the destitute. Sieur Laurent, a wholesale merchant, promised Marie Philibert, a seamstress, to "help her out of her great poverty" and, a few months later, he promised Marie Brossier, a stocking mender, "to be helpful to her in her utter need" (18 ix 59 and 19 iv 60). Geslin, a barge master, "carnally enjoyed" Marie Lebreton "when she was totally destitute, promising to help her in her need" (8 vii 66). Marie Grandmaison, a dressmaker, orphan from birth and twenty years old in 1754, "having no means of subsistence, had given up all hope for herself" (26 viii 54 and comparable cases 19 iv 45 and 1 vii 56).

Some girls were destined for poverty from the very beginning. Magdelaine Boutin was born at Saumur about 1728. Having known neither father nor mother, she was placed in the foundlings' home at the age of two, came to Sanitat at the age of ten, and was in service at twelve or thirteen. She gave many addresses of houses where she had worked, including that of Sieur Querselan, by whom she claimed to be pregnant. She was seventeen years old at the time (26 vi 45). Her story is not unusual and resembles that of other public wards who were "placed" after the death of their parents (28 i 63, 24 ix 84, 24 x 73, 3 iv 51); it is like the story of Marie Allée, whose name is only too fitting, since she was abandoned at the age of two.*

In these cases poverty was the reason for the pregnancy. The pregnancy then compounded the poverty. For a girl in this condition it was even harder to find work. Perrine Ernaud, seven months pregnant, a seamstress by trade "[couldn't] even find work any more" (5 v 48). Another girl, a shirt-seamstress, had no work (14 vi 53). Similarly, Renée Laurent had to give up her work as a seamstress: "since she did not get her

*She was presumably found in a back alley. —Trans.

days of work, she . . . had to learn to spin cotton, like her said mother" (10 xi 61). We know that "spinning for a living" was a poor job indeed. Lodging as well was a thorny problem for these girls. Some of them found a place "through charity," but many had "no asylum," "no fixed domicile," "no place to go" (1 x 41, 5 vi 44, 16 v 45, 4 ix 48, etc.). Many also did not know where to have their child, given that they were so poor (passim, especially in 1743 and 1747). When the registering clerk received a declaration, he made a note of this destitution. He found Anne Marteau "in a house that look[ed] uninhabited . . . on a poor pallet that ha[d] practically nothing but straw on it" (9 viii 54 and 16 vi 57 for an identical case). The girls may have exaggerated the situation, hoping to go to the almshouse or to have their child admitted there free of charge. Perhaps so. But these pleas have a date; broadly speaking, the decade 1740 to 1750. They became increasingly rare thereafter and almost disappeared after 1772.

We must not forget that more than half of these girls were from the surrounding countryside and came to Nantes in search of work. The gamut of possible occupations for them was very narrow indeed. We can be fairly certain that there were not enough jobs to go around. There was little work for these girls outside of domestic service. Furthermore, they were all alone. Little help could be expected from anyone. Under these circumstances, a girl was in a position of inferiority in dealing with every man she met, be he a mason who earned a great deal more than a spinner, her own employer, a merchant [*négotiant*], or his assistant. The expression "has taken advantage of the weakness of her sex," which these documents sometimes employ in its usual sense, thus assumes a tragic social dimension. Such statements as "destitute," deprived "of everything," "of every necessity," "of all help," "of all means," or, reduced "to destitution," "to extreme, utter poverty," or "of notorious poverty" explain the "promises to help her," the "promise to help her with her living expenses," "not to forsake her," "to see that she is taken care of." Promises made in this context were a different matter from promises made to a kept woman.

FROM THE MENIAL RELATIONSHIP TO THE KEPT WOMAN

Menial relationships in the city. While not representing the same percentage of cases of illegitimacy as in the countryside, these relationships were very numerous in the city, especially at the beginning of the century. More than half of the eighty-two domestic servants appearing in the registers between 1726 and 1736 were in a dependent position vis-à-vis the man they named as the father of their child. Even in the city, the master or his associates had rights over a servant girl, or at least the means to apply pressure. Sometimes we hear of violence pure and simple. As in the countryside, these cases were relatively rare, and understandably so, since no further excuse for an illegitimate pregnancy was needed once the master had been named as the father of the child (11 xi 39, 19 xii 42, 14 iv 73 are some of the examples). There was simply no need for such extreme measures. Opportunities for sexual encounters were plentiful on occasions like the absence of the wife (14 x 26) or, especially, during a stay in the country. Thus Sieur Bodichon, a former manager of the royal rope manufacture, took Jeanne Courbet, his servant, to his countryhouse of Pavillon at Mauves and "kept her there with him for two months after the wine harvest" (20 vii 87, and for identical cases, 5 iii 40 and 1 vii 78). Or else we simply hear of "daily solicitations and promises": "promise to keep her permanently as a servant" (7 iv 64), "promise to give her dresses and cast-off clothes," the classic promise of the master (3 iii 62, just one example among many).

These powers extended beyond the master to his sons (12 xii 31, 29 ix 45, 14 vii 55), his brothers (20 ii 38, 19 vi 55), and even to friends and relations. Eighteen-year old Renée Soulard, servant of widow Turpin, yielded to Sieur Terrien (a man, incidentally, who appears twice in the registers) "who took care of the said widow's affairs" (13 xii 79). Perrine Socha yielded to Sieur Rabu, who often visited at her master's house (24 i 63), and Françoise Boitiaud to Sieur Cassard, a frequent guest of Sieur Rollin, her master, "and it happened because she was sent to the said gentleman's house to clean for him" (2 iii 63).

These relationships involved not only domestic servants but all kinds of girls who were hired for the day, such as seamstresses and dressmakers, as well.

We also find many couples in which both partners were domestic servants. This is the closest occupational correlation. But only rarely—in fewer cases, no doubt, than actually existed—do the data inform us that they were working in the same household at the time of the conception.

However that may be, until 1770 these menial relationships were very much the same in town and country. If we compare the seasonal trend of all the illegitimate conceptions in Nantes with the trend among girls from the countryside, half of whom were domestic servants, and if we then further restrict the group to domestic servants and, finally, to those who conceived their child in the house where they were employed, we obtain a secondary peak in the winter. While this peak in the city is less pronounced than that in the countryside, owing to the great variety of cases, it is nonetheless perceptible. It is even clearer by comparison with the total trend of illegitimate conceptions during the last period, 1742–87. By that time, we see no peak for girls from the countryside or for domestic servants. This is an indication, first of all, that there was a decline in sexual relationships between masters and servants; and indeed, they fell from 36 percent in 1737–46 to 9 percent in 1780–87. It was a continuous and regular decline. The evolution of the number of couples formed by two domestic servants is more difficult to evaluate, since only a small number of couples is so designated. Two facts, however, should be noted: the percentage of such couples decreases and the occupational correlation becomes less pronounced, since only 20 percent of the female domestic servants said that their lover was also a domestic servant in 1772–87, compared to 37.5 percent in 1726–66.

For the moment, however, let us consider only the decline in menial relationships between masters and servants. This might reflect nothing more than a change in the law. Earlier, it had simply been to a girl's advantage to designate her master as the father of her child, since her statement was sufficient to saddle him with the financial responsibility. But what was the use of charging him if he was no longer sentenced to paying? However, an evolution in the law is almost always brought about by a change in mores. The master now was no longer responsible for his servant. This fact represents an important change in their relationship. It is tempting to relate this change in behavior to new housing in the city and to the beginnings of apartment dwelling. Such a connection is probable, as long as we keep in mind that brick and mortar do not determine human behavior. The great building activity took place a little later, precisely in response to already existing needs. Nonetheless, the same tendency is evident in all of these areas, namely, an increasingly marked preponderance of the conjugal family and a closer association between sex and married life. And when the menial relationship came to interfere too openly with a morality based on the conjugal family, the domestic servant was replaced by the kept woman—but she was not kept under the same roof as the family.

The Kept Woman. There were kept women in Nantes before 1750 and there were servant girls made pregnant by their masters long after that date. No question about that. The important point is that there was a progressive and never completed shift from one form of illegitimacy to another.

The term *kept* first appears around the middle of the century: "promise to keep her" and, more specifically, "to keep her in a room" (12 iv 63), "to install her in a room of her own" (14 ix 53, and, identical case, 28 ii 58, 1 ix 61). We find more and more promises of this kind as time goes on and by the 1780s men from out of town were keeping their mistresses at Nantes in this manner: a *gentilhomme* from Saint-Philbert-de-Grandlieu (24 xi 83), a merchant from Le Croisic (20 xi 82), a shopkeeper from Angers (24 xi 83).

These illicit affairs were very different from a menial relationship. The lover visited his mistress in the room where he "kept" her. It is one thing to use one's servant, and another to have an affair with a girl one has installed "on her own"; a girl from the lower classes, to be sure, but not from the very lowest. Such a girl was almost never a laundress or a spinner; she was a seamstress or a dressmaker, or even, thanks to her lover, "without occupation." Thus Sieur Deslande, a married man, promised Françoise Bernard, age seventeen, "to take her away from her mother and to set her up in her own room for which he would pay the rent; to pay for her food and all her upkeep in that room and, finally, to give her money so that she would always have everything she needed" (16 vi 53). He really meant it. Such a liaison was one of the ways in which two people could form a real couple. We therefore often find marks of affection. Marie-Louise Pelletier, age twenty, said of Sieur de la Closerie, a merchant [négotiant], that he "was fond of her, paid her rent, and provided her with food and all her needs" (17 vi 48). Similarly, Renée Chopin said of Sieur Roy, merchant, "that he was fond of her" (30 ix 48).

Such unions, while corresponding to the exigencies of a new sentimentality, were nonetheless precarious. A few of them lasted so long that they may have come close to a stable concubinage. Sieur Stock le Holm, a merchant, frequented demoiselle Fey de la Grange, the daughter of a cloth and silk dealer [marchand de draps et soies], "with the greatest assiduity for over a year and a half . . . providing for all her needs in the apartment where she [was] living, and where he continue[d] to show very warm feelings for her," even promising to marry her (6 xii 83). This is an exceptional case, where the difference in social status does not seem to have been very pronounced. Normally these liaisons were short-lived and broken off by the pregnancy. These girls were not, strictly speaking, prostitutes, but they were not far from prostitution. Some had been, or would become, prostitutes. In 1761, for example, Scolastique Beaufreton was kept by Sieur Charon, a man of independent means [vivant bourgeoisement] from l'Isle Feydeau; in 1763 she was kept in lodgings by Sieur Chopin, a married man. But we know that as early as 1756 this girl was an unemployed domestic servant, living with her sister and pregnant by a sailor. We also know that in 1760 she was pregnant by Becot, a master shoemaker who paid her several times to accompany him to his country house at Vertou (12 viii 56, 27 ii 60, 1 ix 61, 12 iv 63).

Also at least close to prostitution was Suzanne Grimaldi, who was kept by Jean Vincent Ferraud, a merchant's clerk [commis de négotiant] (16 ix 87). She was lodging with the woman Desparnay, who, the record shows, had earlier been sentenced for prostitution together with a whole group of prostitutes (Archives municipales, Nantes, FF 272, inquests and sentences of 24 v 79). Jeanne Hubert was in the same situation (6 xii 85). She was lodging with the woman Coullaud, who had been in trouble with the law even longer ago (inquest of 21 vii 61). But this seems to be the normal pattern; first, prostitute, and then, with advancing years, procuress and keeper of lodgings. Men sometimes availed themselves of the services of a prostitute and sometimes kept a girl for a longer-lasting relationship. Sieur Delair, a controller of Le Salorges, appears twice, in 1756 and 1757, as the lover of Louise Le Roy, a shopkeeper. Seven years later he was named as the father of the child of Anne Hérisson, the twenty-seven-year-old widow of a glass-worker, who had already declared one illegitimate pregnancy the year before. During the same years, incidentally, two other Hérisson girls, Janne and Louise, also appeared in the registers. All of them were daughters of the lardmaker Louis Hérisson and of Anne Véquin, so they are clearly identified (6 vii 59, 1 ix 61, 25 ix 63, 23 iv 64, 29 xii 64).

PROSTITUTION

Some of the girls frankly admitted their profession. Marie Le Corre, for example "reserve[d] the right to make a fuller declaration against the said Terasson and others who ha[d] been the cause of her pregnancy" (14 ix 41). Then there are those with a suggestive nickname, such as "the belle of Sainte-Croix parish" (29 i 40). Anne Marie Garnier made it clear when she designated Sieur Coeur de Roy, the choir-priest of Saint-Nicolas: "It is a rather delicate matter, since she cannot deny having had relations with others" (6 xii 84). This declaration, incidentally, seems to be rather old fashioned, harking back to the days when some prostitutes boldly called themselves "women of the world" and refused to give any more information about themselves. By the late century, most gave themselves honorable professions, such as stocking-mender or seamstress. But prostitution can be spotted in various ways, for example, by checking the declarations against the reports of police investigations that give names and show networks of prostitution, and by certain convincing circumstances, such as the presence of a procuress in an indictment.

Many prostitutes were involved with procurers, male or female; sixteen such cases can be identified from our source. Jeanne Artaud was pregnant by Sieur Couder, who had "carnally enjoyed her . . . without making any promises . . . after she was taken to his house by the above-mentioned Gotte who had asked her to go there" (2 xii 65). Half of the girls who were taken around in this manner were from Nantes itself and belonged to this milieu by birth. When the woman Navarre was evicted from her lodgings in the rue de Bigon—and it was her fifth eviction in ten months—she was living with her sixteen-year old daughter, who had declared a pregnancy a few months earlier (2 xii 54). Françoise Christophe, widow Brodu, age forty, dressmaker . . . and fruit peddler, declared a pregnancy by Martin de la Bauche. "They saw each other on a marital basis," as the declaration made by widows put it; and he had been living with her, rue Saint-Léonard, in the parish of the same name (18 iii 43). Two years later, Anne Brodu, of the same address and very probably her daughter, attributed a pregnancy to Sieur de la Prestière, an individual we find often in these registers (23 ii 45). A few days later, proceedings were opened against widow Brodu, still at the same address, for "keeping loose girls" (Archives municipales, Nantes, FF, 271, case of 26 ii 45). One last example: in 1735 we find proceedings against Marie David, widow (another one) of a surgeon, living at Le Marchix. Implicated in this case were, among others, Gilles Baudry and his wife, Jeanne David, and the Montprofit woman. In 1757 a certain Marie David, age nineteen, was taken to Sieur de la Prestière, whom we already know. The girl was living with her aunt, the Montprofit woman. It should also be pointed out that these girls were young, since of the sixteen, six were under twenty and thirteen were under twenty-five years old.

Defined in this manner, the milieu of prostitution would seem to be quite restricted; in fact it was much more extensive. A number of circumstances mentioned in the declarations are unmistakable signs that prostitution was involved, and all of these are found several times. The most usual are the following: rendez-vous in a garden owned or rented by the client; the accosting of a girl in the street—and this is how a grand seigneur proceeded, like Sieur Saint-Mars Carderan, chevalier of the royal and military order of Saint Louis, who, having met Julienne Busson "on the promenade Saint-Pierre and having spoken to her, asked her to come to his house, where he enjoyed her carnally under the false pretext of intending to take her to his countryhouse of Saint-Mars du Désert" (17 ix 74); but the chevalier was certainly not the only one. Possibly because the girls wanted to make the attribution of paternity more plausible, such relations are not depicted as casual encounters but appear to have lasted for several weeks. Other prostitutes can be identified because they made several declarations, naming different fathers from a higher social milieu. This is the case of Catherine Peignon, who made the first of her five declarations at the age of seventeen, and subsequently named five men, all "sieurs," including an English gentleman and a rich Irishman (27 iii 51, 5 xii 54, 1 iv 56, 19 iv 58, 27 viii 59). In this manner we reach a total of approximately 120 prostitutes. This group shows a better age-group distribution, but two facts should be noted: (1) there is a somewhat higher proportion of immigrants from the countryside in this group than in the total group of girls; and (2) within this group of immigrants, there is a somewhat smaller proportion of peasants' daughters who have come to prostitution by way of domestic service and pregnancy due to their employer.

To this group of roughly one hundred, we can add most of those who state that there was "no promise whatever"—indicating that they were honoring a kind of contract. This gives us another hundred cases. Prostitution thus occupies an important place in the illicit sexual relations predicated upon social inequality.

Prostitutes were liable to criminal prosecution.[19] Whenever neighbors lodged a formal complaint concerning scandalous behavior, noise, insults, or violence, proceedings were instituted against the keepers of lodgings or even the owners of the houses, as well as against the girls. Depending on the case, the sentence was prison, eviction, or internment in the workhouse for the keepers and the girls. These sentences always involved dramatic measures: furniture was thrown into the street when there was an eviction; internment was accompanied by the taking of inventory and the placing of seals, as well as the burning of mattresses in the street or in the nearest square. These measures had practically no effect. Many of the prostitutes who had been prosecuted appear again and again in the registers or in subsequent judicial proceedings. Prostitution was simply too much a part of life in the big city. At Nantes, the rise in prostitution can clearly be seen at the time of the great expansion of the city, between the War of the Austrian Succession and the Seven Years' War. The latter, it should be noted, had very little impact on the incidence of prostitution, perhaps because the recession affected the well-to-do group of men who frequented prostitutes less than it affected the lower-class female population of the city.

CONCLUSIONS

There were three kinds of illicit sexual relations between men of higher and women of lower social status. Two of them, menial relationships and prostitution, had a quantitative impact. The third, the liaison with a kept woman, was more marginal but just as interesting, especially since it anticipated the nineteenth century. In terms of our graphs, the two principal forms evolve as follows: regular decline of the menial relationship, progressive rise in prostitution until the middle of the century, declining trend by the end of the century.

Certain social groups appear only rarely among the different milieus involved in these relationships. One of these is the nobility. There is the marquis de Becdelièvre, first president of the Chambre des comptes (28 ii

[19]Archives municipales, Nantes, FF. 271 and 272.

83), the marquis de Lespinasse (8 x 83), a couple of barristers of the Chambre des comptes (27 x 41, 19 viii 75), and a commissioner of audit in that body (29 v 72). One could cite other examples, but the total number would still be small, even considering the fact that this social group represented a small percentage of the total population. This makes the contrast with the world of commerce and the nascent industry of Nantes all the more striking. Sixty-nine merchants [*négociants*] appear in our registers, most of them more than once; in the 1780s, we find almost all of the calico manufacturers: Gorgeras (20 x 78), Huard (24 i 84), Cholt (16 xi 86), Langevin (31 viii 87), and Bourcard or Beauregard—four declarations—(2 x 82, 1 iii 84, 19 v 84, 13 xi 84). Sieur Bodichon, director of the royal rope manufactury, belonged to a similar milieu (20 vii 87).

Generally speaking, however, we note a decline in these illicit relationships between socially unequal partners by 1750, not only in terms of percentage but in absolute terms. This decline becomes more pronounced toward the end of the century; in the period 1780–87 these relationships represent only 4.1 percent of the total number reported in the registers. Does this mean that our document has changed? Or does it indicate less contact between differing social milieus and more adultery among people of the same world? However that may be, the marked rise in illegitimacy at the end of the century was due to the increased involvement of the lower classes.

Illicit Sexual Relations in the Urban Lower Classes

NEW FEELINGS, NEW BEHAVIOR

While we do not have any statistics for Nantes concerning the number of premarital conceptions in the second half of the eighteenth century, we do know that from 1750 on there was a rise in those illegitimate conceptions that can be placed in a context of matrimonial expectations. We cannot, of course, rely only on the formula "under promise of marriage," which, in itself, is rather unconvincing; but there are many cases in which an added detail or a specific formulation make it likely that a girl was justified in taking this promise seriously. Among these is the formula "engaged with the bans published" (28 x 42, 15 iv 52, 29 xi 53, 24 xi 72, 13 xi 75, 2 vi 76, 10 i 76, 29 x 78, 14 xi 78, 5 iii 87) and the promise made before a notary (12 i 73) or in the presence of a third party (1 viii 81, 5 v 83, 27 i 85). One couple had already signed the marriage contract (31 iii 72). In some cases the registering clerk noted in the margin that the marriage had subsequently taken place (19 vi 42, 10 vi 66, 27 viii 77). One of the fathers was waiting for the papers he needed in order to be married (1 x 78). The parents of the child stated expressly that they intended to keep their promise (8 xi 83, 14 ii 84, 29 x 84). Pierre Hubert and Catherine Grosseau were "distressed that the child [would] be born before the marriage" because the papers of the father, a native of the archbishopric of Besançon, had not arrived (13 vii 79). Renoux, a soldier, had asked for a "discharge" (20 iii 84). These conceptions fall into the category of pre-marital conceptions, even if the promise was not kept in the end.

Declarations in which the girl mentions a long-standing association are in the same category. Two and three years are not rare, even five or six. Historians are already aware of the long period of premarital acquaintance. Since the expanding city tended to dissolve the solid sociological structures—village, parish, and family—that had traditionally hemmed them in, it is not surprising that the freedom in which couples experienced the maturing of their love should lead to these results. We hear of some twenty cases of this nature between 1772 and 1787.

Some express themselves with a certain elegance: "The warm feelings they harbored for one another led them to give reciprocal proof of these feelings, notwithstanding the fact that their conduct is contrary to canonic prescriptions and the principles of our religion" (3 i 82). Others put it simply: "Since she believed in these promises, the said Tuaud seduced and took advantage of her, so that she is about seven or eight months pregnant, although she is not really sure of the time" (12 x 72).

A new mentality is also revealed in the couple's refusal to accept the objections of the family. In this area there was undoubtedly a growing gap between the jurisprudence of the Parlement of Brittany and the mores of the people. Sieur Bellanger, a surgeon's helper, had "repeatedly sought to marry Françoise Blineau" by asking the permission of her family, which had put off the marriage several times. He "requested her to enter into his plans by consenting to a carnal encounter, since this was the only way in which they could get married." We learn, however, that this affair did not end well, for his was not a "true promise to marry her" after all (19 iv 48). The same attitude was shown by Jean Jarnoux, who persuaded Jeanne Violain, age twenty, that "unless they went this far, they would not obtain their parents' consent; and that is why she consented to everything" (1 xi 78).

Social inequality sometimes explains the objections of the family. François Heurtin, "who [kept] the post station at Mauves," refused his daughter to Jean Poiraud, the apprentice postillon "who [did] the driving under him" (11 vi 78). The elder Madame Bodichon, widow of the director of the royal rope manufactury, did not give her son permission to marry a twenty-year-old American he had been frequenting for three years. This was the unfortunate side of the requirement for parental

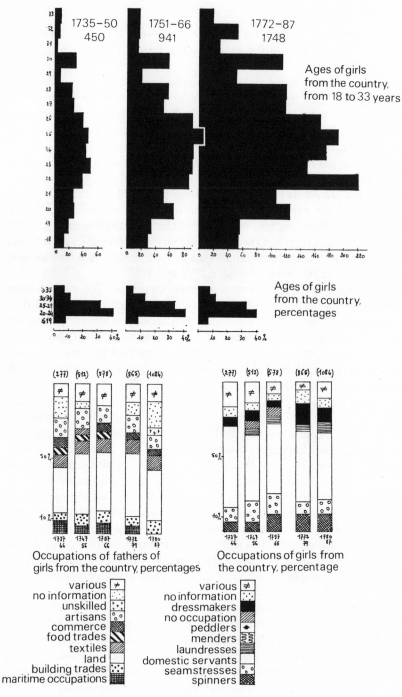

Figure 7.6. Girls from the Country and Girls from Nantes

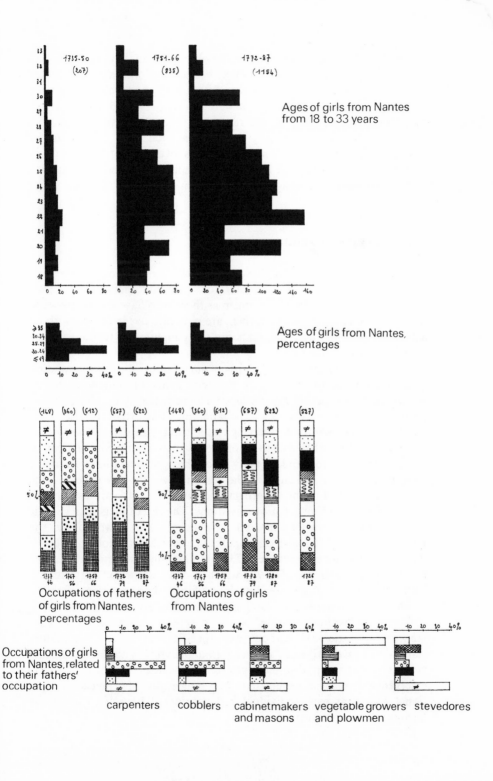

1735-50
(207)

1751-66
(835)

1772-87
(1154)

Ages of girls from Nantes
from 18 to 33 years

Ages of girls from Nantes,
percentages

Occupations of fathers
of girls from Nantes,
percentages

Occupations of girls
from Nantes

Occupations of girls
from Nantes, related
to their fathers'
occupation

carpenters   cobblers   cabinetmakers   vegetable growers   stevedores
                          and masons   and plowmen

consent until the age of twenty-five. Nicolas Chesnais, who accompanied Louise Ollivier when she came to make her declaration, stated that he had been wanting to marry her for a year. "Both have tried their best to make a formal promise of marriage, but were always prevented from doing so by Clément Rousseault, her guardian. . . . Their friendship having become even greater, they finally came to see each other in the manner prohibited by the Holy Canons." He was twenty-eight, and she was twenty-four years old (5 iii 83). "Definitely intends to marry" and "will marry as soon as she is of age" are expressions that occur repeatedly in the documents.

IMMIGRANTS AND GIRLS FROM NANTES

Not counting those who give no information, 40 percent of the girls from the rural milieu are daughters of "peasants" [*laboureurs*]. They present the same vocabulary problem as those who have come to town to have their child. Forty percent, then, are girls who live in the city without a family. Some of the immigrants are the daughters of textile workers, especially weavers [*tessiers*].

The family origins of the girls from Nantes show an evolution corresponding to the changes in the city's economic functions. In the beginning of our period few declarations are made by the daughters of port workers. Families working the land appear as often as those in the building trades; here I am referring to the market gardeners [*jardiniers*] of the outlying parishes such as Saint-Donatien and Saint-Similien. Shopkeeping and the food trades barely reach the 4 percent I have set as the minimum level for inclusion in the statistics. As the city develops, the share of the milieu of the waterfront increases. The girls are usually not the daughters of sailors, but of stevedores. The rise of illegitimacy in the building trade is not as steep, but it is steady. These two milieus, the building trade and the port, account for one fourth of the total number of illegitimate pregnancies between 1737 and 1746; their percentage amounts to almost one-half by 1772-79, which is the last period for which a sufficient number of precise data is available. By comparison, families connected with shopkeeping and the food trades are crowded out. Also, the category "without a trade" begins to appear. It is made up of "day-laborers" [*journaliers*] without any specific mention of occupation, "laborers" [*ouvriers*], and "workers" [*manoeuvres*]. This category bears witness, if not to an absolutely new economic structure, at least to the emergence of a social group that is no longer part of a precise occupational group, as each individual had considered himself to be at the beginning of the century.

For the ages of the girls and for their occupations and those of their lovers, we refer the reader to figures 7.6 and 7.7. Note that the girls from Nantes are definitely younger than those from the countryside. It should also be pointed out that the rise of illegitimacy among girls engaged in a trade, such as spinning, goes hand in hand with the development of the outskirts of the city.

STATISTICAL DEVELOPMENT OF THE TYPES OF COUPLES

We must begin with the raw data, for as illegitimacy was rising, and no doubt because it increasingly involved the lower classes, the declarations tended to provide less and less information.

We wanted to establish separate groups for the semipermanent liaisons on the one hand, and girls who declared several pregnancies on the other, in order to determine their respective share of illegitimate pregnancies. This operation presented us with a small difficulty because of the gap in our document between 1767 and 1771. We felt we needed homogeneous samples and were therefore obliged to make all of them equal to the last period, the time-span of which was dictated by the material. We are therefore using three sixteen-year periods. In order to insure that these three blocks of data are strictly equivalent, we have eliminated the girls whose different declarations overlap the time periods determined in this manner.

The size of the "milieu" of illegitimacy. To what extent were the girls who made several declarations, that is, those whom we might call the *habituées* of illicit sexual relations, responsible for the general rise in illegitimacy? And to what extent were those for whom an illegitimate conception was an episode, in the sense that it occurred only once, responsible? Table 7.1 enables us to measure the share of those who made up the veritable "milieu" of illegitimacy.

The sample that groups together girls who made several declarations confirms the decline of relationships based on social inequality, both in stable unions and in occasional encounters. But above all, table 7.1 shows that the rise in illegitimacy was not due to the girls for whom illegitimate pregnancies were a way of life. The percentage of girls who made several declarations is constantly decreasing. This decline would even be somewhat more pronounced if we had added to the "milieu" those whom we know to be part of it because they are sisters and cousins of certain women who made a number of declarations. However, these relationships are not easy to establish because the Christian names are sometimes ambiguous. The already cited case of the Hérisson sisters is not excep-

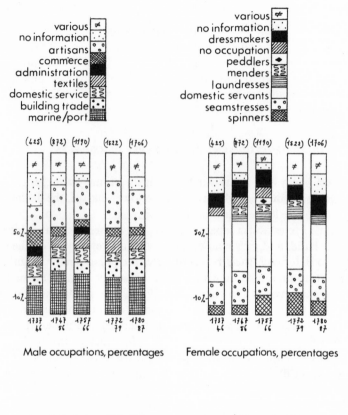

Male occupations, percentages Female occupations, percentages

Lovers of servants girls, percentages

Length of girls' stay in Nantes, percentages

not of domestic milieu
other employees in the same household
servants in same household
members of employer class

6.7 years
4.5 years
3 years
2 years
1 year

Figure 7.7. Illicit Couples in Nantes

1726-66

Columns (left to right): calico workers 3, laundresses 67, spinners 119, dressmakers 173, seamstresses 234, domestic servants 457

Rows (top to bottom): calico workers 3, boatmen 22, roofers 29, weavers 29, carpenters 42, stevedores 51, shipwrights 52, whig makers 56, vegetable growers 62, cabinet makers 63, ship captains 68, tailors 84, cobblers 121, sailors 174, domestic servants 200

OCCUPATIONAL CORRELATIONS OF ILLICIT COUPLES

1772–87

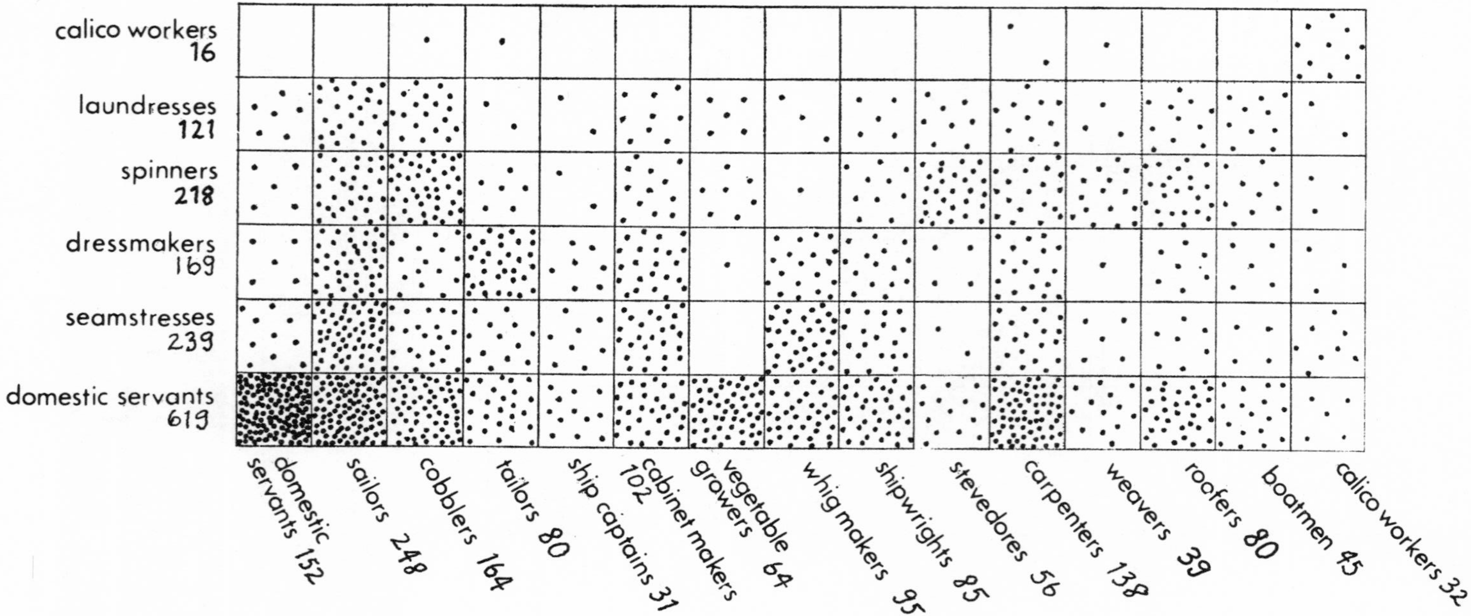
calico workers 16
laundresses 121
spinners 218
dressmakers 169
seamstresses 239
domestic servants 619
domestic servants 152
sailors 248
cobblers 164
tailors 80
ship captains 31
cabinet makers 102
vegetable growers 64
whig makers 95
shipwrights 85
stevedores 56
carpenters 138
weavers 39
roofers 80
boatmen 45
calico workers 32

tional, and thirty-six similar cases could be added to the "milieu" in the first period.

Stable unions. How many children were born to couples who made several declarations?

Table 7.2 shows that unions which lasted a long time and resulted in many children were rare; we have found only six, five of which fall into the last period. Declaring a child every year or every other year, these couples show the same pattern as legitimate couples. Why, then, did they not get married? Some could not because they were already married. In the course of the various declarations made by Marie Landais and Clair Averti, a married man, we can see the emergence of a typical pattern of open concubinage. In the second declaration, Marie Landais is still referred to as the servant of Clair Averti, a married barrel-maker. By the

Table 7.1—Size of the "Milieu" of Illegitimacy

		1735–50		1751–66		1772–87	
		No. of girls	*No. of declarations*	*No. of girls*	*No. of declarations*	*No. of girls*	*No. of declarations*
Social inequality	Pregnancies by same man	6	17	9	18	3	6
	Pregnancies by different men	10	11	29	52	18	19
Within lower class	Pregnancies by same man	11	23	18	36	32	75
	Pregnancies by different men	27	59	49	104	52	106
Diverse	1)		9		21		26
	2)		6		12		8
Total within "milieu"			125		243		240
Total of declarations for Nantes			725		1806		3228
Percentage from "milieu"			17%		13.4%		7.5%

1) Other pregnancies of girls who had a lover of higher social status.
2) Other pregnancies of girls who had formed stable liaisons.

Table 7.2—Number of Children Born to Stable Couples

	1735–59	1751–66	1772–87
2 children	22	18	27
3 children	1		1
4 children			2
5 children			1
6 children			1

third one, it is clearly stated that they have been living together for several years, a statement that is repeated until the sixth declaration (23 vi 76, 24 xii 76, 6 ii 79, 20 i 80, 25 iv 81, 28 iv 82). In another case, Nigre, who has had four children by Michelle Gaboriau, is a calico printer from "Parque" in Bohemia (?) (2 viii 78, 26 x 79, 23 i 81, 7 xii 81). The other men of these couples are one musician, one peddler, and one logger who, by the last declaration, has become a beggar. Were these couples also legally unable to marry or did they not want or rather not care to get married? We have no way of knowing, but it is important to note that there were very few such couples, even considering the possibility that the chronological limits of our samples may have made us lose a few.

To this type of concubinage we should also add the couples who, when making their declaration, insist on the permanent character of their union. An exemplary case is that of Mathurine Maillard, whose husband has perished at sea two years earlier: "She would be married if she had been able to obtain the papers for the death of her husband" (14 ix 59). A similar case, although it involves adultery, is that of the woman whose husband was a prisoner of war in England during the Seven Years' War. Against all legal rules, the child was to be baptized with the name of its real father, "and in the same way as they were living together as husband and wife" (6 x 79). This kind of concubinage was freely admitted. "Staying together," "living together," "with whom she has since that time (three years ago) passed in public as husband and wife," "ordinarily passing as husband and wife" (18 iii 43, 17 ii 78, 28 i 83, 15 i 49, 27 xi 60, 8 ix 63, etc.). In these unions one of the partners, usually the man, belonged to a marginal milieu—peddler (27 xi 60, 8 ix 63,) fiddler (21 vi 66), or sailor between voyages (11 i 83). This was also true for the few girls who were "brought along" from foreign lands. Thus Marguerite Flich of "Wittembourg" was brought along by a dragoon of the Coigny regiment (for other cases of a similar nature, see 29 viii 63, 22 ii 64, 31 i 65, 25 ii 72, etc.). But even if we add these men and these women together, they do not amount to a significant number.

The couples in this group of stable unions, then, usually had no more than two children. These children were born at intervals of fewer than two years in 85 percent of the cases, the most frequent interval being 17 to 24 months. Knowing, as we do, that many of these children were taken to the foundlings' home a few days after birth; knowing, in other words, that the mothers often did not breast-feed them, should we consider these intervals as long? The fact that these couples almost invariably stopped having children after the second pregnancy would be a somewhat safer indication that birth control was practiced, except for the fact that we cannot be sure how long these unions lasted. And if they were dissolved, what became of the women?

Unstable unions. A greater number of girls made several declarations naming different lovers. Let us count them in the same way we counted the girls who entered into stable unions (see table 7.3).

These findings are similar to those we obtained for stable unions. Practically none of these girls had more than two children. It should be kept in mind, however, that girls who have already been counted in one of the previous groups do not appear in this table. Two of these groups also give us the girls who had several children by different men. The first appears in the context of the relationships based on social inequality, especially in the 1750s. Recall the case of Catherine Peignon, who made five declarations. Marie Lebreton made four declarations (1 ii 57, 17 vi 60, 11 iii 62, 7 viii 66). For the period 1751–66, eleven girls declared a total of thirty-eight pregnancies, and for the period 1772–87, seven declared a total of twenty-six. Some of these girls were certainly, others almost certainly, prostitutes; but all of them show that the contraceptive practices of their time were of rather doubtful effectiveness, even in this milieu.

The second of the groups that has already been treated and gives us girls who had a number of illegitimate children by different men is that of stable lower-class unions. Here again, a few examples: Michelle Hamon declared two children by Jean Fleuriau (28 ii 84, 4 iii 85). She had already had, however, four children by four different men (9 iv 78, 2 vi 79, 29 x 81, 6 i 83). But these cases were relatively rare. We find only three for the period 1751–66, including that of Thérèse Largerie, who made seven declarations, two naming the same father and five falling within our time-

Table 7.3—Number of Children Born to Unstable Couples

	1735–50	1751–66	1772–87
2 children	22	38	50
3 children	5	8	2
4 children		1	
5 children			
6 children			

sample (25 v 51, 10 ii 53, 8 vi 55, 6 x 56). Only two girls fit that category in
the last period. Is this also a matter of prostitution? Probably yes,
whenever each one of a number of pregnancies involves a different man.
But if, as in the case of Marie Piou, there are only three pregnancies by
two men, one child by a baker's apprentice in 1779 and then, in 1784 and
1785, two children by Pierre Hubert, a house carpenter (17 vii 79, 1 ix 84,
12 xi 85)—in other words, if we find the same classic interval between
births we have found in the so-called stable unions—we are probably
dealing with two successive semistable concubinages.

What was the interval between births for girls who had two children by
two different men? One hundred cases are insufficient for tabulating these
data, since they would be overly dispersed. Furthermore, especially for
the last period, the only information available is the number of months of
pregnancy as stated by the girl; the date of the baptism is no longer
recorded. Despite these inadequacies we have found that for these girls
the interval between births was longer than for those in stable unions.
Intervals of more than three years were very rare among the latter, while
they were rather frequent for girls who changed lovers. For such girls,
these intervals even became slightly longer. The number of intervals of
more than three years increases from one-third to one-half of the cases,
while shorter intervals decrease. These long delays can only be due to the
time needed to form a new union. But it is difficult to see why this should
take longer toward the end of the century. In fact, one would expect to see
the contrary. This situation may therefore be an indication that the
understanding of contraceptive practices had improved.

All in all, however, we should probably not attach too much importance to this investigation of the girls by groups; it is obviously rather
difficult to manage. We should not attempt to isolate any of these groups
artificially, for we can see that many girls sometimes fall into one group,
sometimes into another. Furthermore, even though our source material is
ample, we soon reach the limit of our sampling technique, since most of
the girls made only one declaration. For this reason, the illicit sexual
relations within the lower classes must also be considered as a whole,
aside from any classification.

Occupational correlation of couples. Figure 7.7 shows that couples
were not formed haphazardly. Certain occupations attracted each other,
while others were incompatible; this was a constant pattern, since we see
little change from one table to the next.

First, there is one classic correlation: the illicit sexual relations of
market gardeners [*jardiniers*] almost exclusively involved domestic servants. Since we have already seen that the daughters of gardners were
destined to become domestic servants or to take up some other poorly

paid occupation, this is another indication that even in the close vicinity of Nantes the rural and the urban milieus existed side by side and hardly intermingled at all.

Many other positive correlations are explained by the working environment. The most characteristic of these is the almost exclusive correlation between the small number of male and female calico workers. There is also a correlation between weavers and spinners, tailors and seamstresses, and between the boatsmen and laundresses whose work brought them together by the river.

In other cases, we see certain cleavages. Why is there a close correlation between the stevedores of the port and the spinners of the Saint-Similien quarter, and between shoemakers and spinners, while the wigmakers are not interested in spinners and laundresses and only take up with menders and seamstresses? Pattern of residence may have something to do with this. Both wigmakers' apprentices and seamstresses probably lived in the center of town. But there were also social criteria. It was a matter of standard or, rather, style of living. The wigmakers were not interested in the "Gervaises" of Nantes. The same was true for the ship captains. Even though not many of them appear in the registers, their choice is clear: their girls were seamstresses and menders, never spinners or laundresses. These choices, then, reveal a kind of social hierarchy. In the lowest stratum, spinners and laundresses formed unions with stevedores and roofers. The carpenter, who was more apt to frequent menders and seamstresses, was somewhat better off. The tastes of the wigmakers were very different from those of the stevedores. The presence of these social criteria makes it appear likely that most of these couples lived together, even if it was not for long. This, then, was a matter of temporary liaisons rather than prostitution or casual encounters.

Seasonal fluctuation in conceptions.[20] Three graphs in the middle of figure 7.8 (nos. 1–3) enable us to compare legitimate and illegitimate conceptions. The two curves are rather similar, much more so than those for region-wide illegitimacy. As we go from the countryside to the city we see, once again, a leveling-off of seasonal variations.

In accounting for the seasonal variations of the first periods we must keep in mind the increased sexual activity of master-servant couples during the winter; these conceptions appear in graph no. 5 of figure 7.8. If they were deducted, the curves of legitimate and illegitimate conceptions would coincide even more closely.

Some modifications appear in the period 1772–87. Since servant girls were no longer as involved in menial relationships as they had once been,

[20]Figure 7.8.

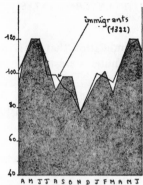

Seasonal distribution of conceptions among servant girls, 1772-87 (761), compared to distribution among immigrants (1,322)

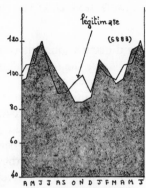

Total of illegitimate conceptions in Nantes, 1772-87 (2,256), compared to legitimate conceptions, extrapolated from data for three parishes, 1771-75 (6,883)

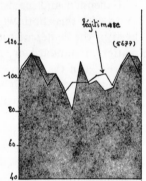

Total of illegitimate conceptions in Nantes, 1747-66 (1,902), compared to legitimate conceptions, extrapolated from data for three parishes, 1750-54 (5,677)

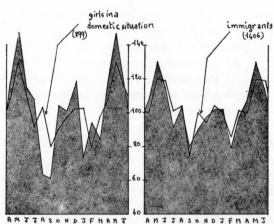

Seasonal distribution of conceptions among girls who concieved in a domestic situation, 1726-66 (355), compared to distribution among all servant girls (899)

Seasonal distribution of conceptions among servant girls, 1726-66 (899), compared to distribution among immigrants (1,406)

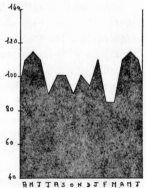

Total of illegitimate conceptions in Nantes, 1726-46 (630)

Figure 7.8. Seasonal Distribution of Illegitimate Conceptions in Nantes

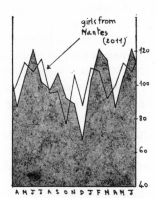

Seasonal distribution of conceptions among girls from Nantes under 20 years old, 1726-87 (488), compared to distribution among all girls from Nantes (2,011)

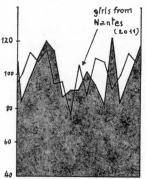

Seasonal distribution of conceptions among girls from Nantes who had a child by a sailor, 1726-87 (488), compared to distribution among all girls from Nantes (2,011)

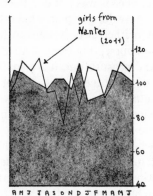

Seasonal distribution of conceptions among girls from Nantes who had a child by a construction worker, 1726-87 (318), compared to distribution among all girls from Nantes (2,011)

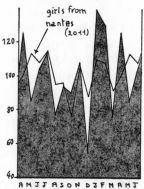

Seasonal distribution of conceptions among girls who had a child by a tailor, 1726-87 (170), compared to distribution among all girls from Nantes (2,011)

they also show the classic pattern of conceptions with a high point in June-July. Legitimate and illegitimate conceptions show a similar pattern. Nonetheless, within the group of illegitimate conceptions, some unusual features are noticeable. Thus, girls under twenty show distinctly seasonal behavior: there is a high point of conceptions in the spring and early summer, but also in January. This pattern appears only after 1772. It is very different from that of domestic servants. Does it indicate that new acquaintances were made during the festivities at the end of the year? Or during Carnival? The enticements of the city were, after all, quite different from those of the countryside. We should also note the distinct high point of sexual activity among tailors in January and the regular curve of the construction workers, who show a remarkable indifference in the spring. As for the sailors, why do they show maximum activity during the summer?

The outstanding feature of this pattern is the regularity of illegitimate conceptions throughout the year.

CONCLUSIONS

Seen as a whole, illegitmacy in the lower classes was not due to stable couples who for some reason were unable or unwilling to marry but otherwise behaved like legitimate couples. But neither does it seem to have been the result of prostitution. It is true, of course, that there is no clear-cut line between temporary concubinage and prostitution. It is also likely that we have missed many of the cases of prostitution because of the addresses given by the girls. However, the majority of the cases involve girls who declared one, at most two, illegitimate pregnancies. Can we explain this fact by contraception? There is no easy answer to this question. It would be surprising if girls who had two children within a rather short time—just like those living in stable unions—completely stopped giving birth even though they continued to live with men. Certain practices may lengthen the interval between births; but can they stop them altogether? It is doubtful; all the more so as we have already seen that these practices proved rather ineffective even for quasi-prostitutes.

In the lower classes, illicit sexual relations were not a matter of prostitution but, rather, of temporary unions formed as the result of the presence of a female population that had migrated to the city in search of work and that of a male population that was not rooted, owing to the rules of the journeymen's associations or new activities such as calico manufacture. It is a striking fact that illegitimate births among girls from Nantes itself increased only when the arrival of girls from the countryside slowed down and leveled off as soon as the influx of female workers accelerated. These lower-class couples did not fulfill the requirements for marriage: the unstable nature of their work, their poverty and, perhaps, the tradition of late marriage ruled marriage out; but this does not mean that no relationships were formed. These liaisons brought together men and women of a comparable social milieu. The eighteenth century often treated this situation realistically by providing ways to abandon children.

General Conclusion

Two figures are of outstanding importance: at the beginning of the century, illegitimate births represented 3.1 percent of all births; by the end of the century, the figure was 10.1 percent. Here we immediately see that illicit sexual contacts became increasingly frequent in the course of the century; at the same time, these figures give us an order of magnitude for the case of Nantes.

Along with this rise in the incidence of illegitimacy, we have found a profound change in the nature of illicit sexual relationships. At the beginning of the century these relations usually involved servant-girls and their masters, except in some particular milieus, such as that of the waterfront; at the end of the century, we find a predominance of temporary unions. This evolution was not a simple one. First, the domestic servant was replaced by the kept woman and the prostitute, but even though illicit sexual relationships became more widespread in a first phase, they still preserved their classic form: men of superior social standing were, in one way or another, using girls of a more humble social condition. The number of people involved in these relationships was relatively small. This type of illicit sexuality conformed to a certain social order, and society acknowledged that order by recognizing the financial responsibility of the man a girl designated as the father of her child, especially if he was her employer. By the end of the century, however, there was a distinct decline in these relationships based on social inequality; it is difficult to decide whether illicit sexual relationships were thenceforth formed more discreetly among men and women of the same social milieu or whether the great merchants of Nantes who, at one time, had tried to imitate the Farmers General,[21] now went in for some kind of morality à la Louis Philippe.*

[21] Yves Durand, *Les fermiers généraux* (Paris, 1971), p. 318.

*The Farmers General, to whom the royal government of the *Ancien Régime* "farmed out" the collection of indirect taxes, made huge profits on these operations and conveyed a public image of general profligacy. King Louis Philippe (1830–48), on the other hand, was intent on disassociating his regime from "aristocratic" profligacy by stressing the virtues of frugality, sobriety, and clean living. —Trans.

By the end of the century illegitimacy was concentrated in the lower classes. Certain indications, such as the relatively advanced age of the girls involved and the presence of social criteria in the formation of these couples, make it clear that these were not simply casual encounters but temporary unions. Couples met in a milieu that was part of the city but not integrated into it. They were journeymen and country girls who had come to the city in search of work. In fact, the girls from Nantes itself were in a comparable position with respect to their work and their dwelling places. The precarious nature of their livelihood is reflected in the precarious nature of their unions; these couples did not marry. Concubinage has already been identified as one of the characteristic patterns of behavior of the "dangerous classes."[22] Can we speak of "dangerous classes" for Nantes as early as the eighteenth century? Stevedores, spinners, male and female calico workers may have belonged to such a class; but we must not forget the very high proportion of domestic servants who hardly fit into that category. A new social differentiation may have been under way, but it was not yet clearly established.

More than anything else, this pattern of behavior reveals a new mentality, especially among women. It is the result of a three-fold emancipation. The first step is the emancipation from the traditional social hierarchy: young servant girls no longer yielded to their employer but instead chose a lover outside the house where they worked. Emancipation from religious morality is shown by the fact that these couples no longer subjected their love life to the requirement of a religious blessing. Finally, we see an emancipation, which may or may not have been intentional, from parental authority when a girl "made" her own life as she saw fit. In conjunction with the premarital conceptions, which were "mishaps" that have left a trace for us, and with the young peoples' demands for the right to form a recognized couple despite their parents' objections (a demand to which the writers of the Code Napoléon paid very little attention), these temporary unions were a corollary to the evolution that was to make the nuclear family, issuing from one couple, the basic unit of the bourgeois society of the nineteenth century, in contrast to the larger groups in which the society of the preceeding centuries had lived. Every new form of legitimacy spawns its own kind of illegitimacy. And the temporary union is no doubt one of the most radical forms of irregularity, since it involves only the couple and excludes the children who, more often than not, were abandoned. And if a society that is based on the family provides the opportunities for abandoning children, does it not seem to acknowledge implicitly that it does not consider these temporary unions to be part of it?

[22]Louis Chevalier, *Classes laborieuses, classes dangereuses* (Paris, 1958), p. 380. English translation by Frank Jellinek, *Laboring Classes and Dangerous Classes in Paris during the First Half of the Nineteenth Century* (New York, 1973).

But what was the situation in the older society? The evolution of illicit sexuality as we have described it here leaves us with two alternatives for the period that shows very little evidence of illicit sexual relations. It was either a matter of more effective contraceptive practices or of different behavior. At present, it is impossible to decide this question. We do not have sufficient information. We know very little about what was involved in abandoning a child, or about the punishments imposed for such an act; and we know nothing about infanticide. Even if we did know, we would also have to find out whether these punishments were actually applied to most of the crimes that were committed or whether the tacit complicity of the offenders' milieu protected many of them. On the other hand, the rigorous sanctions levied against certain ultimate forms of illicit sexual behavior such as sodomy;[23] the practice of court-ordered marriages[24] in defiance of the letter of the Ordinance of Blois, which prohibited marriage in cases of elopement;[25] the upholding of the rights of parents over their children, so evident in the jurisprudence of the parlements; the high regard for priestly celibacy—indeed, its glorification; and the increasing acceptance of the morality of Port Royal, even in the segments of society that were hostile to Jansenism—all these suggest that we should look for a culturally induced sexual behavior that cannot be prejudged,[26] especially in the light of such known facts as the practice of belated marriage, the small number of premarital conceptions, and the possibility that abstinence was widely practiced after the age of forty. For, after all, if illicit sexual relations were common in the seventeenth century, though masked by contraceptive practices, it would be difficult to see why the "deviants" [*irréguliers*] should have abandoned these practices and begun to produce children precisely at the moment when legitimate couples were making the first timid attempts to use them.

[23]People were still condemned to the stake by the Parlement of Paris as late as 1678, 1680, 1692, not counting the very special case of François Deschaufours in 1725. The burning of "sodomites" [i.e., homosexuals] lasted longer than that of witches. See Bibliothèque nationale (Paris), ms. fr. 10969 and 10970.

[24]Isambert, *Recueil des anciennes lois françaises*, 21: 338: "Declaration concerning elopement of 22 Nov. 1730."

[25]A. J. B. Boucher d'Argis, *Ordonnances du roi Henri III* (Paris, 1788), 14: p. 67.

[26]J. L. Flandrin, "Contraception, Marriage, and Sexual Relations in the Christian West," in *The Biology of Man in History*, ed. Robert Forster and Orest Ranum (Baltimore, 1974), pp. 46–47: "Instead, I believe that those who could not afford to have children found an outlet for their sexual impulses in illicit and sterile practises, including both solitary practises and fornication. In short, I believe that illicit relations were not the deeds of restricted groups on the outskirts of society, and that they involved contraceptive measures. Before the massive introduction of contraception into marriage, techniques were learned in 'sin.'"

8

The Seigneury and the Peasant Family in Eighteenth-Century Poland

Witold Kula

The family is a historical phenomenon. I do not need to remind the reader that biological factors play only a minor part in determining the family's size and structure. A discussion of the structure of the family group must involve the number of members, the assigned place each member holds within the group as a whole, and the independent, dependent, hierarchical, and functional links that connect the individual members of the family. Each individual belonging to the family group

Annales, E. S. C. 27 (July–October 1972): 949–58. Translated by Patricia M. Ranum.
Abbreviations:

Instr. I and II = B. Baranowski et al., eds. *Instrukcje gospodarcze dla dóbr magnackich i szlacheckich z XVII–XIX wieku* [Instructions for the Administration of the Estates of Magnates and Lords of the Seventeenth and Eighteenth Centuries] (Wrocław, 1958–63).

Pawlik I and II = S. Pawlik, ed., *Polskie instruktarze ekonomiczne z końca XVII i z XVIII w.* [Polish Economy Handbooks of the Late Seventeenth and the Eighteenth Centuries] (Cracow, 1915–29).

Kutrz.-Mank. = S. Kutrzeba and A. Mankowski, eds., *Polskie ustawy wiejskie, XV–XVIII w.* [Polish Village Laws of the Fifteenth through the Eighteenth Centuries]. Collectanea ex Archivo Collegii Iuridici XI (Cracow, 1938).

KRK = A. Keckowa and W. Palucki, eds., *Księgi Referendarii Koronnej z drugiej połowy XVIII wieku* [Ledgers of Referendaries of the Crown from the Second Half of the Eighteenth Century] (Warsaw, 1955–57), vols. 1 and 2.

Supl. = J. Leskiewicz and J. Michalski, eds., *Supliki chłopskie XVIII w. z archiwum prymasa M. Poniatowskiego* [Eighteenth-Century Peasant Petitions, from the Archives of the Primate M. Poniatowski] (Warsaw, 1954).

SPPP = *Starodawne prawa polskiego pomniki* [Monuments of Ancient Polish Law] (Wrocław, 1957–70), series 2, part 2: *Prawo wiejskie* [Village Laws], vols. 1–7.

occupies a different position within its structure. Thus, these individuals are almost never interchangeable.

The social character of the family has been the subject of scholarly research on numerous occasions. For example, many studies have been made of the process by which the large family is transformed into the small family, and of the various sorts of kinship. In this article I shall study the social factors that shaped the peasant family of eighteenth-century Poland.

A. V. Chaianov has studied similar problems, basing his conclusions upon materials pertinent to the Russian countryside at the end of the nineteenth and the beginning of the twentieth century.[1] His masterly analysis is especially sound since it relies upon the abundant documentation provided by agrarian statistics. Chaianov has shown convincingly how the structure of a given family was gradually modified throughout its existence as a result, first, of an increase in the number of nonactive consumers and, later, of an increase in the number of active persons and a reduction in the number of consumers. Thus, the family experienced a change in its productive strength as a result of the expansion or reduction of the size of its farm through purchases or sales. It also experienced a decrease or an increase in the efforts its active members had to put forth. Chaianov also shows how the family's productive mechanism changed as a result of its adaptation to changes in the family structure over the course of its existence as a unit.

In Poland, the composition and structure of the family seem to have adapted to the unchanging resources of the family's productive strength. It may be that the mechanism described by Chaianov—that is, the adaptation of the land to the family—was also present in eighteenth-century Poland, where land might be leased, be allowed to lie fallow, or be sold when the plowman's widow relinquished a part of her farm because she could not cultivate all the land or perform all the services required for such a large farm. Given the current state of research, it is not possible to say more than this. However, a great deal can be said about the effect of the farm upon the size of the family and the family's adaptation to the farm. Indeed, in this article I specifically intend to describe the methods used by the seigneurial manor to mold the peasant family.

From the viewpoint of the lord of the manor and his administrators, it was important to preserve a virtually constant number of settlers. The manor attempted to achieve this objective through countless ordinances forbidding marriages "outside" the domain. It was generally a matter of preventing girls from marrying boys from another seigneurial domain,[2] for

---

[1]A. V. Chaianov, *The Theory of Peasant Economy*, American Economic Association, Translation Series (Homewood, Ill., 1966).

[2]In the regulations [*Instr. I and II*], *KRK, Supl.*, and elsewhere, numerous ordinances can be found forbidding girls to marry outside the limits of specified domains. Here is an example

in such cases the girls generally moved from their own locality. Yet the manor also opposed a boy's marriage to a girl from "outside" when, because of the dowry, he was obliged to settle in his fiancée's village. These prohibitions were often motivated by the desire to prevent the "exit" of the dowry from the domain—for peasant property belonged to the lord—especially when, as was often the case, the principal component of the dowry was cattle, usually a cow. An individual had greater freedom in choosing his spouse on the large domains than on the smaller ones, since his choice encompassed the entire latifundium. One example among many is the regulation of 1733 for the villages of Zegrze and Rataje, properties of the city of Poznań, which stipulated: "Peasants . . . must not give their daughters in marriage within other jurisdictions but only within the domains belonging to this city."[3]

Since the lord and his administrators opposed marriages that would involve moving to other domains, they should have indicated satisfaction at seeing persons who had married "outside" come to settle on the manor's land. Little proof of such an attitude can be found. Stating such a position openly might have seemed too obvious. In order to justify their refusal to accept persons "from outside," lords gave as a reason the risk of becoming involved in long and costly lawsuits.[4]

However, the general number of peasants was not the manor's chief concern. The population tied to each domain had to have an appropriate structure that would assure the efficient functioning of the seigneurial estate. On this matter—and I wish to stress this point—the manor's aspirations were theoretically identical with those of the peasants.

The demographic structure of the peasant farm assigned each of its members an appropriate place, but the place each member occupied within this structure was individual and belonged only to him; it was not interchangeable. Each member's function within the family community was considered to be qualitatively different from that of the others and, as a result, was not equal. Elements that to us seem to be equivalent because they differ only quantitatively, in a precapitalist economy were, on the contrary and not without reason, considered to be different qualitatively and therefore were not deemed equivalent. This peculiarity was perhaps

chosen from a text at random: "Watch to see . . . that girls, especially rich girls . . . do not marry into other domains; also, it is appropriate to encourage in various manners more frequent marriages and marriage festivities, for which on seigneurial property two quarts of brandy and a keg and thirty-six quarts of beer will be allocated" (*Pawlik I*, 277 [1786]). Such a promise perhaps contributed to hastening the marriage of couples who were hesitating or who had no money for drinks.

[3] *Kutrz.-Mank.*, p. 262.

[4] One exception was the acceptance of men who had taken over a widow's farm through marriage, even if a compensation had to be paid to the bridegroom's former lord. See W. Dworzaczek, *"Dobrowolne" poddaństwo chłopów* (Warsaw, 1952).

most evident for human labor. For example, when death carried off the father—that is, the head of the family on a peasant farm—this empty place could not be filled by several grown daughters. Likewise, when a seigneurial estate lacked laborers with beasts of burden for the corvée, this gap could not be compensated for by an excess number of corvée laborers on foot. The traditional practice of equating one day of corvée with beasts of burden with two days of corvée on foot provides only a very rough idea of the true relationship. In practice, however, there could be no question of equivalence, first, because it was rather widely held that one day with beasts of burden was worth more than two days on foot;[5] second, because it was more difficult to obtain days with beasts of burden; and finally, because for certain field work two or even three days on foot could not replace the corvée with beasts of burden that the seigneurial estate lacked.

In order for the farm to function efficiently and be in a position to fulfill its obligations to the manor, all places had to be occupied and the structure had to be complete. The average life span was short during the period in question; thus, this equilibrium was quite often destroyed, and the manor strove to reestablish it. The short life expectancy, the high mortality rate, and the fundamental role played by the couple on the peasant farm of which it was the keystone necessitated the rapid reestablishment of this equilibrium through the remarriage of the surviving partner whenever the balance was tipped by the death of one of the marriage partners. There is nothing surprising about this, for peasant wills reveal extremely complicated situations in which one of the spouses, and sometimes both, had had children by two or even three previous marriages.[6]

An extremely serious situation was created by the death of the adult working male peasant. In such an event the lord was as strict as compelling circumstances obliged him to be. Often the widow was given a period during which she must remarry—for example, a year—under penalty of losing her rights to the farm. The regulation of Roś drawn up in 1804 stipulated on this point: "Widows of deceased plowmen must remain in possession of all the deceased's property under the surveillance of the councilmen and also of two plowmen . . . who are guardians. . . . It is ordered that the guardians see that the widow remarries within a year, and

---

[5]"Throughout Poland one day with beasts of burden is worth more than two days on foot," we read in the land records of Cracow for 1789, p. 133. The administrators of the primate's property assert that "the entire commune would revert to days on foot if we permitted them to pretend they lacked beasts of burden" (*Supl.*, p. 502). Despite the general practice it does happen that even in the accounts of the seigneurial estate, one day with beasts of burden is considered worth more than two days on foot (for example, in *KRK*, 2: 247, in which an act dated 1781 reckons a day on foot as worth 10 groszy; a day with beasts of burden, 1 złoty. The land records for Plock for 1765 [p. 118] calculate a day on foot as worth 6 groszy; a day with beasts of burden, 15 groszy, with 1 złoty equaling 30 groszy).

[6]However, wills are rarely found for really large families.

she must be warned that if during that period she does not remarry, then at the end of the year, counting from the day of her husband's death, everything will be sold at auction. . . ."[7]

When the heirs were unable to work the farm, to pay the taxes and, most important, to fulfill the obligations due the manor, the equilibrium was reestablished by selling a part of the land.[8] Such transactions were necessary if the peasant was to subsist. Thus, willingly or unwillingly, in the end the manor often approved such sales. However, it preferred to transfer the bereaved family to a smaller farm and to install in its place a family whose composition guaranteed its ability to assume all manorial obligations. In the village of Tacko, for example, a widow and her children initially paid the taxes and did work for the corvée, but it eventually became evident that she was in no position to continue. She was therefore obliged to leave the farm, which was immediately given to another peasant.[9]

If the widow's age prevented her from remarrying, her children were generally already grown. In such cases, the ordinances of great landowners required the adult son to marry immediately after his father's death,[10] in order to assure the proper functioning of the farm and to meet all the required obligations, the chief of which was the corvée.

Since almost as many men as women were widowed during this period, suitable provisions had to be made for either eventuality. The previously cited regulation of Roś of 1804 resolved the problem as follows: "If [the widower] has minor children, the authorities must see that he does not remain wifeless for more than a half year, by ordering him to marry under penalty of being removed from his farm."[11]

On the typical peasant farm, an important place was likewise given to the young working force, the sons and daughters who were able to work and who were still unmarried. The lord of the manor also was concerned with the young. For example, we find this order to punish children who, instead of helping their parents, "rent their working strength out to others. . . . Since children who are capable of working but who are frivolous leave their parents in order to settle and work elsewhere, and as a result act prejudicially against their parents and their own future, sons and

---

[7]Regulation for the commissioner of the Roś domain, 1804, in *Instr. I*, pp. 457 ff.

[8]*SPPP*, Uszwia, p. 110 (1652).

[9]*SPPP*, Tacko, pp. 240–41, no. 654 (1723).

[10]For example, the regulation addressed to the commissioner of the Roś domain in 1804: "Aged widows who can no longer marry as a result of their age must, at the very beginning of their widowhood, be removed from their farm, with the exception of those who have an adult son or daughter who could marry shortly after the father's death. In such a case, it is advised that the marriage be hastened and, when it has been contracted, the entire family may remain on the farm."

[11]*Instr. I*, pp. 457 ff.

daughters are therefore forbidden to hire themselves out to anyone without parental permission; and if a stubborn child should break this arrangement, he must, in full summer season or in any other season, rejoin his parents under penalty of losing his share in the inheritance; and he who refuses will pay the castle a fine of three crowns."[12]

Lastly, let us consider small children, who also had a place reserved for them. For example, priority was given to childless couples when it came to finding guardians for orphans. One of the texts referring to such a situation merits quotation. In a regulation of 1729 for the village of Grabowicz, the following passage appears: "If a peasant should happen to employ a manservant and the latter dies along with his wife, leaving small children, the peasant must raise them. If a childless neighbor asks to take one of them into his house, this will be permitted."[13]

Note that in the above cases the manor was attempting to assure full employment for the family groups within the peasant population. On this matter the manor shared the villagers' desire that each farm be assured its maximum capability to earn a profit. The peasant farm would be threatened if it were unable to supply the seigneurial estate with the quantitative and qualitative work demanded of it; the existence of the seigneurial estate would be impossible if peasant farms could not subsist.

The manor's position concerning the older members of the family is also clearly indicated. The lord respected the rights of the elderly—at least in his declarations, for actual practice is not always so simple—and ordered that they not be considered equals of the landless or of menservants or be forced to work for the corvée.[14] Nevertheless, the manor was chiefly concerned with the younger generation. Consider the inheritance laws.[15] The manor attached considerable importance to these laws and tried to find solutions that would be morally acceptable to the village. In addition, such problems were often very complicated, even if they involved nothing more than the rights of children born of several consecutive marriages. While studying those sources involving inheritances, one receives the impression—and in several instances the sources state this explicitly—that inheritance questions were solved openly, publicly, and in conformity with the moral

[12]Regulation for the starosty of Tuchola, dated 1749, in *Kutrz.-Mank.*, p. 316. Another regulation, dated 1767, addressed to the starosty of Płock contains an almost identical text (ibid., p. 404).

[13]Ibid., pp. 250–51.

[14]"Parents living with their children and having no land must not be forced to work weekly on the corvée, with the exception of warm days during the harvest, if they are able . . ." (*KRK*, 1: 449 [1779]; *KRK*, 2: 230 [1781], 311 [1782], 366 [1783], 463 [1785], 504 [1786], 533 [1786], 568 [1787], 588 [1787], 680 [1788], 710 [1788]).

[15]There is a scholarly Polish work by J. Rafacz on peasant customary laws relative to inheritances, but it does not deal with the problems that interest us. Moreover, in its very approach to the question this work should be revised in the light of the eight volumes of rural court registers that have been published since its appearance [*SPPP*].

judgments of the peasantry in order to satisfy the peasants of the middle generation. Such a procedure was intended to persuade them that by making the most of their farm they were indeed working for their children and that the rights of these children would be protected both by the moral sense of the villagers and by the will of the lord. The regulation of Roś states this clearly: "*In order to encourage people to work in a perfect fashion*, I have decided that the son or the son-in-law (preferably the son) will inherit from the deceased parent if at the moment of the peasant's death either is capable of replacing the father or can become so within the period of a year beginning with the date of his death."[16] It is impossible to be more explicit. This was but one more way of strengthening the peasant's bond to the soil.

The crucial point of the entire problem, however, is that respect for the rights of the children—and even for every one of the children, as was the case in Poland—to the inheritance was in direct contradiction to another policy of the manor that was extremely important to it: the attempt to prevent the large peasant farms possessing beasts of burden from being broken up into smaller units. For several new farms furnishing the seigneurial estate with work on foot could not take the place of a single large farm that provided work with beasts of burden.

The solution—which was not always realized, of course—was a simple one: see to it that the sons of rich peasants would marry the daughters of equally wealthy peasants. If the right to inherit was connected to the dowry, the children of the rich would remain rich. This very ingenious method was, however, rarely realizable, for it placed overly severe restrictions upon the choice of a marriage partner.

Thus, the manor's chief goal was to increase its population by preventing departures from the limits of its territory, by tolerating in certain cases people who came to settle upon lands which were a part of the manor, by seeing that a complete farming structure existed for the peasant farms, and by intervening each time the demographic structure of a peasant farm was weakened. An extremely interesting regulation of 1786 stated this position as follows: "And as for the well-being of the subjects, it is assured by the people themselves through the multiplication of marriages, which occurs only when the people see that they can find enough to eat and to feed their children and when they have considerable recourse to employing aides and domestic workers, whose number, in its turn . . . contributes to increasing the wealth of the peasants."[17]

It is almost as if the author had read the most recent studies in historical demography. Indeed, several of these recent studies reveal that during the preindustrial period, belated marriages were the principal means of

---

[16]*Instr. I*, pp. 457 ff.
[17]*Pawlik*, II, pp. 257–58.

limiting natural growth, while, inversely, early marriages were the principal factor accelerating demographic growth.

The author I have just quoted drew no noticeable distinction between the members of the family in the strict sense of the word and any servants permanently employed on the peasant farm. We are thus confronted with a *familia* in the Roman sense of the word. The large farms were the most important ones for the manor because of the corvée with beasts of burden. In order to function normally such farms could not get along without a stable and salaried labor force, even if such laborers merely cared for the livestock, which were undoubtedly rather numerous, and in addition assumed some of the burdens of the corvée. The problem was one of size, and the administrators of the manor were far from being unaware of this. One of the most frequent peasant grievances during this period centered upon the fact that, in view of the manor's excessive demands, the peasants did not succeed in keeping their menservants.[18] The large landowners would have interpreted such an accusation as a criticism of the administrator or tenant farmer.

The manor was therefore constantly concerned with maintaining the equilibrium between the farm and the labor force and also with reestablishing this balance whenever it was disturbed, as it very frequently was, by a family misfortune. Although this reestablishment of the equilibrium was on occasion achieved by adapting the surface under cultivation to the changes occurring in the active human potential of the peasant family, it was mainly achieved by adapting the size and composition of the family to the needs of the farm. This adaptation was accomplished by an unnaturally high growth in population caused by the early marriages of the children of those owning large farms; by an increase in the practice of taking distant relatives, such as a widowed sister or a dead brother's children, into the home; and by the use of salaried domestic servants. The demarcation line between the latter two groups was undoubtedly nebulous. Members of both groups were certainly equally subject to being exploited as members of the family labor force, as were the peasant's own children. Nonetheless, these relationships assured a roof, family support, and the basic necessities of life.

We might theorize that the large peasant families were that size because their farm was rich. Yet the inverse assertion seems to be at least as true: the farm was rich because the family was large. As long as the absolute minimum of labor was available, an increasing amount of labor could always be invested in a peasant farm to improve family consumption.[19] But such a labor force had to be available.

---

[18]*Supl.*, passim.
[19]K. Kautsky, *Die Agrarfrage* (Hannover, 1966).

In addition, the type of family the manor wanted to impose upon the peasants was chiefly related to the type of farm which the lord was most eager to have. The manor's chief concern was to have farms that could feed several beasts of burden, that had at least one son or a servant, and that were in a position to supply work with beasts of burden for the corvée, sometimes with two persons working. The manor therefore was eager to forbid the division of inheritances, which risked eliminating this sort of farm. "One must not permit subdivision, that is, division of peasant lands among several plowmen," we read in a regulation of 1825.[20] In another ruling, dated 1800, we find that "since the land is the lord's property, none of his subjects has the right . . . to share it among his relatives."[21] Here is the same idea in a more developed and nuanced form:

Since many plowmen demand that each peasant have sufficient land to feed his family; and since, according to an old custom, the lands have long been divided so that in many places they are broken into such small plots that the peasants do not manage to subsist; and although all sharing of lands is forbidden by my previous orders, desirous nonetheless of assuring the peasant a proportionate share of land, I advise the general administrator neither to grant a peasant having fewer than fifteen acres of land materials with which to build a house nor to permit him to build a house. On the contrary, he will take care to prevent any construction on small or subdivided lands, and even any major house repairs. Thus, when the houses built upon the small plots collapse, this land will be granted to another peasant and he will be helped to build.[22]

Here we have the manor's political position expressed in unequivocal terms. The manor wished to stop the widespread tendency among peasants to divide the inheritance among at least all the male heirs. But once the farm could no longer be divided—and while the peasants remained tied to the land and while these interdictions, though frequently broken, were nonetheless in force and prevented peasant sons from going to the city—the family could likewise no longer be subdivided. Indeed, where could those who left the family have gone? And how could the family have cultivated the large unbroken farm without them? In the sources we find opposition to the subdivision of even medium-sized farms, based on the belief that a farm could always use supplementary labor in a productive fashion. An anonymous author (Pawlikowski?) wrote in 1788—as if he had just been reading Chaianov—that when the peasant's children "grow, it is only then, by good fortune, that his affairs improve, since there are more hands to do the work. However, if the peasant has no children or if they have died, he

[20]*Instr. II*, p. 167.
[21]Ibid., p. 91.
[22]Ibid., p. 46 (dated 1798).

will have to live and die in famine."[23] This author was firmly convinced that the labor force on peasant farms was always undersupplied. "It would have been better," he wrote, "for the lords to have given the peasants less land and to have left them more time to cultivate it." He continues: "Which people are chosen as plowmen? Those who have adult children; otherwise, by working the corvée with two persons and two beasts of burden, a peasant would not have enough time in an entire week to work for himself. . . . If he has no children, he must hire domestic servants in their stead. . . . And domestic servants cost so much! . . . Children will go without necessities, but servants demand their due. And after the father's death, the children, wanting to preserve what they have acquired, generally remain together, even on a small farm, and work together in order not to become impoverished."

Another author wrote in the same vein in 1790: "A peasant who lives with his children instead of having separated from them, as long as they are numerous, even though they are not strong, will always manage to cultivate his land in a better fashion and to harvest more than a solitary peasant, without the aid and help of outsiders."[24] It was for this very reason that the regulation of 1773 for the domain of Roś directed the administrator to "establish serious young people upon abandoned farms, separating sons from fathers and brothers from brothers, when they live crowded together in a single house."[25]

Thus we see clearly how the manor attempted to prevent married children or adult brothers from remaining together on the same farm.[26] Now, if such a practice was opposed, it must have been common among the peasants.

Care of orphans and of close, distant, and sometimes very distant relatives was also regulated, generally in conformity with the community's moral judgments. Thus we do not find many normative declarations on this subject. However, the rarer such declarations are, the more interesting they become. There is, for example, a rather late text, dated 1804, but one that is undoubtedly valid for the preceding decades. Addressed to the commissioner of the Roś domain,[27] this regulation stated that the administration had the duty to procure a wet nurse for each orphaned infant and that such a child must then be "brought up until the age when it would be capable of performing some service." The author of this text believed that the

---

[23]*Materiały do dziejów Sejmu Czteroletniego* (Wrocław, 1955), 1: 25–26.
[24]"Not everyone is deceived. Bartek's conversation with a lord explains everything" (ibid., p. 351 [1790]).
[25]*Instr. I*, p. 438.
[26]A similar text can be found in *KRK*, 1: 440, dated 7 May 1779.
[27]*Instr. I*, pp. 457 ff.

newborn should remain with the wet nurse until the end of its first year and that the child would begin to be "capable of performing some service" at the beginning of its eleventh year: "If, after a year has passed, some peasant desires to take a child and raise it, he will be permitted to do so on condition that the child be assured a fatherly protection. . . . If they are raised until the age of ten by the same peasants, such children must, in exchange for support and sturdy clothing, serve these peasants between the ages of ten and eighteen years, and only excessive strictness, poor food, or shameful treatment can dispense them from this obligation. But, when this period of service has ended, the peasant must offer them a wedding feast." A little farther on the text continues: "Foundling children and orphans [in another portion of the text bastards are also included] with no money of their own, when they are in my service will be obliged, like the children raised among the peasants, to carry out services from their tenth to their eighteenth year in exchange for food and clothing."

It seems that, according to the moral judgments of the period, a child was a burden during the first ten years of his life; between the ages of ten and eighteen he repaid the cost of his upkeep and more, since the orphan was obliged to work among the peasants for eight years to repay the care he had received during the first ten years of his life. The prohibition about failing to meet this obligation is a further indication that the upkeep of the child until his tenth year constituted for the peasant-guardian a financial burden that the child had to repay through his work.

We read in the same document that "a widow remaining alone with several children who finds a husband rapidly and remains on the farm has the right to keep her children, especially if they are already of an age to be useful, on condition, however, that she marry a bachelor or a childless widower. If, on the other hand, she marries a widower with his own children, the commissioner must think the matter over and determine, on the basis of their financial capabilities and their need for help and services, the number of children of the two marriage partners that will be permitted to live with their parents, and to distribute the children according to the regulation."

This text confirms unequivocally the thesis presented above concerning the structure of the peasant family, both as a unit of production and a unit of consumption, in which each man occupied an important position, different from the others and not interchangeable with them. For example, too many ten-year-old children on a peasant farm would strain the farm's capacity to provide food; yet if their number fell too low, the peasant's need for "help and services" could not be met. One couple might have a large family while another had no children. One peasant man or woman might marry several times while others married only once. Epidemics might decimate certain families and spare others. Such errors of nature were corrected by the manor, which intervened to subtract children where they were too numerous and add them where not enough were to be found.

The manor attempted to impose upon the peasant family a form dictated by its own needs. Just as these needs required several types of peasant farm to coexist in the village, they likewise required the existence of several types of peasant family. Since the most important type of farm for the manor was the large farm that could do the corvée with beasts of burden, the manor's self-interest led it to make sure that such farms were occupied by large families, with an extended and complete structure. Having the productive forces at its disposal, the manor also attempted to shape the component formed by the peasant and his family. It had to be shaped in such a fashion that the farms would manage to feed the peasant family and provide an adequate amount of good-quality peasant manpower to cultivate the lands of the seigneurial estate.

9

Kinship and Social Organization in the Turko-Mongolian Cultural Area

Jean Cuisenier

The word *Turcoman* (or *Turkmen*) is the natural choice for designating the ancestral type of social organization of Turkish peoples. For the word *türkmän,* composed of the root *türk* and the intensifying suffix *man* or *män,* does indeed signify something like "pure-blooded Turk," "pure Turk," "noble Turk," or "super Turk."[1] Yet there are other than philological reasons for using the Turcomans to character-ize the prototype of social organization of Turkish peoples and the function of kinship within that social organization. We know that, unlike many other Turkish populations who became assimilated to such an extent that they were absorbed into the Persian and Chinese populations they had subjugated, the Turcomans never gave up the traditional forms of their social organization.[2] While it is true that some of their princes

Annales, E.S.C. 27 (July–October 1972): 923–46. Translated by Elborg Forster. The translator is much endebted to Doris Lidtke, who helped her to deal with the mathematical aspects of this article.
See J. Cuisenier, *Economie et parenté, Essai sur les affinités structurales entre système économique et système de parenté.* Book 1: "Le domaine turc," chap. 1, paragraphs 2 and 3 (Paris and The Hague, 1975).

[1]Jean Deny, *Grammaire de la langue turque (dialecte osmanli)* (Paris, 1921), p. 326; Ibrahim Kafesoğlu, "A propos du nom Türkman," *Oriens* 10 (1958): 156.

[2]Carleton S. Coon, *Caravan: The Story of the Middle East* (New York: Henry Holt & Co., 1951) pp. 221 ff.

founded dynasties and induced substantial segments of their tribes to become sedentary and urbanized, others perpetuated the way of life of their most remote predecessors and continued to regulate their social relations according to the pattern of their ancestral system.[3] But above all, the Turcomans and their ancestors, the Oghuz tribes and the Turks of the Orkhon, are not only peoples of the past, a past that was forgotten during the centuries of the Ottoman Empire; they are the cultural ancestors claimed by the present-day Turks in the course of the national revival movement that eventually brought forth modern Turkey from the ruins of the Ottoman Empire. To use the Oghuz Turcomans as the society of reference for a study of kinship and social organization in the Turkish cultural area will therefore serve not only to systematize a century of philology, archeology, and anthropology but also to restore the traits of that past which the modern Turks acknowledge as their own, thus tracing the outline of the nation they wish to be. Any investigation of kinship and social organization in the Turkish cultural area must therefore first accomplish two things: it must establish the range of kinship among the Turks, and it must identify the various social units to which an individual can belong, both in the society of the past they claim as their own and in the entire cultural area they consider related to them.

Kinship and the social units identifiable in the society of reference

The uncertainties in the terminology referring to the various types of social units in ancient Turkish societies have often been noted.[4] Thus the terms *il* or *äl* and *ulus* appear to be used interchangeably in the texts to designate the largest types of tribal groups.[5] Conversely, the word *boy* is mentioned in Ahmad Vefik Pasha's dictionary as referring to one of the smallest tribal subdivisions, while in Kāshgharī's dictionary it designates the great tribal units of the Oghuz.[6] To be sure, we now have Radloff's attempt to systematize this nomenclature. According to him, *ulus*, which he translates as "people," designates the largest type of unit; each *ulus* is divided into *il* or *äl*, "clans"; each "clan" into *ouimac* or *oimak*, "tribes";

[3]Vassiij Vladomirovic Barthold, *Histoire des Turcs d'Asie centrale.* French version by M. Donski (Paris, 1945) (*Collection Initiation à l'Islam,* III).

[4]Paul Pelliot, "Notes sur le *Turkestan* de M. W. Barthold," *T'oung Pao* 27 (1930): 262–63; Claude Cahen, "La première pénétration turque en Asie Mineure," *Byzantion* 18 (1948): 5 ff; Claude Cahen, *Pre-Ottoman Turkey: A General Survey of the Material and Spiritual Culture, c. 1071–1330*, trans. (from French) J. Jones-Williams (London: Sidgwick and Jackson, 1968), *passim.*

[5]Vassiij Vladomirovic Barthold, *Four Studies on the History of Central Asia*, trans. (from Russian) V. Minorsky and T. Minorsky (Leiden: E. J. Brill, 1956–62), 2: 27.

[6]Ibid., 3: 113.

each tribe into *boi*, "subtribes"; and each *boi* into *uruk*, "families."[7] But it seems unlikely that so rigid a terminology was ever used.[8] Indeed, the varying nomenclature of groups and subgroups should be taken as culturally significant, for it shows the fragile nature of the intermediate aggregations located midway between the domestic society on the one hand and the tribal units identified by signs and emblems on the other.[9] Under these circumstances we must find out to what extent the processes by which groups are formed or transformed can be accounted for in terms of coordinated and subordinated groups, in terms of ties of alliance and descent, or finally, in terms of economic considerations involving subsistence, pillage, and exchange.

FAMILY, KINSHIP SYSTEM, AND SUBSISTENCE ECONOMY

Given the natural and cultural milieu in which the ancient Turcomans were operating, the *aul* was the smallest social unit that permitted individuals to organize a viable subsistence economy. A text of Abu'l Ghazi shows this very well:

"I arrived at a village of the Khorasan called Mehine. From there one could see two *auls* at the edge of the black desert and one in the village of Mehine itself. I could see that the stakes of the tents belonging to the *aul* located in Mehine had been made in the Khorasan and that those of the tents by the edge of the sand were made by Turcomans. So I said to my men: 'The two *auls* living by the sand are *auls* of Turcomans from Abul Khan or, perhaps Manguichlaq. The *aul* in the village belongs to Turcomans who are subjects of Quzil-Bach, I can see it by their tents. So let us go to these two *auls*.' When I came to the first of them, I met a young boy. I asked him who lived in this *aul*, and he said that they were *Qizil-Ayaqs* (red-feet). 'But how did you come here?' I asked him, 'for you used to live at Manguichlaq.' 'The Qulmouqs,' he replied, 'attacked and pillaged us; they have taken away all our flocks. Those who were able to escape came here on foot, carrying their young children on their shoulders. We have been here three years and have built real tents (*oï*) only this year; before that we only had *alatchouk* (small tents open on one side).' "[10]

---

[7]V. V. (W.) Radloff, *Ethnographische Übersicht der Türkenstämme Sibiriens und der Mongolei. Besonderer Abdruck aus der vergleichenden Grammatik der nördlichen Türkensprachen von Wilhelm Radloff* (Leipzig: T. O. Weigell, 1883), 1: 1696–97.

[8]Barthold, *Four Studies*, 3: 116.

[9]Arminius Vambery, *Das Türkenvolk in seinen ethnologischen und ethnographischen Beziehungen* (Leipzig: F. A. Brockhaus, 1885), pp. 4–6; Aboul-Ghazi Behadour Khan, *Histoire des Mongols et des Tartares*, publiée, traduite, et annotée par le baron Desmaison, 2 vols. (Saint Petersburg: Impr. de l'Académie des Sciences, 1871–74), pp. 31 ff.

[10]Aboul-Ghazi Behadour Khan, *Histoire des Mongols et des Tartares*, p. 337.

The two-fold function of the aul for the ancient Turcomans is thus very clearly shown. On the one hand it enabled individuals to practice the minimal division of labor required by their techniques of animal husbandry, and on the other it constituted the elementary units—and these were the real core of any social life—of the larger tribal aggregations which, when united, were the basis for even more complex groupings. In its total dependence on livestock for subsistence, the day-to-day existence of the Turcomans followed the pattern of the pastoral nomads of Central Asia[11]—which was precisely the way of life of the Turks of the Orkhon, centuries earlier. Concerning the latter, we read in *Pien-i-Tien:* "Their usual occupation is animal husbandry; they are looking for land where there is water and grass, and they do not always stay in the same place. They live in felt tents, let their hair hang loose, wear the flap-ends of their garments to the left, eat meat, drink milk, and wear clothes made of leather and wool."[12] "During periods of famine," the Chinese historiographer adds, "they try to survive by reducing bones to powder and eating them."[13] The texts concerning the ancient Turcomans and the Turks of the Orkhon do not indicate whether all the members of an aul were kin or not or, if so, which relations of consanguinity or affinity were cultivated among them. Only ethnographic observation and sociological investigation conducted among contemporary Turcoman auls will enable us to see how the structural conditions in which the kinship system and the economic system function determine the make-up of these groupings; a better understanding of these structural conditions could also establish the parameters within which contingencies and events play their part.

Fortunately, at least the eleventh-century nomenclature of kinship as it was recorded by Kāshghari in the *Divan lugat at türk* is known to us with some precision from the texts.[14] This list can be reconstituted as follows:

Vocabulary of consanguinity			*Vocabulary of alliance*		
1. *ata*	father, grand-father	Fa, Fa Fa	1. *kälin*	son's wife, fiancée	So Wi
2. *ana*	mother	Mo	2. *qadïn*	wife's brother	Wi Br
3. *uja*	brother, kinsman	Br	3. *jurč*	wife's younger brother	Wi Yo Br

[11]Lawrence Krader, *People of Central Asia* (Bloomington: University of Indiana Press, 1963), p. 316.

[12]Stanislas Julien, "Documents historiques sur les Tou-Kioue (Turcs), extraits du Pien-i-tien et traduits par S. Julien," *Journal Asiatique* 1 (1864): 351, 352, 493, 495, 514, 531; 2: 203, 230–31, 233, 239, 392, 397, 410, 422. Also published separately as *Documents historiques* . . . (Paris: Payot, 1877). See also Mau-Tsai Liu, *Die chinesischen Nachrichten zur Geschichte der Ost-Türken (T'u-Küe)*, 2 vols. (Wiesbaden: O. Harrassowitz, 1958, 1: 10.)

[13]Liu, *Die chinesischen Nachrichten*, 1: 493.

[14]For a reconstruction, see Krader, *Peoples of Central Asia,* p. 392.

4. *ačïqïm*	older brother	Ol Br		4. *tünür*	in-law (wife's father, mother, brother)	Wi Fa Wi Mo, Wi Br
5. *qardaş*	brothers by the same father but by different mothers	Br		5. *är*	husband	Hu
6. *ikdiş*	brothers by the same mother but by different fathers	Br		6. *iči*	husband's older brother	Hu Ol Br
7. *äkä ajä*	older sister	Ol Si		7. *ini*	husband's younger brother	Hu Yo Br
8. *oğul*	son	So		8. *äkä*	husband's older sister	Hu Ol Si
9. *oğlan*	children	Children		9. *ädä*	wife's older sister	Wi Ol Si
10. *astal oğul*	younger son	Yo So		10. *sinil*	husband's younger sister	Hu Yo Si
11. *qïz*	daughter	Da		11. *baldïz*	wife's younger sister	Wi Yo Si
12. *tağai*	mother's brother	Mo Br		12. *ogaï ata*	stepfather	Step Fa
13. *cïqan*	mother's sister's son	Mo Si So		13. *ögaï oğul*	stepson	Step So
				14. *ögaî qïz*	stepdaughter	Step Da
				15. *jaznä*	older sister's husband	Ol Si Hu
				16. *nämizä*	wife's sister's husband	Wi Si Hu
				17. *jängä*	older brother's wife	Ol Br Wi

We see from this list that the combination of generation and primogeniture is perfectly coherent: no distinction between older and younger is made in the generation before Ego;* order of birth is indicated in the generation of Ego; and younger brothers and sisters are referred to as such in the generation following Ego. There is also a very significant dissymmetry in the use of terms according to sex: the terminology makes a distinction according to sex only for consanguineous relationships —those which in a graph are related to Ego by a single arch—namely, father and mother, son and daughter, brother and sister. But while for brother and sister there is a term indicating who is older, the nomenclature makes such a distinction among the children of the same father or the same mother only for males. The same is true for the other terms

*Anthropologists designate the person whose ancestors are traced in a genealogy as *Ego.*—Trans.

involving the sex of the individual: among the brothers and sisters by the same father but by different mothers and among those by the same mother but by different fathers, only male individuals are identified. The difference, finally, in the distribution of terms designating co-lineality is equally remarkable: among the co-lineal relations for which the distinction between paternal and maternal is pertinent, only the mother's brother and the mother's sister's son—in other words, the maternal co-lineals—are identified. All these indications are confirmed when we study the terms that change depending on the sex of the speaker. On the level of the generation of Ego, these terms make an even more complete distinction between older and younger than does the nomenclature of consanguinity (see table 9.1).

As for the graph showing relatives by alliance, all the possible links of an arc are identified, since every possible lexeme, or complete grammatical form, corresponds to an actually used term, as is shown in table 9.2. Two points, however, remain doubtful: First, Kāshgharī does not state exactly whether the word *qadïn*, "brother of the wife," expresses a category that includes both the older and the younger brother of the wife or whether it refers to the older brother only. Second, *äkä* means both "older sister of the husband" and "older sister of the wife." Also, among the links with two arches, only two of the eight possible relationships are identified: that between Ego and the husband of the older sister and that between Ego and the wife of the older brother. Furthermore, while there is a word, *kälin*, to designate the son's wife, there is no word to designate the wife. Generally speaking, then, this nomenclature is characterized by a remarkable development of the terminology of relations by marriage and by the precision with which the order of birth is indicated at the level of the generation of Ego. These traits have implications for the structure of kinship relations and therefore require a more extensive interpretation.

Assuming that Kāshgharī has exactly reproduced the Turkish terminology in Arabic[15]—and it is very likely that he did—an interpretation of

[15]Frithiof Rundgren, "Teyze und Cicä, Bemerkungen zu den Türkischen Verwandtschaftsnamen," *Oriens* 15 (1962): 325–36.

Table 9.1—System of Terms Designating the Brothers and Sisters of the Husband among the Oghuz Turkman of the Eleventh Century, Following Kāshgharī's Dictionary

	Male speaker			Female speaker	
	Brother	Sister		Brother	Sister
Older	*iči*	*äkä*	Older	*qadïn*	*äkä*
Younger	*ini*	*sinil*	Younger	*jurč*	*baldïz*

the Turcoman system of kinship can be developed only if we take into consideration the determining factors of that terminology, in particular the rules governing descent, residence, and alliances. Concerning alliances, however, the available data are unfortunately incomplete and, moreover, poorly dated.[16] Such an interpretation would also require more knowledge about the economic system than what we can gather from a few allusions; here again, the absence of available source material makes it impossible to go much further. This situation would be completely hopeless if the Turks of the Orkhon or the T'ou-Kioue Turks of the Chinese historiographers were not much better known in certain respects than the Turcomans of the eleventh century. But we can use the available information concerning the oldest Turkish culture known to us, provided the necessary methodological precautions are taken.

Despite an undeniable break in the transmittal of the instruments and signs of the culture, the nomenclature of the terms of kinship that can be reconstructed on the basis of the inscriptions of the ancient Turkish khans exhibits exactly the same structural traits as the kinship vocabulary of the Turcomans of the Oghuz as recorded by Kāshgharī. Here too we find that a distinction is made between older brother, *äci*, and younger brother, *ini*, between older sister, *äkä*, and younger sister, *sinil*; while no distinction is made between older brother and uncle, older sister and aunt. In ancient Turkish, a word like *küdagü*, which is found in both lists, means both son-in-law (husband of daughter) and brother-in-law (husband of younger sister). Thus we see that in both societies an individual's place in relation to the members of his family was determined by order of birth, not by genealogical level. The social cleavages of the system were vertical rather than horizontal. This concept is admirably expressed in a funeral inscription published by Ramstedt. After he has declared his name, indicated his titles, and praised his merits, the deceased khan speaks as follows:

enim yeti, urïm üc, qïzïm üc ärti, äblädim baġlädïm, qïzïmin qalïmsïz bertim, marïma yüzär toruġbertim yegäninim atîmin körtüm.

"My younger brothers were seven, my sons three, my daughters three. I have endowed each of my younger brothers and my sons, I have married my daughters into a tribe. I have given my daughters in marriage without asking for a bride-price. I have granted to each of my preceptors a hundred bay horses. I have lived long enough to see the sons of my daughters, *yegänini*, and the sons of my younger brothers and of my sons, *atîmi.*"[17]

---

[16]Claude Cahen, "The Historiography of the Seljuqid Period," in *Historians of the Middle East*, ed. B. Lewis and P. M. Holt (London: Oxford University Press, 1962), pp. 59 ff.

[17]Originally published by G. F. Ramstedt in 1913, this text was modified by Kaare Grǿnbech in "The Turkish System of Kinship," in *Studia orientalia Joanni Pedersen*

The last sentence of this text is remarkable: it distinguishes the sons of the daughters from those of the younger brothers and of the sons and at the same time places the brothers and the sons in the same category by mentioning their respective sons together. We now fully understand the reasons for the differentiation of terms depending on the sex of the speaker, which was characteristic of the Oghuz-Turkoman nomenclature. Kāshgharī, in his *Divan*, gives the following explanation:

"*yurč* is the younger brother of the wife, and a difference is made between the brother of the wife and the brother of the husband, because the brother of the husband is called *ini* when the former is younger than the latter. But if the former is older than the latter, he is called *iči*. The sister of the husband is called *sinil* when she is younger than he; when she is older than he, she is called *äkä*. The younger sister of the wife is called *baldïz* and the older *äkä*."[18]

Older brothers, older sisters, and younger brothers are, therefore, very precisely identified and named. But it is not explained why there is only one word, *äkä*, for "older sister," whether the speaker is male or female. As we shall see, this anomaly has considerable structural significance.

There are many linguistic proofs to show that the semantic extension of the term *äkä* is indeed wider than the mere study of the nomenclature would indicate. The most important of these proofs is the fact that this term is often used in conjunction with the word *tagai* to form expressions such as *teyze* (in Osmanli), *tay ece* (in Kirghiz), *tay aqas* (in Yakut). When using these words, the Turks mean not only the older sister and the brother of the mother but, in a more general sense, all the "maternal kin." In this manner the two opposing categories *iči/ini* and *äkä/sinil*, for male speakers, and *tagai/yurč* and *äkä/baldiz*, for female speakers, are the expression of an even deeper differentiation. The median term between *iči* and *tagai* is *äkä*, a term that is the real starting point for the fundamental dichotomy between *paternal* and *maternal* kin. We must realize that this dichotomy fulfills a real function in the Turkish system of kinship, a function that becomes clear as soon as one places the nomenclature of kinship into the context of the customary law.

We know from inscriptions found in Mongolia and from the Chinese historiographers that the ancient Turkish law prescribed that after the father's death, the son, the brother, or the nephews should marry their stepmothers, sisters-in-law, or the widows of their uncles.[19] One of the

---

septuagenario (Copenhagen: Munksgaard, 1953), p. 128. It was then reinterpreted and translated into German by Frithiof Rundgren, "Teyze und Čičä," p. 327 (full reference at n. 15, above).

[18]Mahmud Kāshgharī, *Kitab divan lughat al-türk,* ed. B. Atalay (Istanbul, 1915–17), 3: 7. Reinterpretation by Rundgren, "Teyze und Čičä," pp. 328–29.

[19]Julien, "Documents historiques," 1: 352.

specific cases known to us concerns the death of khan Qapghan: "Happily for my mother the khātūn, who resembled the goddess Oumaï," declares the khan Bilgä in the text of the inscription, "my brother Kul-Teghin took the place of her husband."[20] Among the wives of the father, only the mother of Ego was not included in the father's legacy, so that, with this one exception, the law was comprehensive: the widows of an older relative in the paternal line were inherited by younger agnates, or relatives of the male line, who married them. Yet this fate did not reduce the widows to the status of daughters who were chattels to be exchanged by the father within the strategic network of exchanges between lineages. Nor were they reduced to the status of married women whose dowries (*kalym*) could be used to pay fines imposed under the law. The customary law indirectly characterized the status of daughter and that of wife by saying: "For putting out an eye one has to give a daughter, and if there is no daughter, one has to give the property of the wife,"[21] namely, her dowry. A widow who had been inherited by an agnate, while subject to male authority just like a daughter or a married woman, nevertheless retained all her rights as a mother, provided, however, that her son was a minor. For it was the widow and not the man who inherited her who, in the name of her minor son, held all the claims to the inheritance to which the son was entitled. In princely families this was the right to the succession and to the titles; in noble families it was the right to endowments; and in poorer families it was the right to such properties as grazing grounds, livestock, and where applicable, slaves. The fact that a khātūn, the wife of Bidun Bokhar Khuda and mother of Tukshada, ruled Bukhārā for fifteen years shows that princely families still followed that ancient Turkish custom long after the eleventh century.[22] By subjecting widows, through marriage, to the control of the male line of the family in the person of the brother or the son of the deceased, the paternal kin, or "wife receivers" were able to keep a check on any initiative the maternal kin, or "wife providers," might have felt inclined to take through the intermediary of their natural representative in the lineage of their exchange partners. For in the final analysis it was from lineage to lineage, from one "kin of the bone" to another,[23] with each alternately taking the role of

[20]Wilhelm Thomsen, "Inscriptions de l'Orkhon déchiffrées," *Mémoires de la société Finno-Ougrienne* 5 (1896): 141.

[21]Iakinf Bichurin, *Sobranie Svedenil o narodakh obitavshikh v Srednei Azii v drevnie vremena* (Collections of Accounts of the Peoples Inhabiting Central Asia in Ancient Times), 2 vols. (Moscow and Leningrad, 1950), 1: 230, cited by L. Krader, *Peoples of Central Asia,* p. 186.

[22]Mohammed Narshakhi, *The History of Bukhara,* translated from a Persian abridgement of the Arabic original by Narshakhi by Richard N. Frye (Cambridge, Mass: Medieval Academy of America, 1954), pp. 10–11.

[23]Claude Lévi-Strauss, *Les structures élémentaires de la parenté* (Paris: P.U.F., 1949), p. 462. (English translation: *The Elementary Structures of Kinship* by J. H. Bell, I. R. von Sturmer, and R. Needham [Boston: Beacon Press, 1969].)

"provider" and "receiver," that the strategy of matrimonial exchanges was working.

It is not entirely clear, to be sure, whether the rules governing the relationships between lineages in princely families applied to all Turcoman families and whether the outstanding features of these families were due to their nobility or their wealth. But at least neither the Chinese historiographers nor the Arab geographers say anything to indicate that the rules of descent and alliance differed from family to family on these grounds. On the contrary, there is every indication that families were distinguished not so much by the nature of their camping units as by the number of elementary units they could muster and the kinds of allegiance that governed their clan meetings. It seems clear that at the level of the aul—insofar as groupings of this kind have left any trace of their existence—the social organization was indeed a function of kinship relations. The aul, a camping unit made up in such a way that it enabled a group of joint owners of livestock to exploit the flocks it needed for its subsistence, was constantly faced with two dangers: physical extinction if it should prove unable to provide its members with the necessary means of subsistence, and fragmentation if it should fail to establish the proper relations of coordination and subordination among its members. Whenever a society's technology is fixed once and for all—as it was in Turcoman culture in the eleventh century—the danger of physical extinction is inherent in the relationship between man and nature, which is determined by the interplay of demographic and climatic factors. As for fragmentation, it can only be the result of a failure in the functioning of the system itself. Such a failure clearly reveals the state of the relationships between the members of the group, and it should be added that these relationships depend on the manner in which the rules are followed by the members of the group. Since in Turcoman culture the relationships among the members of units just large enough to permit the exploitation of a flock were governed by the rules of kinship, it is not surprising that the logic of descent and alliance, rather than that of production, was also used to forestall the risk of fragmentation. This, then, was the governing principle that gave kinship a structural function within the social system.

But was this also true at another level of social organization, the level of the tribe? What was the logic that governed here and imparted its style to the functioning of the system?

TRIBE, MILITARY SYSTEM, AND THE ECONOMY OF PILLAGE

Given the uncertain terminology concerning the more complex forms of social organization, the only feasible way to explain the reasons for the formation and dissolution of such groupings is to examine the examples indirectly provided by the texts. The same reasons that motivated me to describe the Turcomans as a people showing the characteristic social organization common to all Turkish peoples now make it desirable to choose the group commanded by Seljuk and his descendants as the prototype of a tribal aggregation that was governed by both the principles of kinship and the exigencies of military efficiency.

At the beginning of the ninth century, Seljuk, the son of Dokak, a member of the Kïnïk tribe, was in the service of the *yabgu* (prince) of the Oghuz, at whose court he held the title and carried out the functions of *subāshi* or chief of the armies. He eventually felt threatened by the entourage of the *yabgu* and decided to leave, taking with him all his kin and all his flocks, altogether some one hundred kinsmen (counting only the males), many servants, 1,500 camels and 50,000 sheep.[24] Did this group constitute a tribe (*oba*) or only an unnamed splinter group of a tribe? In the absence of other indications this question is difficult to decide. Whatever the exact nature of such an aggregation, it was a quasi-tribal group that moved off with Seljuk and settled in the region of Bukhārā. Shortly thereafter, other groups from different Oghuz tribes came to swell the ranks of this first group, so that Seljuk's eldest son, successor to the command of the group, Arslan/Isrā'il, was able to assume the title of *yabgu*.

But the very reasons for conflict between the *yabgu* and the *subāshi* at the time of Seljuk himself were to cause discord among his descendants, so that the Oghuz tribes remained profoundly divided. Nonetheless, after 1025 the brothers Tughrïl and Chagrï, grandsons of Seljuk, and their uncle, another successor to the title, were able to play leading roles as *yabgu*. Their victories attracted other tribes, the Ivä, Dogär, Salghur, and Avshar, to them and their tribe, the Kïnïk; these tribes, incidentally, were later to play an important role in the conquest of Asia minor.[25] One of Tughrïl's subordinates held the tribal title of *ïnal* or *yïnal*; he appears to have acted as the chief of a military detachment or as head of the Kïnïk tribe.[26] Even after their victory over the punitive expedition launched against them in 1035 by the Ghaznevid Mas'ūd, the Seljukid chiefs did not conceive of themselves as members of one well-defined social and political entity. After they had defeated the Sultan, they opened negotiations concerning the occupation of Naça, Farawa, and Dehistan with him; but each chief sent a representative, each received an identical set of insignia as governor, and each consented to send a kinsman to his court to act as a hostage.[27] The practice of sharing power was so deeply engrained in these tribes that even in the twelfth century William of Tyre recorded a tradition according to which the representatives of these groups assembled to

[24]Claude Cahen, "Le Malik-Nameh et l'histoire des origines seljukides," *Oriens* 2 (1949): 43.

[25]Cahen, "La première pénétration turque en Asie Mineure," pp. 178 ff.

[26]Cahen, "Le Malik-Nameh," pp. 57–58; Clifford E. Bosworth, *The Ghaznavids: Their Empire in Afghanistan and Eastern Iran, 994–1040* (Edinburgh: University Press, 1963) p. 226.

[27]Bosworth, *The Ghaznavids*, p. 242.

draw lots among the arrows symbolizing their sovereignty in order to determine which one should be in command.

As for the Turcoman army, it was composed of horsemen equipped with bows and arrows who wore clothing made of skins and wool and who moved about practically unencumbered by impedimenta, although they kept their herds close to them. An example of this kind of warrior is the group of 200 men who in 1038 captured the town of Nishapur under the command of Ibrāhim Inal. The first armor appeared in the same year, for we know that it was worn by the 3000 horsemen who entered Nishapur and established the power of Tughrïl there. But it was Ghaznevid armor that had been looted on the battlefield where the Turcomans had defeated Mas'ūd's armies. When Tughrïl himself rode in triumph at the head of his horsemen, he carried the ritual bow and arrows, the ancient Oghuz symbols of authority over the tribe,[28] and when he took over the throne previously occupied by the Sultan of Nishapur, the emblem on his seal (*tughra*) and on his coins was the bow with arrows.[29]

Thus we see that the groupings involved in the historical origins of the Seljukid empire operated on the basis of a set of very diverse principles. Indeed, *oba* designates a group showing the following characteristics:
1. Families and camp groups cluster around an already existing entity that is identified by a name, various emblematic marks, and a legendary genealogy.
2. Power within the group is exercised by a war chief whose titles are inherited through the paternal line but whose real authority is based on talent and success.
3. The fact that families and camp groups attach themselves to an oba does not preclude the formation of larger aggregations made up of splinter groups belonging to different oba.
4. Aggregations of a number of different oba or of splinter groups belonging to different oba usually have a warlike purpose such as raids, pillage in enemy territory, or conquest.

Defined in this manner, the Turcoman oba is clearly the kind of social organization that corresponds point by point to what is called *bod* in the Turkish inscriptions of the Orkhon and *pu-lo* (or horde) by the Chinese historiographers.

We know that each one of these T'ou-Kioue hordes had a name and a chief whose title, in Chinese transcription, was *she* (*shad*); the respective titles for the leaders of smaller segments were in descending order, *K'u-lu-tsho, A-po, Hie-li-fa, T'u-t'u,* and *Sse-Kin.*[30]

---

[28]Barthold, *Four Studies,* 3: 116.
[29]Claude Cahen, "La Tughra seljukide," *Journal Asiatique* 234 (1943–45): 167.
[30]Liu, *Die chinesischen Nachrichten,* 1: 132.

The numerical strength of these hordes was not fixed, but it appears to have been on the order of 50,000 adult persons. *Pien-i-Tien*, for example, reports that in 627 the *Sse-Kin* of the *Sse-kie* arrived with 40,000 subjects to make his submission.[31] This account goes on to say that in the same period the powerful horde of *Shi-pi-Khan* numbered several tens of thousands of men[32] and that in 683 the three hordes of Yenmen included 100,000 soldiers, or approximately 250,000 persons.[33] Even though the horde was sufficiently numerous and well-organized to undertake pillaging raids in China, "international" political relations were not established at this level, but at the level of the khanat. It could happen, of course, that an individual horde might try to place itself under the protection of the emperor, just as it could happen that some splinter group from a horde might seek refuge within the Great Wall or hope to escape famine by migrating south of the Yellow River. Such attempts were possible precisely because it was the policy of the Chinese Empire to divide these groupings by supporting younger brothers against elder brothers or the brothers of a deceased khan against the latter's sons. Still, an aggregate of splinter groups or scattered populations did not add up to a khanat, as the Chinese were to find out around 640. At that time, the Chinese had gathered together various splinter groups of Turkish populations north of the Yellow River and given them as their chief a former khan by the name of A-sse-na-sse-mo, who had declared his submission to the emperor. The Chinese soon saw this population grow to 100,000 persons (40,000 soldiers) and 90,000 horses; but not even three years had passed before they realized that Sse-mo was unable to impose his authority and transform this motley crowd into a real people.[34]

The organizational principle of the tribal group and the forces that certain warrior chiefs were able to call to their aid were so threatening to the imperial Chinese dynasties that they made every effort to destroy the foundation of the Turkish social organization. For their part, the Turkish chiefs continued to place their trust in the fundamental principles of the tribal organization, knowing full well that much of their success was due to the mobilization of splinter groups and that even in the worst difficulties recourse to their fundamental principles of association had enabled them again and again to reconstitute their strength within short order. For this reason the strategy of both the Chinese and the Turks was to remain essentially unchanged between 546 and 745:

[31] Julien, "Documents historiques," 2: 230; Liu, *Die chinesischen Nachrichten,* 1: 196.
[32] Julien, "Documents historiques," 2: 233; Liu, *Die chinesischen Nachrichten,* 1: 71, 113.
[33] Julien, "Documents historiques," 2: 410; on the Yen-men see Liu, *Die chinesischen Nachrichten,* 1: 71 ff.
[34] Julien, "Documents historiques," 2: 392 ff; Liu, *Die chinesischen Nachrichten,* 1: 154 ff.

The Wei, the Tcheou, the Souei, and the T'ang had one unchanging aim, and that was to settle these tribes in the northern part of the empire by attaching them to the towns, which would become courts for the Turkish princes and centers of new agricultural activities for their subjects. If the Chinese emperors permitted these newly rallied subjects to keep their native dress, they certainly made every effort to destroy the foundations of their tribal organization by requiring Turkish princes to serve at court and by conferring Chinese titles upon them. They even went so far as to give them substantial material incentives to settle down. Thus in about 730, emperor T'ang gave the town of Pe-p'ing to Tho-li as a gift, stipulating that the taxes paid by the town's 700 families were to be Tho-li's revenue.[35] In 698 it was decided to give Me-Tchou 300,000 bushels of millet, 50,000 pieces of silk, and 3,000 agricultural implements as an incentive to permanent settlement.[36]

For their part, the Turks were perfectly aware that giving up their pastoral nomadism, their customary law, and the traditional grouping of families into tribes would inevitably mean the end of the groups as such. This is what is meant by khan Bilgä's statement in the inscriptions of the Orkhon: "Because some ignorant people accepted this invitation and came near (the plain in order to settle in China), many of your people are dead. If you go into that country, O Turkish people! you will die. But if you dwell in the land of Eutuken and send caravans and convoys; if you stay in the forest of Eutuken, where there is neither wealth nor trouble, then you will continue to preserve an everlasting empire, O Turkish people! and you will always eat your fill."[37] The subjected Turkish khans who had to live their lives within the confines of a palace or a town were most reluctant to give up their traditional ways. Thus we hear that Kie-li, who was not accustomed to a fixed dwelling, "pitched his felt tent in the middle of the palace, fell into a state of profound sadness, and could not endure his fate. Surrounded by the people of his household, he chanted plaintive airs and wept with them."[38]

But the abasement and the weakness to which the destruction of the khanats reduced the Turks of that period was even more pronounced in the West than in the East. Arab sources indicate that at the beginning of the ninth century the shah of Kaboul was required to furnish to the governor of Khorasan an annual tribute of 2,000 Oghuz slaves.[39] However, those Turkish khans who knew how to make use of all the resources provided by the traditional model of their social organization found ways not only to escape the pressure of the Chinese and to preserve their independence but even to increase their power. An example of such action is Ho-po-chi, an A-sse-na of the Tho-li horde. The (Chinese) historiographer describes how Ho-po-chi, threatened with destruction and death, "took the head of his horde and fled. A thousand horsemen pursued him without success. He went to hide on the north side of one of the Altai mountains, which fell off steeply on three sides and had only one passage for carts and horsemen. He later found a large, flat plain where he settled with all his subjects, 30,000 of whom

[35] Julien, "Documents historiques," 2: 239.
[36] Ibid., p. 422.
[37] Thomsen, "Inscriptions de l'Orkhon déchiffrées," p. 117.
[38] Julien, "Documents historiques," 2: 231.
[39] Bosworth, The Ghaznavids, p. 36.

were soldiers, and assumed the title of I-tchou-tche-pi-khan."[40] All of this amounted to reenacting the legend of A-sse-na, the heroic founder of the horde, in Ho-po-chi's own time. A similar exploit was successfully carried out by Quout-lough, that epic khan whom the inscription of Kocho-Tsaidam extols under the name of Elterich: having broken away with a few of his horsemen, he reassembled the tribes and governed them according to the traditional institutions, thereby restoring, for a time, the empire of the sixth century. Such a feat was unquestionably in keeping with the aspiration of his Turks: "As one man the Turkish populace said: I was once a people that had its own empire. Where is my empire now? I was a people that had its own qaghan. Where is my qaghan now? Thus they spoke, and by speaking thus they became enemies of the Chinese qaghan and renewed their hope of reestablishing and reorganizing themselves."[41]

The principle of tribal organization thus appears to have been the same among the Turcomans of the eleventh century as among the T'ou-Kioue Turks. It was based upon allegiance to a chief who was capable, by using strategies of retreat and ruse, of leading successful raiding expeditions or of rescuing the remnants of camp groups that had been destroyed by war. It is true, of course, that the hereditary functions of the chief were not open to every member of the group; to be eligible for succession a man first had to belong to certain kin-groups. However, while membership in these kin-groups was a necessary condition, it was not a sufficient condition for succeeding to the command of an oba. Among the possible candidates from the various kin-groups—and inclusion in that list was fixed by the rules of descent—the final selection was made on the basis of talent, which was proven by past exploits. This proof, in turn, was twofold, since the command of a tribe involved two functions. One function was military and concerned the conduct of aggressive and defensive warfare; the other was economic and concerned pillage and the accumulation of goods.[42] It should be added that there is no need to ask whether the operations undertaken in such a system were geared toward offensive and defensive warfare or toward profit and capital formation, for in Turcoman society these two objectives were inextricably bound together. For it is a fact that military ventures were almost invariably undertaken with a view to the potential booty and that their success was judged not so much in terms of the numbers of enemies killed, encampments destroyed, or towns sacked as in terms of the numbers of women, livestock, and slaves captured. Conversely, accumulation could only take place by means of aggression, and the culturally accepted, normal way to become rich was to count less on the natural growth of the herds than on

[40]Julien, "Documents historiques," 2: 397.
[41]Thomsen, "Inscriptions de l'Orkhon déchiffrées."
[42]For a list of the raiding expeditions in the Chinese annals, see Liu, *Die chinesischen Nachrichten,* 1: 433–39.

loot from military expeditions and on the profits from the sale of captured slaves. Tribal organization was so essential to the conduct of raiding expeditions that the only groups where this organization was still fully functional eight centuries later, when the nineteenth-century ethnologist Vambery studied them, were the Turcomans of Kharesm, northern Iran, and Khorasan. Their way of life provided the perfect example of an economy depending on livestock and female labor for subsistence and on the capture of slaves for profit.[43] These societies certainly did expect help, support, and participation from kinsfolk and affinity groups; in other words, they looked upon military manpower and female labor in terms of rights and obligations. Yet no one segment within the kin group would call on the aul unless it was necessary to amass a large force for a raiding expedition. Larger aggregations thus had a specific purpose, and the success of such a carefully calculated force could be measured very precisely, namely, in terms of the yield in captives, heads of livestock, ransom, and redemption. So rigorous was this "cost accounting" that the wide variety of operations undertaken was judged by only one criterion: the yield in booty. At the level of the Turcoman oba, then, military and economic exigencies called for identical activity. This *modus operandi* became the distinguishing trait of the culture and imparted its specific style to tribal existence.

And indeed, the oba is the fountainhead of all beliefs and customs, the scene of the primordial epic for the modern Turcomans as well as for those of the eleventh century.

It was, after all, by means of organizations of this type that the Scythians and the Huns, the T'ou-Kioue and the K'itan, the Ouigur, Karluks, Seljukids, Gengiskhanids, Timourids, and Ottomans successively founded empires on a worldwide scale, empires that supplanted the ancient dynasties of Persia and China and were as powerful as Rome itself.[44] In founding their empires the Turcomans and, before them, the T'ou-Kioue Turks were careful never to lose sight of this type of organization, to trust it in difficult times, and to return to it whenever it became necessary to draw from its virtues the strength to restore the fading glory of their empires. And if these empires were ephemeral, as all empires of the steppe must be, they were prestigious enough for many centuries to afford the great variety of tribes the framework they needed for concerted action.

[43]Arminius Vambery, *Voyages d'un faux derviche dans l'Asie centrale, de Téhéran à Khiva* . . . , trans. (from English) E. D. Forgues, abridged and ed. J. Belin de Launay (Paris: Hachette, 1877). For a fictional account, see also Joseph Arthur, Comte de Gobineau, *Les dépêches diplomatiques du comte de Gobineau en Perse*, ed. Jean Hythier (Geneva and Paris, 1859).

[44]René Grousset, *L'empire des steppes: Attila, Gengis-Khan, Tamerlan I et II* (Paris: Payot, 1939), p. 28.

EMPIRE, POLITICAL STRUCTURE, AND THE ECONOMY OF
CEREMONIAL EXCHANGES

Il or *äl*, the term Kashghāri used to designate empire, is an old Turkish
word, whereas the title given to the holder of imperial power, *qaghan*, is
an Iranian word. This dual vocabulary is one indication that there was a
great deal of instability at the highest level of Turcoman social organization. The conflicts that erupted among the Seljuk princes as soon as one
of them aspired to the imperial title also demonstrate that the Turks
themselves felt very differently about a simple rallying of the various
tribes under a war lord, on the one hand, and the integration of these
same tribes into an empire, on the other.[45]

Following his conquest of the towns of Khorasan, Tughrïl-beg remained the chief
of those tribes that had recognized his authority, regardless of the territories
where the groups belonging to these tribes were roaming. At the same time,
however, he also became the holder of territorial powers, the head of an
administration staffed by Iranians and the commander of a permanent, well-
equipped army that included specific means of war, such as mameluks, elephants,
and siege engines.[46] This new aspect of his power was contested by the other
Seljukid princes, eventually even by his uterine brother Ibrāhīm Inal; the rebels
justified their revolt by referring to the traditional rules concerning the allocation
of endowments and the sharing of loot. If Tughrïl-beg, therefore, did not want to
alienate the Turcomans who represented the basis of his power and the principle
of his superiority over the Persian, Kurdish, Arab, Armenian, and Greek armies
he was facing, he was obliged to give them plenty of leeway for their raiding
expeditions; but at the same time he also had to discipline these tribes and confine
them to a common territorial basis. This must have been the origin of the
movement that gradually brought the Turcomans into Azerbaijan, Armenia, and
finally Anatolia. For conquest was necessary to the very structure of the Seljukid
army and, indeed, of the society itself. Armies could only be maintained if their
leaders were given the concession to a territory (*iqta*) whose revenues permitted
them to serve and to keep the requisite number of horsemen. On the other hand,
the holder of political power could not possibly alienate the territories of the state
indefinitely without depleting the very substance of the state. Hence he directed
his forces and the ambitions of their leaders toward the exterior, and this was
precisely the direction taken by the less well-endowed among them, by the
younger sons of princely families and by all those who had lately joined the ranks;
in addition, all were spurred on by the spirit of *ghazwa*, holy war against

[45]P. Wittek, "Le rôle des tribus turques dans l'empire ottoman," in *Mélanges Georges
Smets* (Brussels: Librairie encyclopédique, 1952), p. 665.
[46]Claude Cahen, "La campagne de Mantzikert d'après les sources musulmanes,"
Byzantion 9 (1934): 613 ff.

Byzantium.[47] Claude Cahen has reconstructed the complex interplay of operations and the subtle strategy—a clever blend of political calculation and free rein for the roaming bands—employed between 1054 and the beginning of the twelfth century by Tughrïl-beg and later by his successors Alp Arslan and Malik Shah, both of whom were advised by the Persian vizir Nizām al Mulk.[48] This strategy enabled them to conquer the Sultanate, defeat the Byzantine empire, and transform Anatolia into a region settled by Oghuz tribes. Indeed, so concentrated was the Turcoman population in this ancient province of Rūm that Anatolia, in contrast to all the other regions that experienced Turcoman penetration at one period or another, became the center of Turkish power and remainded so until our own time.[49]

The Turcoman princes, then, substantially modified the traditional Turkish social organization. For the Turks of the Orkhon, empire or *äl* meant political power over the people, *bodun,* or all the tribes. Being the collective plural of *bod,* or tribe, the word *bodun* might be translated as "confederation of tribes" if the term "confederation" did not imply the idea of reciprocal ties between groups, an idea that was totally absent from the Turkish system of values in the early Middle Ages. We know, in fact, that all the tribes that constituted the *bodun* were called by the name of the dominant tribe.[50] Holding court in a brilliant setting[51] and distributing his aid, the khan exercised real political power, a power that was symbolized by, among other things, the distribution of the attributes of power, namely, the arrows the tribal chiefs received from the khan's own hands. The ten tribes were grouped together in two wings or divisions, according to their positions in relation to the south: Five arrows constituted the right or western wing, called Nou-che-pi by the Chinese, and the other five the left or eastern wing, called Tou-lou.[52] This political organization was a legacy of the Hiong-Hu, or Huns; on a larger and

[47]Claude Cahen, "L'évolution de l'Iqta du IXe au XIIIe siècle. Contribution à une histoire comparée des sociétés médiévales," *Annales, E.S.C.* (January–February 1953): 25 ff.

[48]Nizam oul-Moulk, *Siasset-Nameh, traité de gouvernement, composé pour le Sultan Malik-chah, par le vizir Nizam oul-Moulk, texte persan édité et traduit par Charles Schefer,* 2 vols. and 1 vol. suppl. (Paris: E. Leroux, 1891–97).

[49]Cahen, "La première pénétration turque," pp. 5 ff.

[50]René Giraud, *L'Empire des Turcs célestes, les règnes d'Elterich, Qapghan et Bilgä, 680–734. Contribution à l'histoire des Turcs d'Asie centrale* (Paris: A. Maisoneuve, 1960), p. 68.

[51]Menander Protector, "Continuatio historiae agathiae," in *Fragmenta historicorum graecorum,* collegit, disposuit, notis et prolegomenis illustravit Carolus Mullerus . . . (Paris: Firmin Didot, 1851), 4: 200–269.

[52]W. Thomsen, "Turcica. Etudes concernant ;'interprétation des inscriptions turques de la Mongolie et de la Sibérie," *Mémoires de la société Finno-Ougrienne* 37 (1916): 5–6.

more complex scale, it was none other than the organization of a people on the move that pitched its tents looking southward.

However, the functions of the khan of the T'ou-Kioue Turks were not limited to his command over the tribes. On the highest level of social organization he was also in charge of the continued functioning of the system of ceremonial exchanges between the Turks and the Chinese.

The principle of this exchange was immutable. Both sides made gifts of the "noble" goods produced by the country; namely, horses on the one hand and pieces of silk on the other.[53] A large volume of goods changed hands in this manner. In 553, for example, an embassy sent by Ko-lo, the successor of T'ou-men at the head of the T'ou-Kioue, took a present of 50,000 horses to the emperor of China. For his part, the emperor, who feared the incursions of the nomads, sent back to the khan 100,000 pieces of silk and brocade.[54] In 607 the T'ou-Kioue khan Kimin declared his submission and presented the emperor with 3,000 horses. In return the emperor gave him 13,000, later 200,000, pieces of silk. In 619, a Chinese delegation brought 30,000 pieces of silk to the T'ou-Kioue, while in 627 their khan made a present of 3,000 horses and 10,000 sheep.[55] These prestations and counterprestations were made at irregular intervals, since they were inevitably tied to the fluctuating political relations between the two states. We therefore hear of annual prestations in periods when alliances had more or less stabilized and of intermittent exchanges in periods when warlike operations overshadowed all others. Yet these exchanges were frequent enough for the Chinese to note that between 545 and 597 the T'ou-Kioue had sent no less than 370 delegations bearing their presents.[56] Backed by marriage alliances, these exchanges could assume a variety of meanings for the parties involved. They were offerings of gifts, but also payments of tributes; and the function of tribute could loom larger than that of gift depending on the configuration of power at any given moment. They also were donations, no less than means for applying pressure, for they called for a donation in return, which neither the Turks nor the Chinese ever hesitated to demand. The all-encompassing character of these prestations and their precise function in the strategy of both parties can be seen very clearly in a letter written in 584 by the T'ou-Kioue khan Chapo-lio to the emperor of China: "The august emperor of the Soui is the father of my wife; he is therefore my father-in-law. I, the husband of his daughter, may look upon myself as one of his children. Even though we live in two different countries, both of us are equally bound by feelings of affection and by our common love of justice. Now our union is firmly consolidated and it will last without interruption for a hundred thousand generations. The Heavens are witness to my oath; I shall never violate it. All the

[53]Thomsen, "Inscriptions de l'Orkhon déchiffrées," p. 132.
[54]Julien, "Documents historiques," 1: 343.
[55]Ibid., 1: 531 and 2: 203.
[56]Ibid., 1: 514.

sheep and horses in my kingdom belong to the august emperor, and all the silk in his states belongs to me; between us there is no difference."[57]

The most important functions of the ancient Turkish khan, then, were the military command of the tribes and the maintenance of regular international relations. No longer was it sufficient, as it had been when being khan was a matter of leading "ad hoc" agglomerations of tribes, to ensure the material success of raiding expeditions, each one of which was conceived as a separate entity, even though raids were repeated many times. The imperial khan had to make his calculations in a much wider context and had to balance his accounts, as it were, in terms as different as horses and pieces of silk. To be sure, the operations of the imperial khans were far from being of a commercial nature. Yet, despite the solemnity of these exchanges, certain proportional values were bound to become attached to the goods circulating in this manner; in a ceremonial economy of this kind, these values can be considered analogous to the exchange rate in a market economy. But neither party was interested in profit as such. What each expected from an exchange was not a gain that could be evaluated in terms of goods and services, and even less a financial gain, but rather the regularization of relations with other peoples and an improvement in security. But this does not mean that such operations did not have measurable economic consequences. Horses and pieces of silk were, after all, commodities of the market place, and the fact that an imperial khan had a noncommerical way of procuring them did not prevent him from bringing them into the one existing commercial channel where all the goods of that category were circulating, regardless of where they came from. Thus, the exercise of imperial power called for a special combination of procedures. While not neglecting recourse to kinship relations, which provided a valuable tool for political purposes, imperial power, like authority on the tribal level, was primarily geared toward military ends. But while the command of an oba was subject to the constant constraint of producing booty and was consequently unable to undertake any military ventures unrelated to economic considerations, imperial authority could subordinate economic considerations to military aims and gather in whatever the situation warranted, either the profits of war or the tokens of peace.

Of the two functions fulfilled by the khan in ancient Turkish society, the Turcoman princes of the eleventh century assumed only the first

[57]Ibid., p. 495. For a list based on the Chinese annals, enumerating the items conveyed by these missions, see Liu, *Die chinesischen Nachrichten,* 1: 402–17.

—military command of the tribes. Being primarily war lords, these princes gave their tribes free rein in the conduct of their raiding expeditions and made no effort to deal with the sultan in a system of relations analogous to those the T'ou-Kioue had maintained with the Chinese emperor. However, since these princes, too, had certain imperial ambitions, the objectives of their raiding expeditions were geared to their political objectives; furthermore, they did not hesitate to pattern their conduct, at least officially, on the newly adopted tenets of Islam. Having militarily overthrown the power of the Ghaznevids, the Turcoman princes were very careful not to interfere with the structure and the working of the Persian political system, of which they simply became the chiefs. Thus, at this highest level of social organization, the type of system they operated had certain similarities to the most ancient Turkish type, even though substantial differences are also noticeable.

But this difference in attitudes toward maintaining "international relations" is the only major difference between these two types of society. On the three levels of social organization recognized by the Turks themselves, that is, on the levels of the family, the tribe, and the empire, the economic system and the system of kinship functioned in analogous ways among the Turcomans and the T'ou-Kioue Turks. Shaped by the overriding concern for perpetuating and strengthening the group, the auls, insofar as they have left any discernible traces, were essentially regulated by the rules of kinship and descent and dominated by the exigencies of pastoral nomadism. Unfortunately, the data at our disposal are too scanty and too vague to enable us to discern how these groups worked out their strategies in terms of rules and constraints. But there is every reason to believe that in the aul decisions were made not so much in terms of production and exchange as in terms of descent and alliance, since the members of these camp units were kin and descendants of common ancestors, and that the rules governing the ownership of the livestock, the main source of consumable goods, were the very rules that governed kinship relations. At the level of the oba, the materials gathered by scholars are much richer, and consequently the functional rules governing this system can be seen more clearly. At this level the difference between the Turcomans and the T'ou-Kioue is slight. Their culture imparts the same style to the activities of the tribes, and this style is characterized by the need for military efficiency and the booty from raiding expeditions. Here the rules of kinship came into play only in the preliminary stages of a succession to power, since in the interest of the continued success of the raids the actual takeover called for an additional element of allegiance and patronage. At the level of the empire, the inherent logic of the activities undertaken was accepted by both the Turcomans and the T'ou-Kioue. Here again, rules of kinship came into play in the preliminary stages of succession to power only, while the conduct of operations was primarily governed by other principles, such as efficiency in military operations, continuity and economy in diplomatic endeavors, and reciprocity in international exchanges.

It can thus be said that the cultures of the Turks of the Orkhon and of the Turcomans of the eleventh century, while not identical, constitute two forms of the same prototype, a prototype whose chief characteristic is that activities undertaken at every level of social organization are governed by one predominant system of exigencies. If, for the reasons outlined above, we take the Turcomans of the eleventh century as the society of reference, the final step in exploring the problem fully is to find out whether the empirically observable Turco-Mongolian societies conform to this prototype at all and if so, to what extent they deviate from it.

The scope of kinship in the Turcoman prototype of social organization

Stated in these terms, an investigation that would provide satisfactory answers to our questions would demand that the variety of Turkish and Mongolian cultures be treated as the ancient Turcoman cultures have been treated here, namely, with equal attention to form and content, categories of thought and events of history. However, while it would be possible to do this for certain cultures—for example, the Hazara, the Kazak, or the Uzbek—the lack of documentation precludes a uniformly conducted investigation. Consequently, I must simplify my procedure and shall therefore begin by applying the means of comparison elaborated by Murdock and his associates, thus defining the prototype empirically as a set of cultural traits simultaneously observed in the society of reference, kinship being one of the subsets of this set. Then I shall estimate how the Turkish and Mongolian cultures, defined in this manner, deviate from the type. Finally, I shall try to determine the area of applicability and the limits of such a characterization, in other words, the function of kinship in the social organization of the societies observed.

THE TURKISH AND MONGOLIAN SOCIETIES AND THEIR CONFORMITY TO THE TYPE

Following the method outlined by Murdock, the Turcoman prototype of social organization can indeed be defined as a particular constellation of cultural traits. In this context, the documents we have interpreted above suggest that within the Turko-Mongolian language area the phrase *prototype of social organization* should be understood to mean the society that exhibits a combination of the following traits:

[1] The techniques of acquisition, processing, and consumption are selectively geared toward the manipulation of animal nature and are applied to the exploitation of the biological resources of certain species of domestic animals falling exclusively into the ovine, bovine, and caprine categories [Om].

[2] Agricultural techniques are not unknown but are not generally practiced. Cereals and flour are obtained by means of exchange, pillage, or special tributes levied on subjugated peoples [Oo].

[3] Animal husbandry is the dominant subsistence activity. Both men and women milk the animals, but guarding the flocks is an exclusively male occupation [Dn].

[4] Fishing is not practiced [Oo].

[5] Hunting and gathering furnish a large proportion of the subsistence. Hunting is an exclusively male activity [Im].

[6] The settlement pattern is the camp group and the endogamic deme, or dwelling unit [Bd].

[7] The dwelling unit is formed by the extended patrilineal family and comprises several households, one of which at least is frequently polygamous [E].

[8] Residence is patrilineal [Pp].

[9] Polygamy is practiced but in less than twenty percent of cases. The wife or wives are obtained upon payment of the bride-price, the *kalym* [Lb].

[10] The patrilineal kin groups are irregularly segmented, and endogamous marriage within the agnatic line is preferred [Qa].

[11] There are no matrilineal kin groups, but endogamous marriage within the cognatic line is preferred [a].

[12] Marriage with the closest relative from either the patrilineal or the matrilineal kin group is preferred [K].

[13] [58]

[14] Society is not stratified but does include slaves [Hh].

[15] Political integration takes place at the level of the principality or the empire. Succession is patrilineal and favors the son over the brother [Ls].[59]

---

[58] The sources do not permit us to determine what type of nomenclature the Turcomans of the eleventh century used to classify the different kinds of cousins.

[59] The numbers between brackets refer to the pairs of characteristics; the letters between brackets refer to the code of cultural traits used in Murdock's "World Ethnographic Sample." See George P. Murdock, "World Ethnographic Sample," *American Anthropologist* 59 (1957): 664–87.

Table 9.2—Comparison of Twelve Turkish and Mongolian Societies and the Turcoman Society of Reference

Society of reference	[1] Om	[2] Oo	[3] Dn	[4] Oo	[5] Im	[6] Bd	[7] E.	[8] Pp	[9] Lb	[10] Qa	[11] Oa	[12] K.	[13] ••	[14] Hh	[15] Ls
Turks (Anatolia)	-+	--	--	--	--	-+	•	-+	++	-+	+-	+•	••	--	--
Kashgai	++	++	+-	++	-+	+-	•	++	-+	+-	++	••	••	•+	--
Kazak	++	++	+-	+-	--	+-	-	++	--	+-	+-	••	••	+-	--
Turcomans (Merv)	-+	-•	--	++	--	--	+	++	++	++	++	••	••	++	++
Uzbek	+-	++	++	-•	++	-•	-	++	++	+-	++	••	••	++	++
Yakut	+-	++	+-	-•	-+	+-	+	+-	++	+-	+-	-•	••	+-	+-
Kalmyk	++	++	+-	++	--	-+	•	++	++	++	++	-•	••	++	+-
Hazara	-+	--	-+	++	--	--	+	++	++	+-	++	-•	••	•-	-+
Buryat	++	++	+-	++	+-	--	-	++	-+	--	++	-•	••	+-	--
Dagor	-+	--	--	--	++	--	-	++	-+	+-	+-	-+	••	--	--
Khalka	++	--	+-	++	-+	-•	-	++	-+	--	-•	+•	••	-+	++
Monguor	-+	--	--	--	-+	--	-	++	++	--	-+	•-	••	+-	-+

NOTE: The numbers above the columns refer to the *pairs of characteristics*, the letters refer to the *characteristics*. The sign + indicates identity, the sign − indicates difference, and the sign • indicates lack of information. On the scale of similarity to the society of reference, + equals +1, − equals −1, and • equals 0.

227

If, then, we take the Turcoman prototype of social organization to be a combination of the traits described above, we can determine the conformity of any of these Turkish and Mongolian societies to the prototype by determining to what extent their traits do or do not correlate. Table 9.2 indicates that, strictly speaking, none of the twelve Turkish and Mongolian societies listed in the "World Ethnographic Sample" shows all the traits characterizing the society of reference. However, all of them do share four characteristics with the society of reference:[60] the keeping and milking of ovine, bovine, and caprine livestock [1], patrilocal residence [8], marriage by means of the bride-price [9], and absence of organized matrilineal kin groups on the basis of matrilineal descent [11]. The other traits are present in the twelve societies to a greater or lesser extent, ranging from moderate (six societies share trait [14] with the society of reference, while five do not) to extreme (only one society shows trait [6], while ten do not).

This type of measurement still affords only a general indication of a society's degree of conformity to the prototype. These evaluations can be further refined by attaching to each society an index of conformity, R_c indicating its position in relation to the prototype.

Taking C to be the set of cultures, T the set of traits, and $X_{t,c}$ the values observed, we shall count 0 if the culture, c, does not show trait t, and 1 if it does show it, and ½ if we are not sure. We now define $R_c = \dfrac{\overset{\Sigma}{t} X_{c,t}}{M}$,

M being the total number of observable traits.

In this manner each society can be defined according to its degree of similarity to the society of reference. Figure 9.1 shows that the contemporary Uzbek and Qashgai are closest to the Turcomans of the eleventh century, since their $R_c = 0.63$ and 0.62 respectively. In establishing this relation, we have assumed that each of the traits considered is equally important in measuring the similarity to the prototype. One look at table 9.2, however, makes it evident that this hypothesis simplifies matters too much and should be revised. Some of the traits, such as marital residence [8], are insufficient to determine which of the Turkish and Mongolian societies are closest to or furthest removed from the Turcoman prototype. Lack of similarity with respect to other traits, however, such as the techniques of acquisition used [1], clearly sets a society apart. It is therefore necessary to assign a different weight to each of the traits and

---

[60]With the exception of the Yakut who do not share one of them.

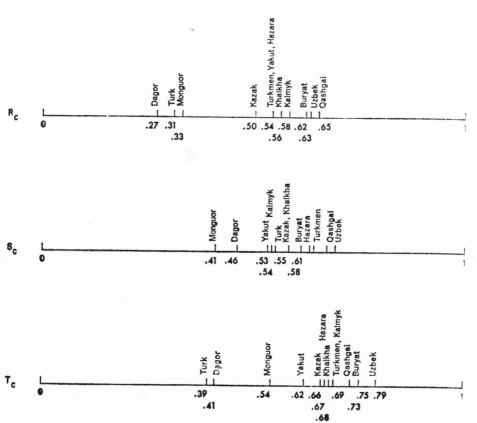

Figure 9.1. Similarity: Values Shown by Indices R , S , T

to construct a weighted index to place these differences in their proper perspective.

The importance of a trait for the degree of similarity of the Turkish and Mongolian societies to the prototype can now be expressed either by the

relationship $\lambda_t = \left| \dfrac{2 \overset{\Sigma}{c} X_{t,c} - N}{N} \right|$,

where N stands for the number of cultures examined, or by the relationship $\lambda'_t = \underset{c}{\Sigma} - X_{t,c} \mid N$.

This equation yields the value 0 when an equal number of agreements and disagreements is observed, and the value 1 in two cases, namely, when only agreements or only disagreements are observed. It is therefore possible to construct an index of similarity S_c between a culture c, and the prototypical culture by establishing the weighted sum of the $X_{t,c}$

using the coefficients λ_t, Σ_t λ_c $X_{t,c}$ and then dividing that sum by Σ λ_t so that it will vary between 0 and 1:

$$S_c = \frac{\Sigma \lambda_t X_{t,c}}{\Sigma_t \lambda_t}$$

Analogously, we will find

$$T_c = \frac{\underset{t}{\Sigma} \lambda_t' X_{t,c}}{\underset{t}{\Sigma} \lambda_t'}$$

With respect to their similarity to type Ic, the values obtained by means of this formula show the twelve societies to be arranged in the following order: (1) Uzbek, (2) Buryat, (3) Qasghaï, (4) Turcoman and Kalmyk, (6) Khalka, (7) Hazara, (8) Kazak, (9) Yakut, (10) Monguor, (11) Dagor, and (12) Turks of Anatolia (fig. 9.2). But this measurement can be refined still further, and it is possible to evaluate not only the total distance from the prototype but also as many differences as there are discernible "dimensions" in each of the cultures under consideration. It is helpful to recall that the factor analyses of Murdock's samples undertaken by Sawyer and Levine[61] show that all cultural traits can be placed into one of three categories: social organization, economic orientation, and social stratification. By recalculating the values of the coefficient R_c for each of these groups of traits, or "cultural dimensions," one obtains some remarkable results. In figure 9.2 the positions of the twelve Turkish and Mongolian cultures are shown on three axes, indicating their similarity to the prototype with respect to social organization, economic orientation, and social stratification.

This operation yields the following results:
1. The positions of the twelve Turkish and Mongolian cultures on the three axes representing three cultural dimensions are widely dispersed, ranging between 0.22 and 0.81; 0.24 and 0.93; and 0 and 0.8 respectively.
2. Relatively speaking, the least dispersion is evident in the dimension of social organization.
3. The pattern of dispersion among the cultures varies from dimension to dimension.

Each in its own way, the twelve Turkish and Mongolian cultures thus differ appreciably from the Turcoman prototype of social organization.

[61]J. Sawyer and R. A. Levine, "Cultural Dimensions: A Factor Analysis of the World Ethnographic Sample," *American Anthropologist* 68 (1966): 708–31.

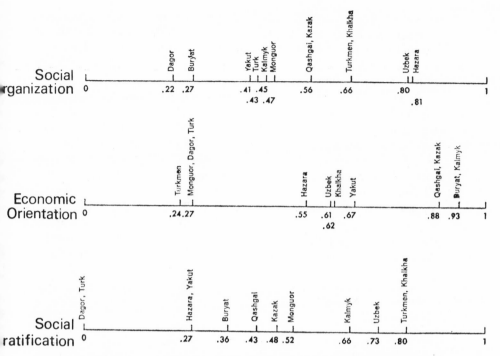

Figure 9.2. Degree of Similarity of Twelve Turkish and Mongolian Societies to the Prototypical Turkoman Society, with Respect to Social Organization, Economic Orientation, and Social Stratification

Once these differences have come to light, they must be explained. To this end, I shall try to pinpoint the respective position of the variables within the range of variation and, in particular, the position of kinship within this pattern.

VARIATIONS IN PATTERN AND VARIATIONS IN FUNCTION

However much we may endeavor to refine our techniques for establishing the similarity to the prototype, we are still faced with two difficulties that interfere with any analysis of this kind. One of these is related to statistical technique, the other to sociological interpretation.

In the formulas we have considered thus far, closeness to the prototype is defined by measuring similarity. But this similarity is always perceived in an identical manner, namely, by adding up the agreements and disagreements observed on thirty unweighted scales between the positions or values found for the society of reference and the positions and values found for the societies that are being compared. Unfortunately, however, this procedure fails to indicate the position of the society of reference within the constellation of values found for all the societies that resemble it. To discover which factors are involved in that system of similarities, a different type of analysis is needed.

A factor analysis of similarities performed according to J. Benzecri's method[62] (fig. 9.3) indicates how, with respect to the traits under consideration, the twelve Turkish societies for which appropriate data exist are grouped in relation to each other and what position each of them occupies in relation to the society of reference. Here we can see how close the Turcomans of Merv are to the prototype, although the Uzbek, Khalka, and Hazar are almost as close. The Buryat, Monguor, and Dagor are far removed, though not so far as the Turks of Anatolia, who are furthest not only from the prototype but also from the other Turkish cultures. Analyzing the system of traits by the same method, we observe a relatively pronounced interaction of the variables. Figure 9.4 also shows

[62]J. P. Benzecri, *Analyse factorielle des proximités* (Paris: Institut statistique de l'Université de Paris, 1964–65).

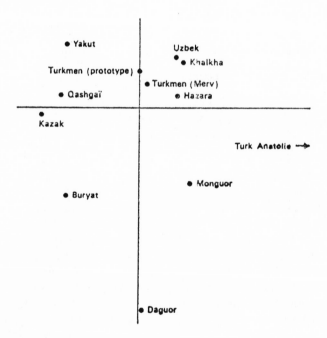

Figure 9.3. Position of Turkish Cultures in Relation to Each Other and to the Prototype

Figure 9.4. Respective Positions of Traits Characterizing Turkish Cultures

clustering of certain traits:[63] [18 b] *marriage by means of bride-price*, [15 P] *patrilocal marital residence*, and [21 O] *absence of matrilineal kinship organization* are clustered together, as are [19 Q] *segmentary lineage organization*, [13 E] *extended family*, [28 h] *hereditary slavery*, [20 a] *marriage with a parallel cousin*, [12 d] *demes or dwelling communities with a marked tendency toward endogamy*, and [23 K] *bilaterally organized kin groups*. By contrast, one trait, [9 I] *hunting and gathering*, is clearly isolated. Finally, the position of trait [02 M], *keeping and milking of bovine livestock*, is unusual: even though it is distant from such technical and economic traits as [03 O] *agriculture absent as subsistence*, [04 o] *agriculture absent as activity*, [01 O] *cereals not cultivated*, [07 O] *fishing absent*, [28 h] *hereditary slavery*, and [05 D] *animal husbandry dominating*, it appears together with certain other traits relating to social organization, such as [19 Q] *segmentary lineage organization*, [21 O] *absence of unilineal kin groups*, and [15 P] *patrilocal residence*.

[63]The traits are identified by the same symbols that were used by Murdock in "World Ethnographic Sample."

If we now superimpose the two patterns, we will be able to evaluate simultaneously not only the degrees of similarity of the cultures within a given pattern of variables, but also the degree of similarity of the variables within a given pattern of cultures. Thus it becomes clear that if the Turcomans of Merv are closest to the Turcoman prototype of social organization, it is because they show few traits that are theirs alone, and most of the traits they exhibit are identical to those of the prototype. Similarly, if the variables [19 Q] *segmentary lineage organization*, [13 E] *extended family*, [28 h] *hereditary slavery*, are clustered in the vicinity of the position occupied by the prototype and by the culture of the Turcomans of Merv, this situation must be attributed to the fact that these cultures and the "neighboring" ones of the Uzbek, Khalka and Hazara specifically show a number of these traits. The position of traits [20 a] *marriage with a parallel cousin*, [12 d] *community of residence organized into endogamic demes*, and [23 K] *bilateral kinship organization* at the extreme right of the figure, where the Turks of Anatolia are also located, makes it appear likely that this culture and this particular pattern of traits are closely related. These two analyses, then, complement each other, because it is possible to express them in "compatible" graphic terms. Their combined use enables us to measure the variations observable in the field and thus to evaluate the manner in which actually observed patterns vary within the system of social organization.

Nonetheless, it is clear that this type of analysis does not provide a measuring device for the variations affecting the *functioning* of this social organization. In a comparative schema of this kind the various terminologies of kinships, for example, would appear to form an identical structural system applicable to all the societies that can be related to the prototype. In the same manner the rules governing matrimonial transactions would appear to be identical throughout the entire area of variation, since these transactions are invariably summarized under the heading "bride-price marriage." But we know from the texts describing the ancient Turcoman society that the same terminologies and the same regulations assumed different meanings depending on whether they operated at the level of the camp group, the tribe, or the empire.

The schematic presentation of the prototype by means of a list of characteristics, such as we have outlined here, is therefore a very useful tool for the identification of types. It provides the means for the morphological analysis of a social *species,* which is the first step in establishing the characteristics of a *genus.*

What is the position of kinship in the Turkish social system? What is its function in identifiable social groupings? To what extent can the Turcoman prototype be applied to the other Turkish cultures? What is the significance of the differences we can discern in this respect between the society of reference and the observed societies? The present study has given some preliminary answers to these questions, but these answers raise as many new questions.

For in choosing the Oghuz Turcomans as the society that must be described in order to account for the origins of the Turkish system of kinship, I was careful not to characterize this *genus* by reference to a social species selected at random, which would be an arbitrarily chosen past. On the contrary, it is a deliberately chosen past, being the one that the present-day Turks recognize as their own. We must therefore realize that referring to a particular society introduces an element of distortion into the morphological analysis, since it gives a specific direction to the study of similarities between the various specimens of the type. Thus, the analysis furnishes more than just the ethnographic and historical framework that enables us to recognize the ancient prototype in contemporary Turkish societies. It also gives us specific tools for investigating the social groupings we can observe today. We might wish to ask, for example, which social groupings in contemporary Turkish societies are analogous to the ancient Turcoman *aul, oba*, and *äl*. And if we should find that these analogous groupings are operating on the same level of social organization as in the ancient prototype, it would be important to know how the categories and rules of kinship had functioned in the ancient prototype.

But since it has become clear that the Turcoman prototype of social organization is not only a constellation of cultural traits or a theoretical model we can use to understand empirically observable systems but the very embodiment of an ideal type for a particular society, we would arbitrarily restrict our comparative investigation if we limited our theoretical ambition to the task of discerning similarities in social organization solely on the basis of summarily established agreements and disagreements. We have already seen that, in the prototype, kinship assumed different functions depending on the level of social organization at which it operated. In the same manner, and even more understandably, kinship patterns exhibit homologous structures but dissimilar functions from one Turkish or Mongolian society to the next. It is quite possible for alliance and descent or production and consumption *as cultural traits* to coincide more or less closely throughout the Turko-Mongolian cultural area; but this does not mean that either the different positions of the system of kinship within the social system or the variety of decisions that can be made within the space of possible strategies necessarily share any real affinity.

Throughout the entire Turko-Mongolian cultural area, then, the categories of kindred and allies and the rules governing descent and alliance provide the members of these societies with two sets of tools that can be manipulated for a wide variety of ends. By means of this tradition of kinship, the Turks can identify with the most glorious cultural ancestors, be they the Oghuz Turks of legend, or Attila, or the Alp Arslan of history; they can also arrange the most fruitful operations, such as raids and the imposition of tributes and taxes. In short, they know that their social organization has given the greatest continuity to Turkish power. After all, the descendents of Othman are the only modern European dynasty that has held power for three centuries without interruption.

10

From Malthus to Max Weber: Belated Marriage and the Spirit of Enterprise

André Burguière

Thanks to a statistical analysis of family fertility, there is no longer any doubt that by the eighteenth century contraception through continence, as recommended by Malthus, had spread throughout the mass of the French population. But the interpretation of this phenomenon remains difficult, for the phenomenon that we view in terms of demographic mechanisms when we spot it in fertility curves only has meaning to the degree that it reflects a more profound and more complex change in mentalities.

We can, of course, isolate the phenomenon from its historical context. The shift to the use of contraception occurs sooner or later in every society along the road to industrialization. In our day, numerous nations of the Third World are attempting artificially to promote birth control in order to hasten their economic development, but the resistance they are encountering shows that the phenomenon goes beyond mere knowledge of contraceptive methods and involves the entire cultural structure of a society. To ask why contraceptive measures spread through France during the eighteenth century and how they came to be invented or reinvented is really to ask a single question. Contraceptive measures—in this case the crudest and most common form, coitus interruptus—were

Annales E. S. C. 27 (July–October 1972): 1128–38. Translated by Patricia M. Ranum.

strictly forbidden by the Catholic Church and were condemned as
unnatural acts.[1] Catholic circles had therefore long considered the
introduction of contraceptive techniques as an impious act. Such an
innovation was explained either as part of a dechristianizing movement
that was impelling one segment of the population to lose respect for
religious morality or, more simply, as a general decline in morality. The
latter position was akin to that taken by the "political arithmeticians" of
the period, those discerning and troubled observers of demographic
transformation. For one of them, Moheau, the spread of "baneful secrets"
was proof that the moral corruption of the cities, already evident in the
increased number of abandoned children, would spread to the countryside.

We know how difficult it is to interpret the indices of morality
provided by demography. The increase of illegitimacy can be attributed as
much to a modification in premarital relations as to an increase in
adultery or debauchery. As for the increased number of abandoned
children in cities—who were automatically considered illegitimate—it
seems that in many cases married couples were limiting the number of
dependents since they could not limit the number of births. Above all, it is
difficult to imagine that an interdict against contraception could be
known and strictly obeyed over a long period. Every prohibition cries out
to be broken. In addition, since the subconscious, reflex attitudes, and
impulses play a predominant role in sexual matters, sexual behavior
demands a stronger constraint than that provided by a simple moral code.

Philippe Ariès,[2] a pioneer in this still barely explored terrain, offers the
historian many interesting perspectives on this matter. He holds that the
interdiction the Church laid upon coitus interruptus was transformed into
a taboo; that is, the interdiction was internalized to the point that it no
longer had to be recalled to be obeyed, and then it was forgotten. It
became "unthinkable." This mechanism of internalization is suitable for
all social behavior in which free will is short-circuited by an implicit
morality, a cultural heritage. Contraceptive techniques did not completely
disappear from actual practice, but they disappeared from memory. One
proof of this forgetfulness is the semantic change in the words used to
designate that particular sin. The phrase *sin of Onan*—Onan was a figure
in the Old Testament incident upon which the Church based its condem-
nation—was originally used by theologians to describe coitus interrup-

[1]The most complete synthesis is in John T. Noonan, *Contraception: A History of Its
Treatment by the Catholic Theologians and Canonists* (Cambridge, Mass., 1965).
[2]Philippe Ariès, "Interprétation pour une histoire des mentalités," in H. Bergues, et al.,
La prévention des naissances dans la famille, Institut national d'études démographiques,
cahier 35 (Paris, 1960); English version in *Popular Attitudes toward Birth Control in Pre-
Industrial France and England,* ed. Orest Ranum and Patricia Ranum (New York, 1972).

tus, but in popular language it eventually came to refer not to contraception, but to masturbation.

Thus, the spread of contraception during the eighteenth century was not related to a sudden and generalized transgression against the interdict but to a change in outlook upon life, an emotional change that made the individual desirous of assuring his children's future through education and improved living standards, rather than of merely begetting offspring, as in the past. This in turn led to an increased concern for the couple and for "civilizing" marital relations. An ethical change also occurred, which led to the dissociation of pleasure and procreation within marriage—although Catholic doctrine only justified the former for the sake of the latter. The apparently paradoxical idea that birth control could be encouraged through an increased concern for children is supported for eighteenth-century France by a great deal of literary and iconographic evidence. "When the French began to become interested in children, they began no longer to have so many," wrote Dr. J. Sutter, summarizing Ariès' thought. This certainly conforms to the logic of the demographic situation. The decline in the infant mortality rate led to birth control as a means of preventing an increase in the size of the family. Parents were thus encouraged to make a greater investment—both materially and emotionally—in their children, whose birth and survival were no longer completely the result of chance.

This point of view is confirmed by those churchmen of the period who seem to have realized the social importance of contraception. In 1842 Monseigneur Bouvier, bishop of Le Mans, observed that contraceptive measures were common in his diocese. In most cases these could be ascribed to good Catholics who did not seem to be aware that they were disobeying the law of the Church. "Questioned by their confessors on the manner in which they exercised their marital rights," he wrote in a letter to the Pope, "they generally appear to be extremely shocked." These good Catholics were shocked both because they were unaware of the interdict laid upon these procedures and because the increased value placed upon married life had caused them to delineate a zone of intimacy and autonomy over which the Church no longer had any say.

An older text, Father Féline's *Catéchisme des gens mariés*, published in 1782, explains this serious deviance within a marriage as stemming from "excessive affection shown by husbands for their wives. . . . They show concern for their excessive delicacy." This latter point permits us to broaden the hypothesis and remove it from the religious context of eighteenth-century France. If the absence of contraceptive practices can only be explained by the interdiction pronounced by the Church, it is hard to see why contraception appeared in France, a Catholic country, much earlier than in Protestant countries, where religious rules were less clear, and also why it encounters such strong resistance today in numerous non-Christian countries of the Third World. A comparison of two recent attempts to introduce birth control—in non-Christian India, where the experiment was a virtual failure, and in Catholic Puerto Rico,[3] where it succeeded—tends to prove that the cultural level, and therefore the type of emotional relationships that govern the couple's life, is more important than religious prohibitions.

Theology has in recent years reasserted its historical position with the publication of J. T. Noonan's important book *Contraception*, which shows a marked evolution in the Church's position during the period under discussion here—the sixteenth through the eighteenth centuries. In certain cases the Church tended to separate the two finalities of marriage, sexual pleasure and reproduction, although it ultimately recognized the intrinsic value of conjugal love. J.-L. Flandrin[4]—relying upon the *distinguo* of Sanchez, the great Jesuit casuist, who appears to have authorized coitus interruptus in extramarital relationships in order to reduce the opprobrium of fornication, although he forbade it within marriage—assumes that two parallel forms of sexual behavior existed as early as the sixteenth century. According to Flandrin, men used contraceptive measures in extramarital relationships which belated marriage must have made more frequent. He asserts that such measures were, however, unknown in marital intercourse, which the Church stressed must be both fertile and temperate. (Theologians condemned amorous "excesses" between husband and wife.) Thus, the revolution that occurred during the eighteenth century simply transferred extramarital behavior to the marriage bed.

Flandrin's hypothesis in a strange way revives Moheau's and Father Féline's moralizing explanation, for the spread of contraception—a conscious transgression of Church laws—indicates a shift in morality. His hypothesis gives rise to several objections. Is such dichotomous sexual behavior imaginable? Can we assume that men familiar with these measures, having tried them on many occasions, would not have been tempted to introduce them into their own marriages? The complete absence of demographic proof makes this hypothesis even more tenuous. Indeed, it is difficult to require such proof for the sixteenth century. But

[3]See M. Brewster Smith, "Motivations, Communications Research, and Family Planning," in *Public Health and Population Change* (Pittsburgh, 1965); for India. T. R. Balakrishnan, "India. Evaluation of a Publicity Program on Family Planning," *Studies in Family Planning*, 1967; for Puerto Rico, see Reuben Hill, J. Mayone Stycos, and Kent W. Back, *The Family and Population Control: A Puerto Rican Experiment in Social Change* (Chapel Hill, N.C., 1959).

[4]J.-L. Flandrin, "Contraception, mariage, et relations amoureuses dans l'Occident chrétien," *Annales, E. S. C.* 24 (November–December 1969); English version in *Biology of Man in History*, ed. Robert Forster and Orest Ranum (Baltimore, 1975).

if illicit sex was as frequent during the seventeenth century as Flandrin suggests, even if we grant that contraception was practiced, a perceptible percentage of "accidents" should have shown up in the baptismal records. For the sixteenth century, Flandrin relies most heavily, aside from theologians, upon Brantôme, who provides an invaluable and racy bit of evidence. But can one generalize on the basis of Brantôme? Suppose the only available evidence about the demographic behavior of Parisians during the last half of the eighteenth century were the works of Restif de la Bretonne; we would be left with an impression of widespread libertinage, while the seasonal pattern of conceptions shows exactly the contrary.*

What then is the value of the evidence provided by theologians? Until the nineteenth century the Church was better informed than anyone else about sexual behavior, first, as a result of its almost obsessive surveillance of sexual activity, and second, through the confessional, a permanently open door to the intimate life of the vast majority of the population. But theology is above all else abstract reasoning. It tries to conform to doctrinal tradition rather than to the social reality. For example, although the penitentials of the early Middle Ages are a precious source of knowledge about the Church's sexual morality, the multitude of exotic and ridiculous perversions to which they refer should not be considered accurate reflections of current behavior. In this case, the unreality, the excessive imagination, and the bookish nature of clerical thought are factors as important as actual behavior. When St. Bernardine of Siena in the fifteenth century exclaimed, "Of a thousand marriages, I believe nine hundred and ninety-nine are the devil's," must we interpret this to mean that virtually all Sienese couples used coitus interruptus?[5]

It is even more difficult to know to what extent the faithful were informed of the Church's attitude toward marriage and sexuality. In this matter, vast religious sources such as inquiries and episcopal letters are still an unexplored field. Until the early eighteenth century, the cultivated public was still interested in theology. Multiple editions of casuistic treatises, like those of Sanchez, were available in France. The scandal they sometimes aroused often makes it seem, as Bayle suggested, that this sort of work served to initiate the public into sexual matters as much as to edify it. But the cultivated public was extremely limited. Its atypical behavior, as studies dealing with the English or French aristocracy have shown, renders it of little value in explaining the spread of contraception during the eighteenth century.

---

*See Jacques Depauw, pp. 185–86 of this volume, for a discussion of such seasonal patterns.—Trans.

[5]Quoted in Noonan, *Contraception,* p. 227.

The most interesting aspect for the historian is not the content, but the evolution, of theological thought. The inflexibilities of doctrine reveal both the pressure exerted by the "spirit of the times" and the efforts of theologians to adapt the Church's morality to new social conditions. To the degree that it reflects a system of values that is capable of evolving, theology supplies a clue by which we can perceive behavior. From this point of view, Noonan's book both enlightens and deceives. It shows the slow gestation of a new concept of marriage and of a new morality concerning the couple. Yet in his concern for reconstituting the itinerary that led the Church to its current positions, Noonan presents this evolution from too chronological a perspective. He stresses the impact of innovative theologians, even if their immediate influence upon the clergy was less than that of strict rigorists.

In the second half of the seventeenth century, especially in France, a very strong theological current existed that opposed the laxity of the casuists. This current included the Jansenists but extended far beyond them to involve men like Bossuet.[6] It dominated the seminaries, controlling the formation of the clergy and through them, the mental framework of the faithful. As Pierre Chaunu (rightly) observed, the contraceptive behavior of the eighteenth century can be traced to this outlook rather than to Sanchez. This connection seems paradoxical. Noonan has recently demonstrated very clearly that a moral doctrine never acts directly upon demographic behavior as if it were a system of propaganda whose orders are to be applied at once.[7] Instead, by modifying mental structures, it either encourages or quashes attitudes it is itself incapable of envisaging. Thus, Jansenism completely reestablished the Augustinian view of marriage, in which sexual pleasure is intrinsically evil, its only justification within marriage being that it accompanies procreation. This total rejection of sexuality, which incited the faithful to seek asceticism within marriage and to limit their pleasure, assured them increased mastery over their impulses. However, Jansenists and other rigorists hovered between two positions: whether to show an inquisitorial concern for sexuality in the confessional in order to forestall or condemn sinful behavior or never to speak of it for fear the mere mention would provoke the sin.

Added to this, for the later Jansenism of the eighteenth century, was an antisacramental attitude that kept the faithful away from the confessional. Thus we see how this moral rigorism could become distorted and could lead to contraceptive behavior. Asceticism, which led to increased control of sexual instincts, was expressed through thriftiness and

[6]The Faculty of Theology of Louvain with John Sinnigh, an exiled Irishman, led the rigorist movement.
[7]John T. Noonan, "Intellectual and Demographic History," *Daedalus*, 1968.

controlled pleasure. The Jansenist refusal to refer matters of conscience to the Church resulted in a lay, private, and individual morality. Sexuality became a strictly private matter between the two spouses. Our greatest difficulty lies in establishing geographical limits for the new outlook. For Normandy, Chaunu has established a relationship between the zones of early contraceptive practices and those that were Jansenist havens.[8] Unfortunately, a precise correlation can probably never be verified for France as a whole or even for Normandy. The ideological terrain is itself vague and extends beyond Jansenism. The important point in Chaunu's thesis is that it shows, as did Weber's for Protestantism, how the distortion of a religious ideology could unexpectedly affect basic behavior. Thus his thesis can account for a phenomenon peculiar to France: the early diffusion of contraceptive practices, not through a hypothetical dechristianization, but through the religious revival of the seventeenth century which, in its late stages and in its most radical forms (Jansenism), was also peculiar to France.

There is nonetheless something disturbing about this for the historian, who is asked to accept the hypothesis that a mere shift in ideology can have caused such a fundamental modification in demographic behavior. The asceticism in which French moral theology was steeped during the second half of the sixteenth century did not accidentally burst forth from some theologian's brain. Virtually the entire society had already become saturated with it. Its way had been prepared by one form of population control—that is, belated marriage—which, because of its emotional consequences, was becoming a veritable training ground for sexual austerity. Strict adherence to the teachings of the Church may well have provided an ideological link between this first form of birth control and the use of true birth-control measures. We might, however, question whether this relay post is indispensable in an explanation of the evolution of demographic behavior.

Although the beginning of the phenomenon of belated marriage is difficult to date, there is no doubt that it existed and intensified progressively until the end of the eighteenth century in a great part of Western Europe. In the Tuscany of the Quattrocento,[9] men married after the age of 30 (the mode was between 30 and 32 years), and almost all girls were married by 20. The average difference in age between husband and wife was about 13 years. In Riana,[10] a village of the diocese of Parma, during

[8]Pierre Chaunu, "Malthusianisme démographique et malthusianisme économique," *Annales, E. S. C.* 27 (January–February 1972).

[9]David Herlihy, "Vieillir au Quattrocento," *Annales, E. S. C.* 24 (November–December 1969); Christiane Klapisch, "Fiscalité et démographie en Toscane (1427–1430)," *Annales, E. S. C.* 24 (November–December 1969).

[10]Cited by J. Hajnal, "European Marriage Patterns in Perspective," in *Population in History*, ed. D. V. Glass and D. E. C. Eversley (London, 1965).

the second half of the seventeenth century the average marriage age for men was 33 years and for women, 25 years. From 1700 to 1750, the average age at marriage for men moved to 34 years; for women, to 30 years. Such a great disparity in the ages of marriage partners was undoubtedly peculiar to fifteenth-century Italy. It had almost disappeared by the eighteenth century. Indeed, by the end of the eighteenth century the average difference in ages in Venice was one year.[11] Note that the delay in marrying involved the wife alone. The contraceptive intent is therefore obvious. Between the sixteenth and the eighteenth centuries, the period of reproductive activity of women was thus decreased by ten years.

Numerous monographs dealing with seventeenth- and eighteenth-century France confirm that belated marriage was widespread. Only a few enclaves remained where custom kept the average marriage age markedly low. In rural areas, marriages occurred around the age of 25 for women and 27 for men. The discrepancy between the ages of husband and wife was slight. In cities, marriages may have occurred even later. In the parish of Saint Pierre in Lyon, during the first half of the eighteenth century,[12] the average age at first marriage for women was 27.5 years and for men, 29. Much less information is available for the sixteenth century. In 1550, Norman girls may have married at an average age of 21 and girls in Lorraine at 22, while a century later they married at 25 and 26 years. The marriage age likewise appears to have been lower in the region of Paris. In some cases we can even trace this gradual change in marriage age from the sixteenth through the eighteenth centuries. Indeed, in five parishes of the Vallage region of Champagne,[13] in which the average age at marriage was 24.8 for men and 24 years for women between 1681 and 1735, and 27.8 for men and 26.3 years for women during the rest of the eighteenth century, we have been able to ascertain a constant increase, decade by decade, in the marriage age during that period.

How can we explain the beginning of such a phenomenon? Here we meet a contradiction common to historical reasoning. Each time we go back to the origin of a complex phenomenon, we find not one specific cause, but a series of possible causes fitting into one another. For a demographic phenomenon, there is a demographic cause. We could explain the delay in marriages at the beginning of the sixteenth century as an effort to reestablish an equilibrium in a period of rising population. While life expectancy remained stable and short, early marriage corresponded to a normal reproductive rhythm. But the increase in longevity at

---

[11]D. Beltrami, *Storia della populazione di Venezia* (Padua, 1954).

[12]M. Garden, *Lyon et les Lyonnais au XVIIIᵉ siècle* (Paris, 1971).

[13]G. Arbellot, *Cinq paroisses du Vallage aux XVIIᵉ et XVIIᵉ siècles,* typewritten (Paris, 1970).

the end of the fifteenth century sharply increased the number of children born of these early marriages. Such an explanation is to some degree tautological. It also credits the demographic system with an exaggerated degree of initiative. However, the delay in inheritances—another consequence of increased life expectancy—seems to have played a more important role. Regardless of the legal system, an abrupt increase in the average age at death upset inheritance procedures both in the rural areas and in the cities. Thus, belated marriages may have been a response to the delay in becoming established.

But must marriage be considered in terms of an establishment? At the beginning of the sixteenth century, the increase in population growth was paralleled by a change in mentality, which evolved in the direction of a new viewpoint regarding marriage and the family. This evolution can be discerned on several levels. On the theological level, Noonan has clearly shown that the laxist concepts of sexuality that won out among seventeenth-century casuists stemmed from a redefinition of marital relationships, from a valorization of the couple that appeared at the end of the fifteenth century. Martin le Maistre, the Parisian nominalist, seems to have been the most important architect of this regeneration. We also see among the humanists and reformers a general questioning of marriage both as a sacrament and as an institution. In 1472 the German humanist Albrecht von Eyt published a treatise entitled *Ob einem Manne sey zu nemen ein eeliches Weib oder nit* [*Whether a Man Should Take A Wife or Not*] while Rabelais' Panurge asked the same question in a comical fashion [*Gargantua . . ., *book 3, chap. 9]. Such literary excitement about this problem shows the importance of the unrest that permeated the entire society.

Social pressure was perhaps most notable in the field of law. Emmanuel Le Roy Ladurie has elucidated for the province of Languedoc the increased power of the lineage and of the various forms of family regrouping—such as *affrairement* [the creation of a *frérèche*, or joint family of siblings and their families]—which seems to have been the predominant if not general trend during the "century when men were scarce." The increased birth rate of the sixteenth century made these regroupings more economically fragile and also increasingly constrictive. It caused people to question patriarchal authority, and it gave rise to laws promoting emancipation. At the same time, the farm and the family broke down into smaller units. There was a gradual shift from the marriage-as-alliance to the marriage-as-establishment: the marriage integrated into the lineage was replaced by the marriage that established a new family unit and a new unit of production. Belated marriage was the price paid for this emancipation.

A study of the matrimonial system for the region of Bordeaux during the sixteenth century[14] shows that strict provisos, such as *affiliation*,* gradually disappeared from marriage contracts and were replaced by the associative formulas of the "community of acquests."† But between these two extremes we can see "universal joint property between spouses"—the form of ownership most opposed to the rights of the line-age—appearing and spreading in the cities and among the lower classes during the first two decades of the sixteenth century. Marriage contracts sometimes called this joint ownership the "household," asserting that the couple was an indivisible entity. Thus the joint-property movement of the fifteenth century promoted the marriage-as-establishment in two ways:by creating centrifugal forces that viewed marriage as the means of dividing authority and property, and by supplying the model unit that could guarantee the couple's autonomy and establishment as a household.

Indeed, the sixteenth century shows contradictory trends concerning marriage. Both the indissolubility imposed by the Church and its weak social status were criticized. Contrary to a rather widespread idea, marriage in the sixteenth century was not a sclerosed institution, but an underdeveloped one. The Church had on the whole been forced merely to "baptize" the marriage contract drawn up under Roman law or under customary law and to impose moral obligations upon it. It did not administer the sacrament, which was carried out through the *copula carnalis*; it simply recorded it. Thus disparity existed— and was deplored by many, from the state on down—between the ease with which this obligation could be assumed and the seriousness of the obligation itself. This gave rise to numerous abuses—abductions, clandestine marriages, and so on—that violated the free choice of the spouses or the guardian-ship of the parents. In France as early as 1556 an edict of Henry II gave parents the right to disinherit sons under the age of thirty and daughters under the age of twenty-five who married without their consent. The

---

[14]J. Lafon, *Régimes matrimoniaux et mutations sociales; les époux bordelais (1450–1550)* (Paris, 1972).

*The old matrimonial system involved a strict separation between husband and wife. The husband was the protector of his wife's rights, while she played a passive role, having very few rights of her own. (Cf. E. Le Roy Ladurie, in chap. 4 of this volume, for the role played by the portioned child who had left the family circle.) The bride became "affiliated" or adopted by the family. Thenceforth the husband, or the male head of the household, retained the administration of her dowry, although she might in some cases regain possession of it upon her husband's death. Nor did the wife generally have any rights to dispose of any acquests acquired through the couple's efforts during their married years.—Trans.

†The "community of acquests" means the joint ownership of acquests—i.e., any possessions, and the income from them, acquired "through the labor, industry, and management" of the couple. This joint association, or "community," formed by the couple did not include property inherited by either partner.—Trans.

Church hoped to strengthen its control over the institution of marriage through the obligatory presence of a priest, and at the same time to ensure the couple's free decision. The decisions of the Council of Trent attempted to meet these two demands. These decisions gave belated marriage a legal and moral foundation, even though they were not immediately accepted everywhere—especially in France, which refused to accept them at all.

Therefore we shall risk hypothesizing an evolution that occurred in two stages. First, during the sixteenth century belated marriage became common as the result of the double conquest of the couple's moral autonomy and its economic independence. Until the 1580s this process served chiefly to sustain and brake the demographic upsurge. Then, during the seventeenth century, belated marriage became consolidated as the keystone of an ascetic outlook upon life. From 1580 to 1730 the population remained stationary. Belated marriage guaranteed this stability. Asceticism became part of the mores, as society's response to a constrictive economy and also as the ascetic ideal. Asceticism alone justified continuing so frustrating a practice. All the Church's efforts to strengthen the celebration of marriage were aimed at disciplining sexual life. In this respect the strange history of the betrothal perfectly reveals the moral strictness that the Church progressively made a part of her customs.

There were a thousand reasons why the betrothal, an old institution of Roman law but even more vital in certain customary laws, displeased the Church. This premarriage symbolized the marriage contract, an arrangement between two families. In the minds of many the betrothal laid too much emphasis upon the contract to the detriment of the religious ceremony itself, which was limited to simply recording the fact.[15] In particular, the Church denounced two unfortunate results of the betrothal. First of all, an agreement between the families preceded, and often even neglected to take into consideration, the agreement between the future marriage partners, and canon law stressed the consent of both partners. Second, being promised in marriage inaugurated a period of tolerance during which the fiancés often began to live like a married couple, long before the religious ceremony of marriage. Instead of attacking the betrothal head-on, the Church strove to transform the practice into an instrument of moral correction, as it often had done when confronted with pagan practices.

In France the post-Tridentine Church made the betrothal ceremony general and obligatory wherever the institution had remained prevalent among the lower classes, transforming it into an essentially religious ceremony. On the other hand, it forbade or neglected the betrothal

---

[15]For example, in the case of *matrimonia praesumpta*.

wherever that practice had fallen into disuse. Thus, we can draw up a map of betrothals based on synodal statutes that clearly separates northern from southern France.[16] The betrothal became both a means of verifying the free consent of the fiancés and a preparation for marriage. But the statutes often repeated the strict prohibition against fiancés living together or even residing under the same roof, a sign that acceptance did not come about without some difficulty. The date of the betrothal, at first obligatorily set before the publication of the marriage bans, was gradually moved closer to the marriage date until it finally merged with the wedding ceremony. The betrothal gradually disappeared. Like a film being shown at slower and slower speeds until the picture finally stops completely, the austere betrothals of the seventeenth century became fossilized and were transformed into folklore rites. Such a practice as the *"nuit de Tobie,"*[17] which forbade the newlyweds to consummate the wedding on the bridal night and imposed upon them a further delay of three days, is undoubtedly a vestige of this institutionalized asceticism. Indeed, this medieval custom was encouraged and spread by the Church after the Council of Trent. It could still be found at the beginning of this century in certain French provinces.[18] Other rites such as the "hidden bride" or the "flight of the bride" represent the same sort of survival.

Are a religious institution and a juridical arrangement capable, on their own, of keeping a social habit like belated marriage alive for such a long time? In our society, where choice of marriage partner is dictated by no official rule other than the prohibition imposed by the Church involving consanguinity, a multitude of economic constraints, customs, and trends contribute to obliterating freedom of choice. A simple numerical imbalance between males and females can unexpectedly postpone marriage age, as, for example, when the difference between the ages of husbands and wives remains stable and a sharp increase in the birthrate brings a large number of girls into the marriage market. Their marriage partners would normally come from an older age group, which is naturally less numerous, so a portion of these girls will be obliged either to marry a younger husband, which is not deemed proper, or else wait until the larger male contingent reaches a suitable age. The marriage age for these girls will thus be delayed.[19]

This mechanism may have played its part during the sixteenth century in Italy, where the difference in the ages of the partners was very marked.

[16]See C. Piveteau, *La pratique matrimoniale en France d'après les statuts synodaux,* typewritten (Paris, 1957).

[17]See A. van Gennep, *Manuel du Folklore français contemporain,* vol. 1, pt. 2: *Mariages-Funérailles* (Paris, 1946).

[18]Especially in Brittany-Normandy, Bresse, and Savoy.

[19]Concerning a similar phenomenon affecting presentday France, see the study of Louis Roussel, "La nuptialité en France," *Population* 26 (1971).

But it is difficult to postulate its universal and prolonged influence. Here the historian is tempted to use the same reasoning as the geneticist faced with the proliferation of a congenital birth defect. If the defect continues despite its harmful aspects, it is because it has been selected by the natural or the social milieu. It has become useful. As in genetics, chance may have created the necessity for late marriage. "Chance" was the demographic imbalance that may initially have modified mores. "Necessity" was the phenomenon of general accommodation that by degrees mobilized legal procedures, canon law, and religious morality and created a behavioral pattern. But it seems probable that without social demand, without the slow gestation of a new concept of marriage that is evidenced among theologians by the fifteenth century, an increasing population would not have permitted belated marriage to become permanently implanted.

We are confronted with a sort of Weberian demographic model. Like Max Weber for industrial capitalism, J. Hajnal has proposed the idea that the "Western marriage pattern," with belated marriage and a rather high proportion of unmarried persons, was the historical exception.[20] It is not found before the twentieth century, either in Eastern Europe or in most other civilizations. Its originality may lie first and foremost in the fact that it imposes an antinatural behavior and increases to the maximum the distance between instinct and institution. All cultures impose a period of waiting between puberty and marriage, in order to ritualize this rite of passage; but the period is generally brief.

On the contrary, beginning in the sixteenth century Western Europe set out upon the road to asceticism, and this moral resolve brings us back to Max Weber. Despite Flandrin's hypothesis of a dual sexual behavior, there is little doubt, at least for the seventeenth century, that a widespread asceticism exalted by the Church and confirmed by parish registers existed and that it resulted in a dearth of extramarital sexual intercourse and of contraceptive measures. Why must we believe that the impulses repressed by the social system had to have a sexual outlet? Freud showed us that active neuroses can very effectively absorb these impulses and channel them toward other goals. In the social dynamism of this austere era, we can trace both a very extensive process of sublimation and the spectacular neuroses such as sorcery, hysteria, and other savage forms of peasant culture described by Le Roy Ladurie.

The other Weberian characteristic of this model is its social efficacy. In addition to regulating population growth, belated marriages freed additional cheap manpower. The surplus of women increased the productive forces and favored the earliest or "primitive" accumulation of wealth. But, as was the case for Weberian puritanism, it was from the social

[20]Hajnal, "European Marriage Patterns."

values crystallizing about it that belated marriage gained the most effect. We can see how the society of the *Ancien Régime*, by delaying the time of marriage, identified marriage more and more clearly with becoming established. In the countryside this autonomy often took the form of the couple's installation in a separate dwelling. This would presuppose funds from an inheritance (which was frequent in the world of shopkeepers or artisans), from an estate, or simply from the possession of enough money to cover the costs of setting up housekeeping. This autonomy progressively substituted the spirit of enterprise for the young married couple's love and for the spirit of the marriage alliance that had traditionally inspired family strategies. The couple's main preoccupation was no longer simply to create a family but to know how to direct it and to preserve and improve its social status, which had become its principal goal.

Sexual asceticism plays the same role in this spirit of matrimonial enterprise that the sense of thrift played in the spirit of capitalist enterprise. Is this just an analogy? Historical demography today is exploring this meeting ground of mentalities and behaviors of which Max Weber was unaware. For this reason he was unable to establish a continuous link between capitalism and the ideal of austerity. Here we must be wary of saying too much or too little. It would be absurd to try to reduce the industrial adventure of Europe to the mere choosing of birth control, but some importance must be given to the existence of this choice. Not only did European populations meet the first "preconditions" of industrial growth—a calibrated population and an increased life expectancy—they also served as an archetype for economic behavior. Between belated marriage and contraception—even if the order is changed or the system of values seems gradually to become inverted—we remain within the same cultural logic: the instinctual life must be inhibited in order the better to serve reality.

11
Differences or Changes in Family Organization

Françoise Lautman

Several types of families coexist within any one society. The coming together of many social forces aids and then later works against the supremacy of one type over another, according to the period or a given family's social position. But, although they fade away, the preexistent forms do not disappear totally, nor do they disappear at the same rate in each of the various social groups.

Theoretical Perspectives

The nuclear family that settles in a new location has been shown to be a phenomenon that existed before the industrialization of Europe. The nuclear family was already the predominant type along the entire Atlantic seaboard in those regions that were the first to become industrialized and that were the chief source of emigrants to the United States. Having long disregarded the previous existence of this type of family, certain scholars today do not hesitate to assert that its triumph through industrialization and emigration represents a survival rather than something new.[1]

The search for the causal relationships or the correlations that develop between each society and its preferred type of family structure often results in a failure to note the importance and the meaning of the

Annales E. S. C. 27(July–October 1972): 1190–96. Translated by Patricia M. Ranum.
[1]J. Mogey, "The Family and Community in Urban Industrial Societies," in *Handbook of Marriage and the Family,* ed. Christensen (Chicago: Rand McNally, 1964).

simultaneous presence of one or several other forms of family organization.

Recent work in family history and demography is oriented toward Mogey's and Goode's finding that in most societies, or at any rate in those that preceded our industrialized ones, the extended family was found only among the ruling or wealthy classes. The "result of power, wealth, and mobility,"[2] it already represented a minority of the population.

However, we have an idealized image of the family, which we believe provides unconditional solidarity, homey affection, and a satisfying place for a moderate amount of sexuality. Continually obliged to admit that the image does not correspond to reality, we find that we can give it more substance by projecting it into the past. Thus the family serves as both a haven and a symbol. It is a rallying point for ideologies: "The traditional family is not, as we might believe, a mere survival; it is a warhorse."[3] Goode agrees with this opinion and asserts that the traditional Western family, like the traditional Chinese family, is a myth that never corresponded to any reality.

In many ways, the same is true for the conjugal family, which is an ideal type in the Weberian sense of the word. The conjugal family is also an ideal, since a large proportion of families accepts it as a suitable norm. Lastly, it is an effectively functioning sociological fact. With regard to industrialization, it also plays the role of an ideal goal, the aim of which is to facilitate the adaptation of the individual.

It has been tempting to view the newlywed couple's opportunity to settle down away from its ascendants as an adaptation to the mobility demanded by the system of industrial production. It has been equally tempting to conclude that family ties were weakened by the physical separation thus imposed; that the egalitarian division of inheritances facilitated the mobility of capital for investment purposes; and that the more fluid definition of roles in the more egalitarian family gave each person more ways in which to organize his family life and, therefore, a better chance to adapt to all the demands that industry made upon him. Viewed thus, the conjugal family is no longer the family *in* an industrialized society, but the family *of* the industrialized society.

We can logically reverse these assertions and say that industrial society became possible as a result of modifications in family organization. This reversal immediately reveals all the ambiguities of the interpretation I have just described. In addition, both the harmonies and the dissonances revealed by empirical studies continue to raise serious questions about the

[2]W. Goode, *World Revolution and Family Patterns* (Glencoe, Ill.: Free Press, 1963).

[3]J. Stoetzel, "Les changements dans les fonctions familiales," in *Renouveau des idées sur la famille,* under the direction of R. Prigent, (Paris: Institut national d'études démographiques, 1954).

fundamental meaning of the alleged affinity between the family system and the system of production employed by industrialized society. The relationship is the inverse of what we might expect. Far from being more closely associated with the well-to-do social groups, which one would think ought to adjust more successfully, the nuclear family is seen to be the lower-class family. The family of the ruling classes has preserved a certain number, if not all, of the characteristics of the traditional family (the continuation of a more extended network of kinship, a more effective system for helping its members, a greater stability in marriage, and a longer period of supervision over children but also an increased period of dependence on their part).

The conjugal type of family was already predominant in the lower classes, for the extended family offered the members of this class few advantages and was not a part of their way of life. On the other hand, although kinship no longer, or only rarely, permitted an individual to transmit power, among the upper classes it remained the chief means of transferring the material possessions and especially the cultural possessions (education and ambition) that assure access to power. Privilege results from an individual's social condition rather than from his possessions, but it is always facilitated by the family. Maintaining privilege helps assure a closed system: "The family appears as the social institution that controls and distributes opportunities for upward social mobility and brakes backward movement. . . . It thus assures a certain degree of permanence within social structures despite changes that occur within society, especially those changes that modify the potential of the various groups."[4] The real structure and function of the family have not changed. The change lies in the way society views a certain ideal that the ruling classes once practiced effectively and that on the whole they continue to act out.

We might wish to investigate the nature of the resulting relationship between family types and social classes, but to do so we would have to depend upon a double typology of families and communities that does not really exist.

Is the relationship all that simple? Did it not rather result from a common reference to older and deeper characteristics? Kooy shows that in Holland the family has always been nuclear or nonnuclear depending on the province, and Mogey then hypothesizes that a bilateral system of kinship and of inheritance-sharing preexisted in those regions that have long had nuclear families.[5]

---

[4]A. Girard, *Le choix du conjoint,* (Paris: Institut national d'études démographiques, 1962).

[5]Mogey, "The Family and Community."

Moreover, granting that the kinship system is more or less broad according to the social class and that the family has more or less numerous and well-defined functions within it—the rich family serving its members for a much longer time and at the same time socializing them much more effectively—we must expect that behavior will not have the same purpose in every class and that what is considered deviant for one class is normal for another. We can cite countless cases of such behavior: the early financial independence of adolescents or the separation of leisure activities according to sex are but two examples.

The criterion of normality for each type of behavior lies in the family rules that permit the best possible integration into society as a whole. Moreover, any specific category of behavior can be more or less advantageous for the individual who conforms.

Previously formulated hypotheses should therefore be examined in the light of A. K. Cohen's theory of social disorganization and deviant behavior.[6] Such a condition is not a static state, for a system can change as long as it persists. Indeed, disorder involves the breakdown or disorganization of a system. In either case, there is a place for deviant behavior, since any social system simultaneously generates both the means of its own survival and the types of deviant behavior that permit individuals to find escape-hatches from conformism.

These deviant phenomena have often been considered all too hastily as indices of the degree of disorganization. On the contrary, they can signify a restructuring insofar as they constitute alternative solutions for the renewal of the system when it is no longer in tune with the social organization as a whole and fails to provide the individual with the optimum conditions for social acceptance through conformity. We have seen that these conditions can vary considerably from one social class to another.

Thus, divorce was long considered a sign and a measure of the loss of the sense of family, chiefly by those sociologists to whom moralists had communicated their notion of good and the habit of making normative evaluations. However, divorce is increasingly coming to be recognized as related to the enhanced value placed upon marriage (failure is not well-accepted) and the family. The increase in the divorce rate chiefly involves childless couples and affects them primarily as individuals. On the social level, in the United States for example, it has been accompanied by an upsurge in the birthrate.[7] Divorce can therefore be considered an example

[6]A. K. Cohen, "The Study of Social Disorganization and Deviant Behavior," in *Sociology Today,* ed. R. K. Merton (New York: Basic Books, 1959).

[7]T. Parsons and R. F. Bales, *Family, Socialization, and Interaction Process* (Glencoe, Ill.: Free Press, 1965).

of the sort of deviant behavior that can lead to a restructuring of the individual and of the general system.

The relative frequency of divorce in the United States is much greater among black families than among white families; but the number of black divorces must be compared with the number of black marriages. Marriage had little reality for this population until the beginning of the twentieth century, owing to the disorganization resulting from slavery and also to the remnants of old African social structures. Blacks rarely married; the free and temporary union was the rule. Family organization was centered around the mother, the only stable member. In addition, to become legitimized this organization, which could be considered reactive, was obliged to accept general rules of marriage that were based on family structures that were alien to it in origin and nature. The expectation was that as a result blacks would become adapted to white society; yet in other respects society did not offer blacks many favorable opportunities for acceptance and success.

In our discussion of divorce, we can also mention the higher divorce rate among the lower classes of Western society and recall both the importance given to the free union and the decreased number of marriages within the working classes at the end of the nineteenth century.[8] At that time divorce served to increase the flexibility of the institution of marriage, permitting marriage once again to become a satisfying form of family organization among social classes that had either turned away from or never been interested in it. The argument that from these very brief marriages legitimate children would henceforth be born was explicit among legislators, as evidenced by the parliamentary debates that accompanied the Naquet law of 1884 in France. From this perspective, divorce appears as an institution that helps society at the least cost to maintain the institution of marriage by modifying its functions.

Illegitimacy even more than divorce is the sign of breakdown, for—according to Sprey[9]—one of the basic objectives of marriage is the reproduction and socialization of children—situating individuals, as they appear, within the society of which they are a part, in other words, making legitimate children. If we look beyond the process of family breakups and envisage the results, we must ask in what way the structure of the interpersonal relationships that form a family system becomes inadequate, for an inadequacy of the structure is involved here, rather than the deviant behavior of any one member (such as desertion). Indeed,

---

[8] Louis Chevalier, *Classes laborieuses et classes dangereuses à Paris pendant la première moitié du XIXe siècle* (Paris: Plon, 1958).

[9] J. Sprey, "Family Disorganization: Toward a Conceptual Clarification," *Journal of Marriage and Family Living,* 1963.

one family member can fail, and a marriage can end in divorce, but the role and utility of the family need not be called into question.

Yet in the case of disorganization, it is the norms and values forming the structure of the social institution that fail to provide a meaningful model for the participants' actions. To use Merton's terminology, the cause of disorganization is the ambivalence that comes from the tension or the disharmony between cultural themes and the institutions through which culture is practiced. Lower-class black families in the United States can be used an as example of this type of disorganization—which is not to say that all black families present phenomena of deviance or of disorganization but only that the causes of this sort of disorder result from incompatibilities within social structures.

Incompatibilities between family participation and social participation[10]

During the past two centuries the evolution of the family's functions and size in industrialized countries or in countries in the process of becoming industrialized suggests an incompatibility between the optimum development of the entire society in which we live and that of the family group.

The family has been reduced to a tiny nuclear group of parents and small children. In exchange for a greater degree of sociability, it has been deprived of its economic foundation, its selective functions, most of its educational functions, its role of solidarity toward the old and the sick, and its concern with providing for the future. Yet the family has indisputably preserved two functions: the socialization of the child and the channeling of the adult's sexual and affective needs. These two functions even seem to have assumed increased importance and to have reinforced one another. The new interest shown in the child corresponds to a change in the advantages that adults expect from family life.

Professional life, which has become increasingly bureaucratic, offers individuals fewer and fewer chances to assert their personality. Prosperity as we know it—in which nothing belongs to us personally, in which

[10]The notion of social participation to which I and most of the authors quoted are referring means participation in the established society and indicates the opportunities presented to any specific category by that society rather than its supposed aptitude for sociability.

Participation is generally measured with the help of indices taking into account the nature and the number of the different behaviors and indicating among other things the extent and density of the network of interrelations; activity within the cultural, religious, political, or trade-union groups; and professional life. Cf. H. L. Wilenski, "Orderly Careers and Social Participation: The Impact of Work History on Social Integration in the Middle Class," *American Sociological Review,* 1961.

consumption is centered about objects that may also appear in a friend's house, on a stranger, or in a shopwindow—leaves the family as the only refuge for the need—a holdover from Romanticism—to feel irreplaceable. The family becomes the place where the greatest value is placed upon the individual's personality.

Although the satisfactions thus offered by the family and society as a whole theoretically complement one another, we have reason to ask whether the differences between the individual qualities demanded by the family and by society do not result in an antagonism and whether the individuals most able to obtain satisfaction from the one are also those most apt to be satisfied by the other.

The conflict between devotion to the family and devotion to society is illustrated historically by the insistance of certain religions that the clergy remain celibate, by the requirement during certain periods of history that teachers remain celibate, and by the struggle to bring about the disintegration of the family in societies like revolutionary Russia and the Palestine of the kibbutzim, which ardently wish to occupy the fundamental place in the life of their members.

Certain empirical studies support the thesis that this antagonism between family and society does influence effective participation in one or both areas.

Blood and Wolfe's study of family life in the United States was later carried out in a comparative manner in several European countries. These studies reveal that in each country there is a correlation between the mature years—which involves the most intense participation in social and professional life (long working hours, as well as increased responsibilities and interest)—and a decrease in time spent at home, in role-playing within the family, and in participation in its decision-making.

Naturally this decrease is especially evident among the ruling classes, whose social life is more intense. Although not the sole reason, decreased participation in family life has a great deal to do with diminished satisfactions with marriage, which correlate with the same stages in the cycle of family life described by Reuben Hill.[11]

Scanzoni's study provides a good example of the reinforcement of the conflicts between conjugal and professional roles in the families of Protestant ministers.[12] Those ministers who belonged to small sects,

[11]For the purpose of this analysis, family life is divided into segments indicating the appearance of children, the ages of the children, and their departure from the family; childless couples are divided into two separate categories, young married couples and truly childless couples. Cf. R. Hill, "The Eddyville Story: Family and Personal Adjustments to the Rapid Urbanization of a Southern Town," in *Recherches sur la famille,* ed. Vandenboeck (Tübingen, 1958).

[12]John Scanzoni, "Resolution of Occupational-Conjugal Role Conflict in Clergy Marriages," *Journal of Marriage and the Family,* 1965.

which form more integrated units and which are more demanding about participation, experienced more conflicts than their counterparts who were members of more established churches.

Thus, according to one's age, the demands of one's profession, and the resources one has available for participation in society, we can conclude —although we can be less specific for each social class in particular —that a virtual incompatibility exists between a high level of participation in society as a whole and participation in the family.

Mutual Reinforcements

It has also been shown, however, that a low level of participation in one form of sociability is limited to a low level in other forms, although it is not always possible to decide which came first.

The previously cited study by Blood and Wolfe shows that American blacks in the Detroit area are clearly less well-integrated into society as a whole than are whites in terms of shared values and the gratifications they can expect from society. And, at least in the sample, blacks more frequently have a marginal job such as that of common laborer, which provides no stability, no personal recognition, and no career opportunities. These blacks show a lesser degree of participation in family roles and decision making, a less satisfactory degree of communication with family members, and a higher divorce rate than do whites at a comparable social level.

If we accept the thesis that these are the reasons why the members of the lower classes in general participate less in society than do members of the ruling classes, we can relate this to the increased weakening of the bonds of kinship, the early liberation of children, and the decreased share in family roles evident among these classes. In addition, the services rendered by this less extended, less powerful, and less educated family are very inadequate.[13] This impoverished family socializes the individual less and at the same time gives him fewer reasons to become attached to the family itself.

It is among the lower classes that Morsa found the greatest number of women who knew nothing about their husbands' professional life[14] and that M. J. Chombard de Lauwe found the lowest degree of awareness concerning the changes occurring in family life and in the way the

---

[13]Goode, *World Revolution and Family Patterns.*
[14]G. Morsa, "Notes sur la famille dans une localité du Brabant Wallon," in *Recherches sur la famille,* ed. J. C. B. Mohr (Tübingen, 1956).

marriage partners perceived each other.[15] In support of this thesis, it has been shown that among these classes, even a partial strengthening of the bonds with the community brings about increased participation in family life.

On the economic level, if the father of the family is better paid and his employment more prestigious, he will exert a greater influence upon family life and participate more in decisions concerning the family.

Active church membership in which special attention is paid to one's role as head of the family causes the father to place greater value upon his position in the family and to become more interested in his duties. Frequent contacts with friends, especially if they are also married, increase the social pressure needed if he is to respect his family obligations.

Although optimum social integration brings about increased participation in family life, we can also cite cases in which a coherent family life permits the most rapid and most adequate adaptation to a changing society.[16] At Eddyville, a small town in the southern United States, the families that adapted best to the rapid industrialization of the city and the sudden increase in population that resulted from the installation of a military complex were those in which communication among members was most effective and in which the greatest number of decisions were made together. Those families that were beset by conflicts adapted least well.

We must therefore reexamine the thesis that the institution of the family is being asphyxiated by industrial society. Durkheim's hypothesis that the family would disappear if confronted by a vaster organic solidarity born of trade or function can be countered by the hypothesis that a correlation exists between participation in the family and participation in society as a whole. This correlation would resemble that which Wilenski, in reworking Durkheim's[17] and Mannheim's[18] theses about careers, established between participation in professional life and participation in society as a whole.

This conflict over the degree of participation seems to intervene only when there is a high level of participation in both social and family life. This presupposes an intense social life and a very coherent family structure. We have seen that this combination is most often found in the upper classes; the lower classes seem to be socially unengaged as a result

[15]M. J. and P. H. Chombart de Lauwe, *La femme dans la société* (Paris: Editions du C.N.R.S., 1963).
[16]Hill, "The Eddyville Story."
[17]Emile Durkheim, "La famille conjugale," *Revue philosophique,* 1921.
[18]Wilenski, "Orderly Careers and Social Participation."

of a less marked degree of integration, which leaves a rather large margin for potential development that may be triggered, wholly or in part, by such material reinforcements.

If this hypothesis were confirmed, we would have to determine at what point these forms of sociability begin to compete, regardless of where they may be situated along the continuum of intensity of participation and of social hierarchy.

Or do conflicts make their appearance in a broader sphere? Would it be possible to concentrate upon this sphere in elucidating the form of sociability that would play the determining role in the process of competition?

Is it therefore necessary to test the hypothesis that social status is a variable capable of concealing or revealing the convergence of various sociabilities, and to determine the point at which the influence of this variable changes direction? The result would of necessity be the formulation of new hypotheses about the interactions among the various social structures. These hypotheses would then lead us to question comparisons between the images and the practices of family life that are followed by each group.

The ruling classes and the lower classes have shown very different types of family behavior for a much longer period than we had thought. However, along the imaginary line running from one type of behavior to the other type, the middle class, contrary to its name, is not always in the middle, and the variety of its options is a sign of the complexity of the situations involved. For example, middle-class people are almost as young when they marry as are the workers; but the working class produces fewer children than the bourgeoisie, although in general the number of children is positively linked to early marriages.[19]

The higher divorce rate among the lower classes played its part in reinforcing the stigma of family deviance that was already attached to it. Why are certain differences seen as simple variants and others treated as deviance? We may have grounds to assert—and a first estimate seems to support this thesis—that differences accentuating those characteristics found among the families of the ruling class are generally well tolerated, while the attitude is exactly the opposite when the difference lies in the other direction and appears to compromise the social order, even when an adaptive phenomenon is involved. The analogy between this hypothesis and a tested principle of the sociology of crime should be stressed: "The criminality censured by the penal code forms only one part of criminality

---

[19]S. Calot and J. C. Deville, "Nuptialité et fécondité selon le milieu socio-culturel," *Economie et Statistique,* October 1971.

as a whole, namely, the criminality that is generally found among the disinherited classes, who are the victims of the power wielded by in society."[20] The existence of different forms of family organization multiplies the number of possible misunderstandings about behavior and respective images and consequently strengthens the tendency to formulate analyses and sanctions purely in terms of the social order.

[20]D. Szabo, "Introduction," *Déviance et criminalité* (Paris: Colin, U2, 1970).

Library of Congress Cataloging in Publication Data

Main entry under title:

Family and society.

    (Selections from the Annales, économies, sociétiés, civilisations; no. 2)
    CONTENTS: Belmont, N. Levana; or, How to raise up children.—Duby, G. Lineage, nobility, and chivalry in the region of Macon during the twelfth century.—Klapisch, C. and Demonet, M. "A uno pane e uno vino", the rural Tuscan family at the beginning of the fifteenth century. [etc.]
    1. Family—History—Addresses, essays, lectures. I. Forster, Robert, 1926–   II. Ranum, Orest A. III. Annales, économies, sociétiés, civilisations. IV. Series.
HQ503.F316   301.42'09   76-17299
ISBN 0-8018-1780-3
ISBN 0-8018-1781-1 pbk.